RELIGION AND THE PSYCHOLOGY OF JUNG

Religion and the Psychology of Jung

by

RAYMOND HOSTIE, S.J.

Professor of the Faculty of Theology of the Society of Jesus in Louvain

translated by

G. R. LAMB

SHEED & WARD—NEW YORK

840 BROADWAY
NEW YORK, 3

LIBRARY OF CONGRESS CATALOG CARD NUMBER 57-6049

De Licentia Superiorum

Imprimi Potest, Mechliniæ, 12–4–56
Can. Van den Dries, Censor
Imprimatur, L. J. Suenens, Vic. Gen.

MANUFACTURED IN THE UNITED STATES OF AMERICA

CONTENTS

I

ANALYTICAL PSYCHOLOGY AND RELIGION

JUNG is a doctor and quite rightly proud of the fact. For the first ten years of his medical career he was attached to the Zürich canton hospital, Burghölzli, first as assistant, then as second-in-command and finally as principal. In addition he was for eight years in charge of the psychiatry course at the university in the same town. Even at this early date he gained world-wide renown through the writings he published about his experiments in the matter of the "association of ideas", as it was called. These experiments led to the discovery of unconscious "affective complexes" and also to a period of close collaboration with Sigmund Freud, from 1907 to 1913. In 1911–12 he published his first full-scale work, *Wandlungen und Symbole der Libido*. It is a remarkable book, enthusiastically written throughout, though in places still showing signs of immaturity of thought, and it raises all the problems that Jung was to go on investigating for the next forty years. However, it was too personal a work to find immediate acceptance. In fact, it led to a definite break with Freud. Jung thereafter devoted himself exclusively to psychotherapy, and this forms the background to all his theoretical writings. For the sake of psychotherapy he gave up his university teaching in 1913; he had relinquished his post at the psychiatric clinic in Zürich in 1909 for the same reason.

His isolation during the succeeding years only increased his passionate absorption in his work. The enormous number of facts that he collected—he himself says that he has interpreted between two and three thousand dreams a year—widened the scope of his activity considerably. In his determination to gain a better understanding of man as he actually is, he studied the lives and customs and ideas of primitive peoples on the spot, both in Central Africa (in 1921 and 1926) and in North America (1924–5). During these years, with the help of his friend Richard Wilhelm, he gained some insight into the hidden meaning of the religions and philosophies of China, Tibet and India. In about 1930 he began to realize that both the Ancients' "gnosis" and medieval alchemy contained a great deal of instructive data. And more recently still, especially since 1935, he has made some of the central dogmas of Catholic teaching the objects of psychological study in one book after another. Whilst the writings Jung published between 1915 and 1935 were almost entirely concerned with his analytical psychology, his more recent works are devoted primarily to an examination of alchemy, gnosticism and Catholic dogma from the psychological point of view.

This brief biographical introduction is sufficient to show that the problem of the relationship between analytical psychology and religion is not one imposed from outside but has been brought increasingly into the foreground by Jung's own researches. It thus becomes a first necessity to attempt to define "analytical psychology" and "religion" so as to explain the scope of the two topics that we are to investigate. I shall then give a sketch of the data we have at our disposal to enable us to compare and contrast these two things. Finally, I shall need to show how all this data can best be appreciated.

Very early in his career, in 1915 in fact, Jung had given the name "analytical psychology" to the psychological science that he was developing on the basis of his painstaking observations of the human soul or, to be more precise, psyche. His aim was to make a clear distinction between his own ideas on the one hand and both classic psychiatry and experimental psychology on the other. According to Jung both these latter branches of study made a mistake in trying to explain phenomena in a purely physiological way. The first derived all mental troubles from some organic lesion generally located in the brain; the second split up psychic behaviour and then submitted what were taken to be its simple elements to artificial examination in the laboratory. Jung, for his part, was concerned with the soul in its entirety.

He fully realized the ambitious nature of such an undertaking, but his patients forced him to embark upon it. By describing his own kind of psychology as "analytical" he acknowledged by implication that it was based to a considerable extent on psychoanalysis. For many years he was one of the most enthusiastic supporters of psychoanalysis, being both the founder and first president of the *Internationale Psychoanalytische Gesellschaft*. When the final break with Freud came in 1913, bitter reproaches and unjustified criticisms were bandied about on both sides; nevertheless, Jung has never failed to recognize that his collaboration with Freud did a great deal to enrich his own thought. The very name of his psychology shows this.

In 1935 Jung introduced a second term: "complex psychology". Unfortunately this expression is ambiguous: it was meant to describe the complex, universal character of his psychology, but it gives the general impression that his psychology is a psychology of "psychic complexes". Perhaps it was for this reason that the new term was only used in German. Even in the case of the Jung Institute in Zürich, which in German is officially known as the *Institut für Komplexe Psychologie*, the old form has been preserved in the French and English translations of the name: *Institut de Psychologie Analytique* and Institute for Analytical Psychology. In the present book I shall keep to the phrase "analytical psychology" to cover Jung's whole system of ideas.

"Analytical psychology" is a thing that can easily be defined in a single sentence, but the same is not true of "religion". In Jung's books this word is often merely a synonym for "religious attitude" or "subordination to some higher (psychic) power". In other cases it is applied to various religious denominations, as codified in definite dogmas and forms of ritual. Occasionally, for the sake of clarity Jung describes these denominations as "confessions" (*Konfessionen*). And then again the word "religion" can mean either Christianity as a whole or Catholicism in particular.

The fact that Jung so often speaks with open admiration of Catholicism should not blind us to the fact that by birth and education he was a Protestant and still gives himself out to be such today. In the following pages we shall have occasion to inquire into the real reasons for this paradoxical attitude, and its exact significance.

The problems that arise around the relationship between analytical psychology and religion derive from ideas actually put forward by Jung himself. This being so, it would be a mistake to examine the relationship in itself and then go on to criticize it on the basis of inessential data—for instance, by detailing the contents of some particular religious denomination and then contrasting this with the conclusions reached by analytical psychology. This would lead to an endless series of misunderstandings, all due to the fact that there was no common basis in the first place. It is therefore necessary to decide first upon the precise significance of the data provided by analytical psychology that come within our present scope. Only after a careful examination of these data can we decide what exactly "religion" means to Jung, and then go on to a serious comparison of the psychological and heological data that exist on the subject of religion.

It is therefore necessary to study the whole of Jung's work if one is to achieve a balanced view of it—a thing that he himself has never done, driven as he has been by an insatiable desire to penetrate ever more deeply into the hitherto unexplored regions of psychic life. Nevertheless, in this book I have only included those elements that are directly relevant to our subject, so that there shall be no overloading. Thus my silence, for instance, on the matter of Jung's typology, does not mean that I am unaware of it. I believe that for Jung himself it has a real importance. The only reason why I have not made any attempt to deal with it and other matters of a like importance here is that they seem to have very little relevance to the subject under discussion.[1]

The present critical study is based on an analysis of Jung's work as a whole—all the score of volumes and hundred articles of which need to be studied in their entirety. The theoretical

[1] Anyone who desires further information on these matters will find a good deal of enlightenment in the excellent introductions to Jung's work that have been published by two of his women collaborators: Toni Wolff, "Einführung in die Grundlagen der Komplexen Psychologie", an article published in the *Jung-Festschrift, Die kulturelle Bedeutung der Komplexen Psychologie*, pp. 1–168; and Dr. Jolande Jacobi, *The Psychology of C. G. Jung*.

points cannot however receive their full value unless they are examined in the light of their practical applications. Repeated personal contact with Jung and his closest collaborators is absolutely essential for a proper understanding of his actual writings. However, though entirely convinced of the need for this, and though I have been able to enjoy such contact, I have based my argument in the ensuing pages solely on Jung's official publications—feeling obliged to limit myself to his writings so as to avoid any over-personal interpretation on my part and also so as not to run any risk of including any of the ideas of his collaborators and pupils, who, though they may start from certain fundamental ideas supplied by their leader, can hardly avoid developing them in their own particular way. For the same reason I have refrained from making use of any of the many unpublished typewritten notes taken at Jung's study groups held at the *Eidgenössische Technische Hochschule* (E.T.H.) in Zürich. These lectures were written up by members of his audience and they are not lacking in interest, but they do not contain any theoretical points that are not treated fully by the author in his own writings, though they provide very valuable practical corollaries to them. I have strictly avoided using them, more particularly as Jung himself declines to accept any responsibility for them.

The foregoing considerations have led me to divide this book into two parts. The first contains an account of Jung's main ideas. This is absolutely essential, Jung himself never having published any general bird's-eye view of his psychological ideas to which reference can be made. Through his researches he has gradually accumulated a vast number of empirical facts and psychotherapeutic experiences. Anyone who aims to pass judgment on him is obliged in the first place to follow the development of his ideas. Otherwise, one ends—and this has often happened—with biased or contradictory conclusions, because one has failed to grasp his work as a whole as it has developed through the years. In an effort to avoid this major disaster I have paid scrupulous attention to the chronological sequence of Jung's writings, even including their sub-divisions, introductions, etc., whenever these date from a different period—and I have kept to this principle both in the body of the book and in the notes.[1]

We shall thus examine the empirical character of the method proper to analytical psychology. With a clear understanding of this "empiricism"—jealously defended by Jung—we shall be able to appreciate the fundamental insights of his science at their true value.

In the light of the conclusions reached in the first part, I shall endeavour in the second to determine what Jung means by "religion" or "religious attitude", and then investigate what function he ascribes to religions, in the sense of "confessions". From then on, genuine criticism will be possible. And I shall finally be able to test the implications of analytical psychology, which extend into the fields of dogmatic and pastoral theology.

[1] So that there shall be no doubt about the chronological order, to the reference that follows each quotation I have added in brackets the date of the year in which Jung first published the quoted passage. The reader should remember that this date will not always be the same as the date when the book in question first came out, particularly in the case of collected articles or a revised edition. The quotations themselves have been taken from English translations of Jung's works wherever these exist.

PART I

II

THE EMPIRICAL METHOD IN ANALYTICAL PSYCHOLOGY

It is no easy matter to decide exactly what method is followed by any new science. No doubt the innovator himself is aware, implicitly, of his own manner of proceeding. His real merit, indeed, lies not in bringing some hitherto unknown object to light, but in discovering a new way of looking at it, so that, having for centuries formed part of the heritage of human knowledge, it can be examined anew and the laws governing its structure and behaviour be revealed. Nevertheless it still remains true that the innovator is almost entirely concerned with results, and has very little interest in the irritating people who come along and ask him questions about the basis of his method or its implications. The best they can hope for from him is some casual reply such as: "Watch me while I'm at work." If they persist, and ask him why he has chosen this particular method, back comes the answer, like a flash: "I work like this because it brings results. You can try it if you want to make sure . . ."

Throughout his life Jung has followed a very definite method, but he has never thought it necessary to burden posterity with a treatise labelled *De Methodo Psychologica*. This is due not only to the fact that most of his time has been taken up with applied psychotherapy, but also in equal measure to his own personal aversion to any kind of systematization. He has for instance protested most energetically whenever anyone has presented his psychological views as a "system". Nevertheless, as is only to be expected, his books include a large number of passages that shed a great deal of light on one or other of his ways of proceeding in the matter of method. With the help of these I shall attempt to establish as rigorously as possible the empirical character of this method. Having thus delimited the theoretical side of his work, I shall go on to inquire, from his own point of view, into what exactly he means by "psychic". This practical approach will help us to grasp the full significance of his method whilst at the same time bringing out what he is actually aiming at.

I. A Non-Experimental Empirical Method

Both as doctor and as man of his age Jung has been too deeply affected by the natural sciences not to adopt their traditional way of procedure, aiming to establish necessary laws by generalizing from hypotheses proved by scientific experiment. The difficulties inherent in such a bold endeavour have with the passage of time caused his immediate claims to be expressed with increasing modesty. After fifty years of patient, painstaking research, his conclusion is: "Our psychological experience is still too recent and too limited in scope to permit of general theories. The investigator needs a lot more facts which would throw light on the nature of the psyche before he can begin to think of universally valid propositions."[1]

This—unfeigned—modesty is the result of an increasingly clear understanding of the difficulties inherent in psychological observation. The complex nature of the psychic phenomenon itself, and also the psychological observer's inevitable involvement in the phenomenon he is studying, make any investigation in the field of depth-psychology singularly difficult. As early as 1928 Jung pointed out these two obstacles, in his view well-nigh insurmountable. "The complex psychic phenomena that we are concerned with," he wrote, "are all outside the experimental field. The guinea-pigs of experimental psychology, the chronoscopes and cymographs, are of no use to us. The psychologist's observations are all personal observations, and his judgments all come from his own experience. In this field every theory is ultimately a subjective personal statement."[2]

[1] *The Practice of Psychotherapy*, p. 115 (1951).
[2] "Die Struktur der Seele," p. 27 (1928).

Later, Jung explained in even clearer terms why the psychologist desirous of establishing a science of the whole psyche cannot possibly be helped by experimentation.

"An experiment consists in asking a definite question which excludes as far as possible anything disturbing and irrelevant. It makes conditions, imposes them on Nature, and in this way forces her to give an answer to a question devised by man. She is prevented from answering out of the fullness of her possibilities since these possibilities are restricted as far as practicable. . . . If we want to know what these workings are, we need a method of enquiry which imposes the fewest possible conditions, or if possible no conditions at all, and then leaves Nature to answer out of her fullness. . . . The disadvantage, however, leaps to the eye: in contrast to the scientific experiment one does not know what has happened."[1]

Analytical psychology can therefore never be experimental except by sacrificing its very *raison d'être*, which is to study the psyche as a whole. Nevertheless, Jung insists on the empirical nature of his science. Now the empirical method is concerned to give an exact description of observed facts. When these facts are correlated with each other, hypotheses can be established, and these can both help towards a better understanding of subsequent observations and also reinforce the facts themselves. Thus the main, immediate aim behind Jung's empirical method remains the development of hypotheses. It is through them that he has laid the foundations of a positive science. But he has carefully abstained from making any prophecies about the development of this science, though nursing a hope that some day his pioneer work will be crowned by fulfilment. We shall take a closer look at the methodological significance of the scientific hypothesis.

An "hypothesis" in Jung's sense of the word, it may be worthwhile recalling, has nothing to do with a mere unproven assumption, though the familiar phrase, "It's a pure hypothesis", might lead one to think this. An hypothesis is an intellectual insight made in response to certain demands, the one that at some particular

[1] *The Interpretation of Nature and the Psyche*, 1951, pp. 49–51. Cf. *Allgemeines zur Komplextheorie*, pp. 6–7 (1934).

point in the research affords the simplest, fullest and most likely explanation of all the facts under review. As such it is not simply a statement of fact, nor is it any final intellectual acquisition; it is simply an intellectual tool to help subsequent research, and therein lies its whole justification. As the science advances it can just as easily be cast away as preserved: this can only really be decided by the—unforeseeable—development of knowledge in the field in question. Let us see what follows from this definition of the scientific hypothesis as conceived by Jung.[1]

It is clear, in the first place, that the facts we discover and the hypothesis we put forward to explain them condition each other to some extent. It is with this in mind that Jung agrees with Maréchal that to ask for a complete absence of prejudice or preconceived ideas is absurd, because impossible. "Assumptions are unavoidable, and this being so, it is wrong to pretend that we have made no assumptions."[2] To say that we have no preconceived ideas is to say that the mind is quite without previous knowledge, which means doing away with the very possibility of science, and empirical science in particular, based as it is on a series of observations. However, we can agree that there is indeed a kind of

[1] It may be worth while comparing Jung's latest conclusions with those reached in a study published by J. Maréchal in 1912: " Empirical Science and Religious Psychology " (to be found in *Studies in the Psychology of the Mystics*, London, 1927).

Maréchal divides scientific procedure into three stages—the establishment of observed empirical facts, the application of the laws of induction, and the theory, the statement of the reality (pp. 8–27). He goes on to make a criticism of the illegitimate claims advanced by scientific determinism in each of these three stages. In the first stage in particular he shows what great margins of error may exist, both quantitatively and qualitatively. Qualitatively, this is a result of the unavoidable influence exerted by the observing subject: " To observe a ' fact ' is at once to introduce it into a pre-existing mould, to class it to some extent, and to grasp not so much its original and individual features as those which it shares with other facts " (p. 8). Quantitatively, it is a result of the objective impossibility of an absolutely cast-iron quantitative measurement: " Particular observations have always to be ' corrected ' by a certain amount, however small, in order to follow the curve that expresses the law " (p. 10). Thus some sort of latent interpretation comes before any research has been engaged upon: " No observer is without ' prejudices ' and no one ever allows the facts to ' speak for themselves ', purely and simply—it being the nature of facts to be mute " (p. 11).

Jung's own view of the hypothesis exonerates him from Maréchal's strictures. Psychic facts, being perceived by a conscious subject and too complex to be grasped fully, remain hypothetical even in the final scheme into which—well or badly—we incorporate them.

[2] *Modern Man in Search of a Soul*, p. 142 (1929).

attitude that may be described as absence of prejudice. This comes into being when we regard our preconceived ideas simply as hypotheses in Jung's sense of the word; for by doing this we neutralize the ideas, and instead of tyrannizing over us without our being aware of it, they become a conscious help to us in the general framework of our researches.

Next, it follows from this that no hypothesis will ever be final, since it is essentially incomplete. If it is not invalidated by new facts, it will be enriched by new insights and obliged to undergo modifications. Aspects that have been over-emphasized will lose some of their weight and allow others to come forward into the limelight. On the other hand, it is not beyond the bounds of possibility that new discoveries will lead to a completely new presentation of the theory. But that is exceptional. An hypothesis will very rarely be found to be radically false, even though new data often oblige us to rethink our former views from the very beginning. The new synthesis will still be hypothetical, like the preceding one, but it will have a closer grasp of the observed facts. It may also happen that an hypothesis that has been abandoned for perfectly good reasons may be taken up again provisionally because the advances that have been made in the meantime have made it clear that two parallel hypotheses are required to explain the various aspects of some highly complex reality.

Now that we thoroughly understand this matter of the scientific hypothesis we shall no longer be amazed at Jung's obvious indifference to the contradictions and right-about-turns that so frequently occur in his work. These are particularly disconcerting to readers brought up on philosophy, who can usually only regard them as signs of a confusion of thought, an inability to create any system, or a complete disregard of logic. These people generally quite fail to recognize the truth behind Jung's words when he says to them, quite frankly: "Give me a better hypothesis, and I will come over to your side like a shot." They smile at this as though it was a joke, or else complain of his lack of a proper sense of gravity. But Jung cannot imagine anyone criticizing a hypothesis without having something better to put in its place. To reject a hypothesis for reasons that have nothing to do with the science in question is not, in his view, a very intelligent thing to do. Such a rejection only shows that the hypothesis is not absolutely true—which in fact is the essence of any hypothesis—and does nothing to safeguard the element of truth in it which is its very *raison d'être*. That is why Jung regards such condemnations as valueless, whereas when any new and fuller hypothesis is introduced he is always on its side at once. With the calm assurance of a seeker after truth who has grown old in its service, he can say: "Work in this field is pioneer work. I have often made mistakes and had many times to forget what I had learned. But I know and am content to know that as surely as light comes out of darkness, so truth is born of error. I have let Guglielmo Ferrero's *mot* about the 'misérable vanité du savant' serve me for a warning, and have therefore neither feared my mistakes nor seriously regretted them."[1] This passage, first published in 1942, does not appear in the earlier editions of *Über die Psychologie des Unbewussten*; nevertheless it reflects what has been Jung's attitude for a period of over thirty years. The passage from Guglielmo Ferrero was put at the front of *Wandlungen und Symbole der Libido* in 1911. The same passage reappears in the revised edition published in 1952. It thus dominates all Jung's incessant activity and patient labour, and gives the answer to the problem of all the contradictions that have been made so much of by the less perceptive critics of analytical psychology.

The passage is indeed important and significant enough to be quoted in full:

> Therefore theory, which gives to facts their value and significance, is often very useful, even if it is partially false, for it throws light on phenomena which no one observes, it forces an examination, from many angles, of facts which no one had hitherto studied, and it gives the impulse for more extended and more productive researches.
>
> It is, therefore, a moral duty for the man of science to expose himself to the risk of committing error and to submit to criticism in order that science may continue to progress. A

[1] *Two Essays on Analytical Psychology*, p. 116 (1942).

writer has attacked the author for this very severely, saying, here is a scientific ideal very limited and very paltry. But those who are endowed with a mind sufficiently serious and impersonal as not to believe that all that they write is the expression of truth absolute and eternal, approve of this theory which places the aims of science well above the miserable vanity and paltry "amour propre" of the scientists.[1]

If Jung remains faithful to his principles, then, his work will show an endless series of fluctuations. This is what makes his books so hard to follow unless they are seen in the light of the general development of his thought. Hence my determination to discover the exact chronological sequence of his main statements on every important point. If this procedure is not adopted it becomes all too easy to manufacture an impressive list of "flagrant contradictions", as some critics have done most enthusiastically, unfortunately, however, only demonstrating thereby their complete failure to understand Jung's method, which aims at absolute scientific honesty and hence refuses to regard itself as infallible. In a number of the ensuing chapters, particularly those concerned with archetypes and religion, an attempt will be made at this kind of chronological interpretation.

The kind of attitude favoured by Jung is not an easy one for the scholar to appreciate—nor for anyone trying to study Jung's thought and reduce it to an intelligible, if not a final, systematic form. But as it is the consequence of a sincerely held scientific position we should be delighted that Jung has held on to it so firmly and been so modest about the results it has yielded. "No practical science," he says, "can get along without its tricks of the trade [*Handwerksregeln*]. That is the way to look at anything I may say about the structure of the soul. There is no question of my producing incontrovertible truths—they are simply ideas thrown out in an attempt to bring a bit of order into the bewildering conglomeration of psychic realities. . . . All our present psychological theories are subjective assertions which we defend jealously,

[1]This passage, taken from G. Ferrero, *Les lois psychologiques du Symbolisme*, p. 7, is reproduced at the front of *The Psychology of the Unconscious* (1911) and occurs again in " The Unconscious in the Normal and the Pathological Mind " (1942) (in *Two Essays on Analytical Psychology*) and *Symbole der Wandlung*, p. 2 (1952).

in a highly partisan spirit, because they echo powerful currents in the human soul. When we have amassed something like all these assertions we shall be able at some future date to compare them together and so reach a deeper understanding of the nature of the soul. In the meantime the founder of any psychological theory must try to reconcile himself to the fact that he will be not only a founder but a martyr as well . . ."[1]

The real aim behind Jung's researches, then, is the establishment of scientific hypotheses on the basis of observed psychic facts.

II. The Object of Analytical Psychology

This outline of the theoretical side of Jung's method needs to be complemented by an investigation into the way he has applied it in practice. With this end in view, I shall now try to discover what Jung conceives the object of his science to be.

Jung practises psychology. Now in his view psychic reality is a kind of absolute. Here again he is only putting forward an hypothesis. He regards the realm of the psychic as *sui generis*, since he is not aware of any valid proof that the field of the psychic can be reduced to that of the physical. Not that he denies that the two fields interact: he has often come across cases of this that have left him in no doubt about it whatsoever. Body and soul, the physical and the psychical, condition each other, undoubtedly. But the how and the why of this interaction are not in his view available to us in the present state of our knowledge, and for this reason he prefers not to make too much of the fact or put forward any unproved assumptions—being content to leave this thorny problem to the psychologists of the future. So long as there is no proof to the contrary, he will continue to regard psychic reality as a thing specifically different from physical reality. "The materialistic hypothesis is too daring altogether: it goes beyond the available data and slips over into 'metaphysical' arrogance. In the present state of our knowledge all we can assert with absolute certainty is our total ignorance of the actual essence of psychic reality. This being so, it would be quite ridiculous to regard

[1] "Die Struktur der Seele", pp. 28 and 27 (1928).

psychic reality as a secondary product or an epiphenomenon, when we have good reasons for regarding it, hypothetically at least, as a factor *sui generis* . . ."[1]

The essence of psychic reality, then, escapes us for the moment; but we can still get some idea of what is involved in it.

There is, to begin with, human consciousness, that is to say man's power to relate situations, people, things, to his own ego. But to narrow the idea of psychic reality down still further, we must add that more precisely it is whatever in these situations, people and things relates to the ego, and in so far as it relates to it—no matter what particular mode of existence these psychic realities may have when they are regarded from another angle—from the angle of medicine, for instance, or philosophy. As soon as these things, which may be inside or outside the subject, exert any psychic influence, they are psychologically real.[2] Anything that has any influence on the subject, then, is real in a psychic sense: "Das was wirkt, ist wirklich".[3]

Jung therefore has no difficulty in accepting the philosophers' view that the spirits that haunt the world of primitive man do not exist, if in their own field the philosophers give valid proofs that this is so. But he would still go on to maintain that these "non-existent" spirits are real from the psychological point of view because they have a harmful or beneficent influence on some patient of his. In the same way, he will accept a doctor's diagnosis that a patient is suffering from an imaginary cancer, and agree with the surgeon who as a result of this refuses to perform an operation for it, but he will still assert that the cancer is a "psychic reality" for the patient, and that the patient needs an "operation" of a psychological kind at the hands of the psychotherapist. The fact that a spirit may be a projection and a cancer imaginary does not affect their psychic reality, which can only be judged by the particular individual concerned.

In these two examples we are faced with a psychic reality of

[1] " Über den Archetypus ", p. 263 (1936).

[2] Jung often says that these psychic objects are psychologically *true*. I have avoided using this word and chosen " real " instead, so as to avoid sowing confusion in anyone's mind: " true " is usually taken to be synonymous with " objective ", i.e., " existing independently of the knowing subject ".

[3] " Über das Unbewusste ", p. 550 (1918).

a subjective kind, that is to say, a reality known to a certain individual and only referring to his own particular case, so that we cannot draw any conclusions or inferences from it with regard to other individuals of the same species. But if the same kind of view about a particular psychic reality is found in a great number of individuals, we have a consensus of opinion on that particular point. In that case there is a psychic reality of an objective kind, constituting an undeniable fact. A striking example of this kind of objective psychic reality, and one which Jung returns to again and again, is the idea of God. All peoples at all times have had some sort of conception of God, says Jung, in this agreeing with the latest findings of comparative religion. The idea of God is therefore a psychic reality, whatever the philosophers may have to say about it. As early as 1911 Jung had stressed this point: "When an idea is so old, and also generally believed, it is probably true in some way, and, indeed, as is mostly the case, is not literally true, but is true psychologically."[1] In 1939 he said again: "The imagination itself is a psychic occurrence, and therefore whether an 'enlightenment' is called 'real' or 'imaginary' is quite immaterial . . . Yes, even if all religious reports were nothing but conscious inventions and falsifications, a very interesting psychological treatise could still be written on the fact of such lies, with the same scientific treatment with which the psychopathology of delusions is presented . . ."[2] In the revised edition of *Symbole der Wandlung* Jung still maintains his position of 1911 when he says, "When any idea is so old and universally admired it must be true in some way or other, particularly *psychologically true*."[3]

These individual and collective psychic facts—the first, in Jung's terminology, being subjective, the second objective—form the starting-point of all his research. It is essential to grasp this point before one can understand anything about depth psychology. Many people, when they try to find out what an "archetype" or a "complex" really is, will often scrutinize one group of external realities after another. They find nothing bearing the slightest resemblance to either of these things, any more than a surgeon

[1] *The Psychology of the Unconscious*, p. 4 (1911).
[2] Introduction, in Suzuki, *An Introduction to Zen Buddhism*, p. 15 (1939).
[3] *Symbole der Wandlung*, p. 10 (1952). Jung's italics.

comes across a human soul when he is operating on a human body, for the simple reason that psychic realities belong to a different order from external objects. Unfortunately in some cases they can seem to become identical with some particular object, for instance, in the case of a mother complex, with a real mother. It is one of Jung's greatest achievements to have managed, throughout all the chances and changes of his investigations, to hang on to the specific nature of psychic phenomena. In doing so he has fought a successful battle against the scientific materialism of his age, which tends to regard all such phenomena as, fundamentally, simply transformations or later developments of something essentially physical in origin.

This opposition to scientific determinism led Jung to try to prove amongst other things that the idea of God is a psychic reality. He was astonished to discover that this roused a wave of opposition from the side of believers—particularly those of the Protestant persuasion—who rushed to the conclusion that he was saying that the idea of God is nothing but psychological. In their view any assertion of psychic reality was equivalent to a denial of ontological reality. It does indeed seem as though in the early stages of his career Jung was content to be an agnostic so as to allow himself a certain latitude, and by so doing he laid himself open to the charge of psychologism which has ever since been made against him. In later life, however, he has more than once sharply attacked this interpretation of his attitude as being grossly mistaken. In his commentary on *Das Tibetanische Totenbuch*, which was edited by his friend Wilhelm, he took up the cudgels against his two brands of opponent: "Metaphysical utterances are utterances made by the soul (psyche) and hence psychological. But the Western mind takes this truth, which is self-evident, to be either something too obvious to be worth mentioning, in the sense that with a resentment only too well-known it is delighted with such an explanation because it gets rid of the object, or else it takes it to be a denial of metaphysical truth, and hence unacceptable. For the people of the Western world the word 'psychological' always seems to mean 'only psychological' . . ."[1]

[1] Introduction to *Das Tibetanische Totenbuch*, p. 18 (1935).

Jung therefore wants on the one hand to bring out the special, specific nature of psychic realities; and on the other hand he insists that this tells us nothing either for or against the ultimate ontological reality of the things in question.

So far I have been describing psychic reality by reference to human consciousness. This may seem surprising, in view of the fact that we are discussing the object of depth psychology. But it must not be forgotten that this science was obliged in its early stages to define itself by what it was setting itself up against—the psychology of human consciousness. The reason for this is perfectly simple: all new discoveries appear as denials of or exceptions to what has been previously known. The initial discovery made by analytical psychology was the presence of disturbances in association experiments. When Jung went more deeply into this he found what Freud had found: the existence of "affective complexes" showed that the realm of the psychic did not merely include what the person consciously related to his ego but everything that by its nature—and before any conscious reference was made—related to the ego. This gave Jung his first glimpse into the unconscious, the realm to which depth psychology was to devote all its attention, determined to get to the bottom of it. Previously this vast field, being as it is well nigh inaccessible to direct inspection, had only been vaguely divined and had never been explored systematically. To this field both Freud and Jung gave the name of "the unconscious", though they gave the word a very different meaning in each case; and to it can be applied all the more strongly all that has been said about the psychic reality that is actively connected up with consciousness: it is an irreducible whole, independent of ontological or any other considerations. As Jung's investigations proceeded he realized more and more that the attempt to describe the psychic through its connection with the ego was worse than insufficient: it was mistaken.

Freud had conceived the unconscious as a composite of repressed psychic elements, which because they were repressed acted independently of the ego. Jung's view, on the other hand, was that besides this unconscious, which he accepted unhesitatingly as the "personal unconscious", there existed a more fundamental level still, common to all men and hence properly to be described as the "collective unconscious". This collective unconscious was not the result of any repression but lay at the very root of consciousness as its non-activated *a priori* form. This hypothesis, of a general or collective unconscious independent of the ego, obliged Jung to postulate some higher instance able to synthesize these two elements, the ego and the unconscious. If there were no such power there could be no possible interaction between the two. Jung called this power the *Selbst* or "self", and justified his use of the word as "a term on the one hand definite enough to convey the sum of human wholeness and on the other hand indefinite enough to express the indescribable and indeterminable nature of this wholeness".[1]

The "self", as the "total personality, really present [*vorhandene*] but unable to be grasped in its totality",[2] refers to the psychic realm as a whole. It is therefore the principal object of analytical psychology.

It will probably be objected that this way of going about things brings singularly little light, the psychic being described as everything that relates to the "self" and the "self" itself being the psychic realm as a whole; but this kind of objection is not always valid in psychology. Jung, as an observer of empiric facts, is not concerned with giving definitions: he gives a name to the psychic realities he finds by analysis, studies their conscious significance and tries to discover their unconscious activity. A moment comes, usually after decades of patient, painstaking comparison of the facts,[3] when he decides that it looks as though he can produce some more general rule or fundamental concept. Then he is prepared to risk giving it a name, without suggesting, however, that he has said the last word on the subject. All his

[1] *Psychology and Alchemy*, p. 18 (1944).

[2] *Aion*, p. 18 (1951).

[3] In his written work Jung only refers explicitly to the *self* after 1930, but he has assured me privately that he began to glimpse the importance of this psychic power as early as 1915. It took twenty years' thought and experiment before he could produce a satisfactory description of it. He refers to a similar maturing process in the case of the archetypes and the collective unconscious (*Two Essays on Analytical Psychology*, pp. 121–2), the four main functions (*Psychological Types*, pp. xi, 20), the mandalas (*Psychology and Alchemy*, pp. 94–5) etc.

definitions, which never reach the essence but are concerned solely with the functions of psychic realities, are really only descriptions growing increasingly closer and more subtly shaded.

To Jung, as to Freud, Binswanger's remarks about the various outlines of depth psychology apply with equal force: "Freud's psychic scheme might be compared, superficially, with those sketches of the organs of the body upon which lung and heart specialists plot their medical data. But these people only need pencil and paper to draw the particular organ in question, whereas Freud had first of all to imagine the organ itself at the end of numerous experiments which could only be brought into any sort of order after much thought . . . The psychic apparatus is as much an organ as a medical sketch."[1]

It is in this way that the self is to be understood—as a transcendent psychic reality postulated by experience but not directly accessible to inspection, subsuming all the other realities and ensuring their unity. Only those who study Jung's empirical material according to the method that he himself inaugurated can appreciate the accuracy of this description and be in a position to make any criticism of it that is not irrelevant to its subject because unaware of its method.

It is clear from the preceding pages that Jung's method can never be experimental, because it aims to study the realm of psychic reality as a whole. It is nevertheless an empirical method because it aims to create scientific hypotheses on the basis of observed fact.

The first of these hypotheses is concerned with the irreducible nature of psychic reality. Psychic reality is, on the one hand, neither a derivatory form nor an epiphenomenon of physical reality; on the other hand it is quite independent of any metaphysical or ontological view of existence. As long as we stick to this specific nature of psychic reality, all the "organs" of the psychic apparatus conceived by Jung will retain their own very definite meaning, not only when they are referred to in obviously technical terms—collective unconscious, archetype, self—but also

[1] Ludwig Binswanger, *Ausgewählte Vorträge und Aufsätze*, pp. 171–2. Cf. Jung's preface to V. White, *God and the Unconscious*, pp. xx–xxi (1953).

when they are described in everyday language—soul, image, idea. To avoid any possibility of misunderstanding or ambiguity, through the present work these latter expressions will be replaced as far as possible by their technical equivalents—psyche, imago, representation. Great care will need to be taken if we are to avoid being led astray by the inevitable ambiguity of certain terms that will be used. How are misunderstandings to be avoided if some technical term, say "soul", for instance, which is used as a synonym for "psyche", is confused with its clearly defined philosophical and theological equivalent, or, worse still, its vague, equivocal equivalent as used in common speech? Our sciences, specialized as they are to an extreme degree but by no means synthesized into a general whole, force us to a fundamental probity if we wish to come to any real understanding or make any fair judgement.

To avoid as far as possible the rocks of ambiguity, we must now go on to investigate the main fundamental views of analytical psychology as they have gradually developed. Our enquiry into Jung's empiric method should have provided us with a solid basis for our later considerations.

III

THE FUNDAMENTAL VIEWS OF ANALYTICAL PSYCHOLOGY

BEFORE we go on to the actual subject of this chapter we must pause to consider a question that arises immediately. How does Jung stand in relation to Freud?

The usual answer only seems to take into account the matter of their respective birthdays, whereby Freud is presented as the innovator, the master, and Adler and Jung begin by being his disciples and end up as rebels.[1] This answer undoubtedly has the advantage of being brief; but it is far too gross a simplification of the actual facts of the case, and so obliges us to go into the matter in rather more detail.

Freud was incontestably the pioneer of genius to whom all forms of depth psychology owe their existence and a considerable proportion of their actual development. Nevertheless, Freud's greatest claim to fame is not the discovery of the unconscious as such—others before him, philosophers rather than doctors, had suspected the existence of some unconscious zone[2]—but the fact of having drawn the attention of people in general to practical methods that could lead to the discovery of its structure and activity. Freud was the first person to bring out the importance of dreams and free association and to break through to these

[1] Jung's view of this is slightly different. He says that Freud's exclusivism led Adler to react in a diametrically opposite direction, and he himself synthesized their two partial attitudes. Later, in Chapter IV, I shall examine this view of the affair.

[2] Jung himself includes in his list of these " predecessors " Leibnitz, Kant and Schelling, and, more particularly, Dr. C. G. Carus. It is worth noting that the first three, whose works Jung had read in his youth, were quite unknown to Freud. Moreover, they never bothered with any empirical psychology. Even Carus only went in for purely theoretical speculations, which came to the forefront again as a result of the discoveries made by depth psychology. His book, published in 1846, had fallen into oblivion, and it was only republished in the nineteen-twenties. Cf. *Introduction to a Science of Mythology*, p. 98 (1940).

hitherto impenetrable manifestations of psychic life. After a series of minute observations he succeeded in enumerating the mechanisms that have ever since formed the principal weapons in the arsenal of every kind of psychotherapy. Repression, condensation, displacement, dramatization, symbolization, are all so many keys to the meaning of dreams and other unconscious products. But Freud was not so much interested in the make-up of these mechanisms as he was in finding the real causes that lay behind hysteria, the psychic disturbance that formed the starting-point of all his researches.

Freud believed that he had found by analysis that the last link in the causal chain of psychic illness was always some disturbance in the invalid's sexual development. In the beginning he attributed these disturbances to external causes such as seduction by adults; later he attributed them almost entirely to internal causes like arrested development at an infantile stage of sexuality. These disturbances, he thought, especially when grafted on to some hereditary tendency, were repressed into the unconscious until some cause or other made the tension they caused intolerable, whereupon they suddenly burst out in the form of neurosis. He believed that the repression was in fact exerted by a factor later defined as the censorship of the super-ego, which prevented the real cause from making any direct appearance. The neurosis thus took a form that hid the original disturbance—the sexual trauma itself, and all its subsequent activity, remaining buried in the unconscious. The only thing that could emerge into consciousness was the camouflaged form. Freud did not exclude hereditary tendencies and external circumstances from the genesis of neuroses, far from it; but in his view the decisive and essential factor was sexual disturbance.

As Freud's first aim was to make his work scientific, he applied the laws of cause and effect, as understood by the natural sciences, to his experimental data. Inevitably, then, if the cause was a sexual one, the effect must be assumed to be of the same order, and if it was not obviously so, this must be because it was hidden behind some sort of disguise—a real but camouflaged sexuality. Freud held firmly to this principle throughout all the changes that took place in his various explanations—and indeed there is no avoiding this conclusion if one adopts a realist point of view. Seen realistically, the causal explanation requires that the cause itself shall be ontologically—or as a *Ding an sich*—what it seems to be in any given relationship. These two points—the "reification"[1] of sexuality, and its prime importance in explaining neurosis—became the focus of Jung's attack, even during the years of his most intense collaboration with Freud.

Jung was not in fact a pupil of Freud's in the strict sense of the word. He says again and again that he discovered the unconscious and the complexes independently of Freud, as a result of his experiments in connection with the matter of word-associations. During these experiments, which are described in detail in his *Diagnostische Assoziationsstudien* (1906–7), he had been struck by mistakes made in repeating words and anomalies in reaction times which were to a large extent due to inhibitions or persistences. Generally speaking the people who were the subjects of these experiments were quite unaware of their errors, and when they were conscious of them they had no idea what caused them. It was not long before Jung realized that these mistakes and anomalies revolved round certain centres that were very highly charged affectively. These centres became known as "affective complexes" (*gefühlsbetonte Komplexe*).[2]

Encouraged by his own discovery of the complexes that influence man's psychic life, Jung began to study Freud's writings on psychoanalysis, particularly his *Interpretation of Dreams*. He has acknowledged his debt to this book: he took his analysis of dreams from Freud, and he also accepted the psychological importance of transference. We shall even see, when we come to the part played by religion in his philosophy, how he follows in Freud's footsteps in his explanation of the genesis of religion—in one of his earliest essays, "The Significance of the Father

[1] "Reification" means regarding sexuality as an independent entity (a *Ding* or *res*) and not as an element in a higher whole.

[2] See "On Psychology and Pathology of so-called Occult Phenomena" in *Collected Papers on Analytical Psychology* (1902); "Reaction Time in Association Experiments," in *Studies in Word Association* (1905); "Über das Unbewusste," p. 541 (1918); and *The Development of Personality*, p. 67 (1924).

in the Destiny of the Individual" ("Die Bedeutung des Vaters für das Schicksal des Einzelnen," 1909).

But despite his sincere admiration for Freud, he was never one of his orthodox disciples. Even when he was taking most of his theories and nearly all his technique from Freud he still claimed to be an independent investigator. He was quite ready to be inspired by Freud's work and discoveries, and to go on to develop and, where necessary, rectify them, but as early as 1906 he was making serious reservations about some of the most important points. "Fairness to Freud does not, however, signify, as many fear, conditionless surrender to a dogma; indeed, independent judgment can very well be maintained beside it. If I, for instance, recognize the complex mechanisms of dreams and hysteria, it by no means signifies that I ascribe to the infantile sexual trauma the exclusive importance seemingly attributed to it by Freud. Still less does it mean that I place sexuality so preponderantly in the foreground, or that I even ascribe to it the psychological universality which Freud apparently postulates under the impression of the very powerful role which sexuality plays in the psyche. As for Freud's therapy, it is at best a possible one, and perhaps does not always offer what one expects from it theoretically. Nevertheless, all these are quite incidental and completely vanish beside the psychological principles, the discovery of which is Freud's greatest merit."[1]

It would be more accurate to present Jung as a collaborator, then, rather than as one of the great man's disciples. The above deferential way of referring to Freud occurs several times in his writings round about 1911–12—the result, perhaps, of his fear that some sort of break was imminent? For the difference of opinion that had first appeared in 1906 was still there underground. When the final break came in 1913 it was largely due to differing attitudes towards the libido. "When Freud publicly declared that psychoanalysis and his sexual theory were indissolubly wedded, I was obliged to strike out on a different path: as I was unable to endorse his one-sided views."[2]

[1] *The Psychology of Dementia Praecox*, pp. iii–iv (1906).
[2] *The Development of Personality*, pp. 96–7 (1924).

I. The Energic Conception of the Libido

Jung was sceptical about the sexual libido from the beginning. This was not because of any longing for arbitrary simplification or groundless generalizations. He was quite aware that Freud's theory came after much patient observation of hysterical neurosis. But Freud's terminology seemed to him unacceptable, although at the beginning he did his best to sugar the pill. "Freud's terms should not be always regarded as strictly united concepts, but rather as occasional expressions of a language rich in new forms. Those who write about Freud should avoid logomachy but should keep in mind the essence of the thing."[1]

Soon, however, Jung had to give in. Freud was quite certain about the truth of his own ideas, and he endowed the libido with a sexual significance which, if it was not absolutely all-inclusive, was very pronounced indeed. Jung rejected this unjustified extension of the term categorically. "The term 'sexuality' is quite firmly established and its meaning is so precise that the word 'love' cannot possibly be identified with it. Yet Freud often means 'love' when he says, 'sexuality', as can easily be seen in a large number of passages."[2]

In his first book of any considerable scope, *Wandlungen und Symbole der Libido* (*The Psychology of the Unconscious*). Jung made one last attempt to salvage the sexual libido, at the same time manhandling Freud's theory until it was barely recognizable. Not surprisingly, Freud, conscious of the way Jung had mutilated his theory, rejected the proffered olive branch categorically. This attempt at a resolution of their differences in fact revealed the fundamental opposition between the two investigators, and thereafter Jung continued his researches entirely on his own. But his own theory provoked a good deal of misunderstanding, due in part at least to a lack of precision in his presentation of it. Another fifteen years passed before, in 1928, he returned to a purely theoretical treatment of his ideas of 1913 and he then formulated them

[1] "Psycho-analysis and Association Experiments," in *Studies in Word Association*, p. 297 (1906).

[2] "Über das Unbewusste", pp. 542–3 (1918). Cf. *Contributions to Analytical Psychology*, p. 111 (1928).

clearly in the "energic" theory he put forward. And so, before going on with the practical differences of 1913, we must now examine this work, published under the title *Über die Energetik der Seele.*[1]

Jung, like Freud, relies on the methods used in the natural sciences, but he tries to get away to some extent from the mechanistic point of view. In point of fact the natural sciences are not unaware of the energic point of view themselves. Jung gives an excellent description of the two complementary conceptions. "The mechanistic view is purely causal; from this standpoint an event is conceived as the result of a cause, in the sense that immutable substances change their relationships to one another according to fixed laws. The energic view-point on the other hand is in essence final; the event is traced from effect to cause on the assumption that energy forms the essential basis of changes in phenomena, that it maintains itself as a constant throughout these changes. . . . Both view-points are indispensable for the comprehension of physical phenomena, and therefore both have attained a general recognition . . . The predominance of the one or of the other standpoint depends less upon the objective behaviour of things than upon the psychological attitude of the investigator. . . . Both tendencies are liable to the error in thought of hypostasizing their principles because of the so-called objective facts of experience. They make the mistake of assuming that the subjective concept is identical with the behaviour of things . . . We must always bear in mind that, despite the most beautiful coincidence between the facts and our ideas, our explanatory principles are none the less only points of view, that is, phenomena of the psychological and aprioristic conditions under which thinking takes place."[2]

Clearly, it is not Jung's aim to eliminate the mechanistic or causal point of view. But he is afraid that it has taken up too big a place, with the result that no one in psychology ever imagines that there might possibly be another side to the question just as important as the first. And Jung emphasizes again that it was

[1] The bulk of this work is published in *Contributions to Analytical Psychology.*
[2] *Contributions to Analytical Psychology,* pp. 1–4 (1928).

through having lost all sight of the energic view-point that Freud had come to see nothing but the sexual element in his analysis. Though his conclusions are based on a large number of observations, which may themselves be able to be explained entirely by his own particular theory, he plumps for a one-sided, and therefore false, attitude. This attitude is all the more dangerous in that it inevitably reifies sexuality and is in fact based on a *petitio principii*. "The reduction of a complex structure to sexuality is only a valid causal explanation if it is agreed beforehand that we are interested only in explaining the function of the sexual component in complex structures. But if we accept the reduction to sexuality as valid, this can be only with the tacit presupposition that we are dealing with an exclusively sexual structure. To assume this, however, is to assert *a priori* that a complex psychic structure can only be a sexual structure, a manifest *petitio principii*!"[1]

Let us, then, take a closer look into what is involved in this energic point of view. In its analysis of physical or psychic processes it leaves out everything connected with substance, and cause and effect, and concentrates on the amount of energy in the particular process in question. No matter what the cause, therefore, it only discusses its energic relationships—whatever the thing in question may be. The quality of the thing does not enter into it: all that is measured is the quantitative intensity of the energy. This energy is itself a pure concept, or, to be more precise, an abstraction that has no existence in itself at all. In the thing this purely quantitative energy only exists in connection with objects which carry it along and get rid of it: "In my view, this concept is synonymous with psychic energy. Psychic energy is the intensity of the psychic process . . . I do not hypostatize the concept of energy."[2]

What new horizons does this open up?

In the first place the energic theory makes real development possible, as a result of genuine displacements of energy. Jung devotes a considerable number of chapters in *The Psychology of*

[1] *Contributions to Analytical Psychology*, p. 22, n. 1 (1928).
[2] *Psychological Types*, p. 571 (1921).

the Unconscious to this problem, in an effort to escape from the unavoidable consequences of postulating a sexual libido.

In Freud's system, says Jung, discussing the Three Essays, there is indeed a displacement of the libido. But as the libido itself is essentially sexual, any sublimation of it is in fact a more or less obvious distortion of it and fails to hide its true nature from the expert eye of the analyst. The gulf between its fundamentally sexual character and the ethical, or aesthetic, or religious disguise it may wear, condemns any sort of sublimation as something essentially false. Freud recognizes, however, besides the libido or the sexual instinct, the existence of instinctive forces whose precise nature is not yet known: "Freud's original conception does not interpret 'everything sexual', although this has been asserted by critics, but recognizes the existence of certain forces, the natures of which are not well known; to which Freud, however, compelled by the notorious facts which are evident to any layman, grants the capacity to receive 'affluxes of libido'. The hypothetical idea at the basis is the symbol of the '*Triebbündel*' (bundle of impulses), wherein the sexual impulse figures as a partial impulse of the whole system."[1]

Freud was nevertheless quite convinced that the pathological manifestations of neurosis that he had had under observation derived essentially from displacements of the libido. He himself says so quite clearly: "The energy of the sexual instinct is not merely one of the forces that bring on morbid manifestations. I emphasize expressly that in neuroses it is the only constant source of energy. It is also, beyond any shadow of doubt, the most important."[2] This theory, which regards the "libidinous" contributions to the other instincts, themselves irreducible, as essentially, indeed entirely, responsible for neurotic disorders, Jung calls "descriptive".

In *The Psychology of the Unconscious* Jung makes no attempt to dispute the value of this etiological explanation, in the matter of neurosis. But it gave him no help in explaining the genesis of

[1] *Psychology of the Unconscious*, p. 77 (1911).

[2] S. Freud, *Three Essays on Sexuality* (*Drei Abhandlungen zur Sexualtheorie*, in *Gesammelte Werke*, V, p. 62). Quoted by Jung in *Psychology of the Unconscious*, p. 77.

dementia praecox, which he had studied more closely than Freud. "In *dementia praecox*, on the contrary, not merely that portion of libido which is saved in the well known specific sexual repression is lacking for reality,[1] but much more than one could write down to the account of sexuality in a strict sense."[2] In an attempt to discover an explanation of this kind of mental disorder Jung resolutely embarked upon a new route, encouraged by the fact "that our teacher also, when he lays his hand on the delicate material of the paranoic psychology, was forced to doubt the applicability of the conception of libido held by him at that time."[3]

Against Freud's "descriptive" theory Jung set up a "genetic" theory which allowed him to identify the libido with psychic energy. On the one hand he accepts the fact that the reality function is only to a small degree made up of sexual libido and is mainly constituted by other instincts of an irreducible kind, but on the other hand he asks whether "philogenetically the function of reality is not, at least in great part, of sexual origin."[4]

The pages in which Jung develops his theory are more like a lyrical flight than a description of empiric fact. He suggests that the libido in the course of its genetic evolution appeared in the beginning at the sexual level only, i.e., in the reproductive instinct, "in the form of an undifferentiated sexual primal libido, as an energy of growth, which clearly forces the individual towards division, budding, etc."[5] It produced millions of ova and sperms in one single tiny creature. Bit by bit, first in the higher animals, then in man, it changed. The energy which had been restricted to feverish reproduction—without there being any security measures for that which was reproduced—rose in the higher animals to some sort of cultural level at which male and female sought each other out, recognized each other's existence and helped each other in looking after their less numerous progeny. As soon as man appeared, this ascending movement took on a still wider reference. New displacements of the libido led to

[1] The reality function is taken by Jung from Janet, whose lectures he had attended in Paris.

[2] *Psychology of the Unconscious*, p. 79 (1911).

[3] Ibid., p. 79.

[4] Ibid., p. 80.

[5] Ibid., p. 82.

genuine culture that could transcend nature. The various forms of this culture, however, despite their great degree of differentiation, still preserve traces of their origin in the more or less hidden sexual symbolism that even today accompanies the production of fire and working the earth.

This "daring assumption"[1] posits a proto-libido that appears exclusively at the level of procreation. As soon as it breaks up into different elements it becomes desexualized, for it loses its original function—the formation of ova and sperms—and is incapable of rediscovering it. This evolving process, therefore, consists of a progressive absorption of successive libidinous affluxes by other instinctive mechanisms. It is thus impossible, in Jung's view, to put this desexualized libido—either in animals or in man—in the category of sexuality. "A similar nomenclature would then lead us to classify the Cathedral of Cologne as mineralogy because it is built of stone."[2]

The movement of sexuality from the libido to secondary functions continues today. When it succeeds Jung calls it sublimation; when it fails, repression. And he sums up his account of the matter as follows: "The descriptive Freudian standpoint of psychology accepts the multiplicity of instincts, among which is the sexual instinct, as a special phenomenon; moreover, it recognizes certain affluxes of libido to non-sexual instincts. Quite otherwise is the genetic standpoint. It regards the multiplicity of instincts as issuing from a relative unity, the primal libido; it recognizes that definite amounts of the primal libido are split off, as it were, associated with newly formed functions and finally merged in them." And, says Jung: "In this way we attain an insight into certain primitive conditions of the function of reality. It would be radically wrong to say that its compelling power is a sexual one. It was a sexual one to a large extent."[3]

Jung is thus able to identify the libido with the sense of reality genetically, whilst at the same time presenting each as *sui generis* in its present condition. Nevertheless a real feeling of dissatisfaction remains after struggling through these tightly-packed

[1] *Psychology of the Unconscious*, p. 81.
[2] Ibid., p. 80.
[3] Ibid., p. 83.

pages—which, as the author himself confesses, gave rise to a great deal of misunderstanding. These misunderstandings originate from the ambiguity centring round the phrase "undifferentiated sexual libido". Most likely Jung had no desire to clear up this ambiguity, for fear of making his disagreement with Freud even more obvious than it was already! But what exactly is this "proto-libido"? Is it, quite simply, the sexual instinct, as one is tempted to infer from the fact that it is said to become desexualised? Or is it merely the ultimate undifferentiated force that informs all the various instincts in turn? Whatever the answer to these questions may be, it is quite certain that for Jung this proto-libido is everything. One is almost tempted to hazard a paradox and say that Freud rejected Jung's explanation so as not to be accused of pansexualism! But it is just as likely that he reacted so violently because he realised quite clearly that reducing everything to the libido meant depriving the libido of its specifically sexual nature. This was what in fact happened in Jung's case when, free from all remaining obstacles, he made his position quite clear by emphasizing the importance of the energic point of view. Thereafter, the libido lost all its sexual significance, retaining only a quantitative value and becoming synonymous with psychic energy.

When, nearly forty years later, Jung returned to *The Psychology of the Unconscious*, intending to bring out a new and completely revised edition under a new title, *Symbole der Wandlung*, he made no changes in his account of Freud's ideas. But he brought his own ideas up to date by mentioning the energic theory. "The libido clearly signifies uncontrolled psychic impulse and is wide enough to include all human tendencies. It becomes *the idea of 'tendency' pure and simple* [*ein Begriff des Intendierens überhaupt*]."[1]

The energic point of view thus helps us to understand how Jung's theory differs from Freud's.[2] Nevertheless, Jung went on

[1] *Symbole der Wandlung*, p. 225 (1952). Jung's italics.

[2] In the above account, Freud's ideas are presented as he developed them on the basis of his own observations up to 1912. His later development, though interesting, does not come within the scope of this book. I have restricted myself to the points that are relevant to the study of Jung, and the reader should remember this: it applies to all the remarks about Freud that will be found later on in the book.

using the term, even though Freud used it to mean something very different, because in his view its meaning as "tendency" or "impulse" corresponded exactly to the force of the Latin word.[1]

Jung's energic theory of the libido forced him to reconsider his original agreement with Freud about the etiology of neuroses. Following Janet and Bleuler, he regards dementia praecox as a disturbance of the reality function. Similarly, neurosis is in his view the result of a failure of adaptation. As soon as any obstacle arises to prevent the energy from following its normal course the psychic development is checked. First the energy begins to mount up; then, as the pressure increases, it seeks an exit; but as the normal channel is blocked up it goes back up-stream and returns along its own tracks. In doing so it reactivates earlier or infantile states. When there is a failure of adaptation to the adult world, the accumulated energy takes the form for instance of a regressive reactivation of the parent image. Such a reactivation is not simply a going backwards, however; it is also a sign of a longing to go forward. There is thus a twofold mechanism, in fact, in all regression. Negatively, it represents failure in the face of reality; but positively it is an attempt to find a solution, though unfortunately by infantile or outmoded means.

Now if the causal view is able to cover the first element in the failure by finding the cause of it, a mother- or father-fixation, for instance, it is not the same when we come to the second element, which it is obliged to ignore. Anyone who reads Freud's analysis of the Dora case[2] carefully is quite overcome by his inexorable logic. But at the same time one cannot escape a feeling of oppression under this retrospective analysis that offers no outlet for the future because it systematically ignores any sense of ends. Whatever positive values may be contained within neurosis remain hidden from any causal view of it. The energic view, on the other hand, brings out precisely these positive values; what is more, it makes use of them to help patients to recover

[1] Cf. *Psychology of the Unconscious*, pp. 75–6. These pages are repeated without any alterations worth mentioning in *Symbole der Wandlung*, pp. 213–17.

[2] Cf. S. Freud, "Fragment of an Analysis of a Case of Hysteria" *Complete Psychological Works*, vol. vii, pp. 7–112.

their psychic equilibrium. "A psycho-neurosis must be understood as the suffering of a human being who has not discovered what life means for him. But all creativeness in the realm of the spirit as well as every psychic advance of man arises from a state of mental suffering, and it is spiritual stagnation, psychic sterility, which causes this state."[1]

The tension between the adult attitude that is wished for but remains unrealized and the infantile attitude that has been realized but is undesirable lies at the basis of neurosis. Like a fever, it is a symptom of lack of equilibrium, but at the same time it is an attempt at recovery. In the neurosis itself "the patient is looking for something that will take possession of him and give meaning and form to the confusion of his neurotic mind."[2]

To succeed in this task he must manage to rise up from the lower level not only by unblocking the libido but above all by directing it along new channels. Jung has found that the most effective psychic function for this is some symbol. A symbol is in fact something that expresses an analogous condition on a lower level although it actually belongs to a higher one. For this reason, Mother Church for example can release psychic energy that has collected at the infantile level in a mother fixation and raise it to the religious level. Symbols form a bridge by means of which the libido, which as mere intensity is not bound to any particular level, can achieve a genuine situation at the higher level, even when it still retains traces of the lower one. The psychological part played by symbols, and the question of their exact importance, are interesting enough for the subsequent part of this chapter to be devoted to them.

In Jung's idea of neurosis as symptomatic of a failure of adaptation, sexual troubles are consequences rather than causes. He does not deny their frequency or their infantile character. He is quite prepared to accept the traumatic effect of juvenile experiences. But he regards the majority of sexual troubles as being repercussions of the psychic situation as a whole.

Let us try to sum up for a moment the main results reached so far.

[1] *Modern Man in Search of a Soul,* p. 260 (1932). [2] Ibid., p. 260 (1932).

The energic theory assumes by hypothesis that psychic energy is different from physical energy, and, until there is any proof to the contrary, utterly separate from it. This psychic energy, or libido, can in no wise be hypostasized like the reified sexuality of the causal theory. In Jung's view it is simply the quantitative intensity of the psychic process. This is what enables it to spread and appear at quite different human levels without being changed or changing or vitiating the higher levels.

Jung did not solve this problem all at once. In *The Psychology of the Unconscious* he first of all tried to present the libido as something genetically sexual. By this he meant something that first appeared entirely at the sexual level of procreation and then became desexualized later as it communicated itself to the higher instinctive functions as these gradually developed. Freud was not taken in by this attempted compromise, for it struck at the roots of his theory of the sexual libido as the origin and cause of neurosis and reduced the libido to an undifferentiated form of psychic energy. Jung refused to give his ideas up. From then on he regarded neurosis as a psychic effort, in the face of a failure of adaptation to the world of normality, to find a solution—inevitably unsatisfactory—in an infantile stage of development. This being so, troubles in the sexual sphere—which Jung has never minimised—became reflections rather than causes of the lack of equilibrium.

In 1929 the *Kölnische Zeitung* invited Jung to explain how his views differed from Freud's. He accepted the invitation and pointed out in the most emphatic terms that Freud knew nothing at all about religious experience and so quite failed to understand it, whereas he himself did know something about it and could estimate it at its true value. This is true. Jung, however, only explains the difference between them by a very vague reference to different "fundamental presuppositions".[1] In my opinion the difference arises from different conceptions of the libido. The sexual libido makes every kind of sublimation, even religious sublimation, a camouflaged manifestation of sexuality. The energic libido, on the

[1] Jung's article was republished under the title "Freud and Jung, Contrasts", in *Modern Man in Search of a Soul*.

other hand, does not affect the genuineness of these things in the least. In the second part of this book (Chapter IV) I shall discuss this matter in detail. I have thought fit to mention it here in passing, however, for it shows how the technical inquiries in Part I lead slowly but surely to the very heart of our subject.

II. Imago and Symbol

The symbol is the cardinal element in analytical psychology. And so, not surprisingly, Jung only managed to achieve an exact description of it after a good deal of effort. Before venturing upon a detailed study of his gradual approach to it, we must pause for a moment to consider an idea closely connected with it—the imago. Jung estimated this at its true value from the beginning. The definition he gave of it in 1921 is in no way different from his description of it in 1951. He has frequently substituted for *Bild* or "image" the corresponding Latin word *imago* to emphasize the fact that at some particular point in his argument it is being used as a technical term with a very precise meaning.[1]

The imago, as Jung says again and again, is not a copy of any external object, lodged in some part of the brain. It is the concentrated expression of the psychic situation as a totality activated by an object. This activated totality or constellation is the result of the activity of the unconscious as well as the conscious attitude.

The imago thus has two sides to it, joined in a single psychological reality. It is both objective and subjective: objective, because it is nourished by the object, though not identical with sense-perception of it; subjective, because at the same time it expresses the subject's reaction, with all the unconscious elements totalized or constellated around the perception. Because of its dual nature, the imago, having its own independent vitality and relative autonomy, remains unconscious for as long as it coincides more or less with the object's own life. Parents, for instance—whose objective existence, with reason, Jung has no wish to deny!—

[1] The word itself is taken from Spitteler. Cf. *Collected Papers on Analytical Psychology*, p. 322 (1907). Its technical meaning is firmly established in *Psychological Types*, pp. 554 and 599 (1921).

leave an impression, an imago, upon their children. This represents the parents, but as seen and known—almost, one might say, as "lived"—by the child. As the child usually knows of nothing outside its own immediate experience, it is not aware of bringing anything subjective to the imago. And as its parents are undoubtedly real, it identifies the objective reality with its subjective vision. And so the parents are given an exaggerated psychic plus value, either positively or negatively. This psychic plus value is based entirely on the projection[1] of the imago on to the object, or, in other words, on the identity, postulated *a priori*, between the imago and the object.[2]

Any observer who keeps his eyes open has no difficulty in seeing this mechanism of the projection of the imago at work in all living experience. Are we not all inclined to judge the world around us as though it were actually what it seems to be from our own particular point of view? Don't we all naïvely imagine, in the same way, that people are what we imagine them to be? Today we have adequate ways of discovering whether our subjective impressions of the physical world correspond with the actual facts. We may talk of the sun rising and setting, but we know very well that in fact the earth goes round the sun. Unfortunately we have not so far managed to discover any satisfactory way of guaranteeing that our psychological knowledge has the same objectivity. As a general rule we simply project our own psychology on to the things around us. In normal people most of these "imaginations" correspond more or less with reality and do not conflict with it unduly. In neurotics, however, this is not so. The "imaginations" they form are still projected on to the object but they bear no likeness to the objective reality whatsoever. These "unhingings" give rise to attitudes in the neurotic that to sensible people seem "incomprehensible", "unreasonable", "mad" even. The neurotic himself is unaware that he is attributing his own

[1] Jung defines projection as the unconscious process that attributes a subjective but unconscious element to an object in such a way that the element in question seems to be a part of it. Freedom from the projection is achieved as soon as it is realized that the projected element forms part of the subject. Cf. *Über den Archetypus*, p. 265 (1936).

[2] Projections are analysed a great deal in Jung's works. Cf. *Über die Energetik der Seele*, pp. 174–5 (1928) and *Introduction to a Science of Mythology*, p. 110, n. (1940).

subjective reaction or imago to the people or things concerned. He thus remains firmly convinced that his judgments are objective, and acts in accordance with them. By doing so he gets further and further away from reality and becomes locked up in an imaginary world. If he is to be got out of this blind alley, it is not sufficient to tell him that his attitude is illogical. From his own particular point of view, indeed, it is only too logical. He therefore has to be helped to realize, bit by bit, what subjective or imaginary reactions are determining his attitude. Then he will be in a position to grasp the real nature of things and persons and react sensibly to them.

The idea of the imago thus enables us to find meaning in neurotic behaviour. It also helps us to get a better grasp of a point that Jung introduced in his interpretation of dreams. We are all quite prepared to admit that dreams are products of the imagination. But when someone dreams about a certain Mr. X., he is quite certain that it is the Mr. X, who was his friend, the person he had such a great regard for because of his intellectual qualities and whom he has always remembered with affection since he died several years ago. But is it in fact as simple as that?

Freud had already stressed the fact that the image presented by the dreams is really an expression of something other than itself. The dream calls it a church tower but means the phallus, he had slyly suggested, thereby considerably scandalizing the respectable. In this way he drew a contrast between the manifest content of any dream and its latent content. In his view only the latter was of any importance. To make his interpretations he delved into the implications of oniric representations. Jung, on the basis of his analysis of the imago, pursued a similar course but in the opposite direction. He believed that it was essential not to ignore the obvious content of the dream—that it was in fact Mr. X. who figured in the dream and not someone else. But what makes me interested in Mr. X.? Is it not in point of fact his intellectual qualities? And why am I struck by those qualities? Is it not because I lack them myself? No doubt the person involved is Mr. X., but because he interests me. In my dream it is not so much my friend who is concerned as myself. What Mr. X.

represents is primarily my subjective reaction or imago. And Jung concludes: "A dream is a theatre in which the dreamer is at once scene, actor, prompter, producer, author, public and critic. This quite simple truth lies behind the kind of interpretation which I describe as 'on the subjective plane' [*auf der Subjekt-Stufe*]. This regards all oniric figures as personified characteristics of the dreamer."[1]

It should be noted however that this dream analysis on the subjective plane which Jung presents as his own discovery by no means excludes the analysis on the objective plane that he took explicitly from Freud. And, says Jung: "When I speak of interpretation upon the objective plane, I am referring to that view of a dream or phantasy by which the persons or conditions appearing therein are referred to as objectively real persons or conditions."[2]

As Jung accepts both these ways of analysing dreams, a crucial question arises: what decides in actual practice which of the two is to be preferred? Jung gives valuable pointers to the answer to this here and there, but he never provides any really satisfactory standard of judgment.[3] On his own word and that of his collaborators most qualified to speak, the question is not the sort that can be settled once and for all. In each individual case the therapist has to make his own decision as to which method to adopt.

It seems to me that this theoretic distinction between analysis on the objective plane and analysis on the subjective plane shows, precisely because it leaves us unprovided for in practice, some sort of failure of method; but as this chapter is meant to be devoted entirely to Jung's basic views I shall leave all criticism of these points for the next.

And now, after this considerable digression, we are in a position to tackle our real subject—the symbol. After the first feelers, which appeared in the article entitled "Über das Unbewusste", Jung gave his own definition of the symbol for the first time in

[1] *Über die Energetik der Seele*, pp. 162–3 (1928).

[2] *Psychological Types*, p. 572 (1921).

[3] *Über die Energetik der Seele*, pp. 163–5. These pages may not get us much further with regard to applying the two kinds of analysis, but they provide an excellent example of the wise moderation and wary circumspection that characterize Jung's psychotherapeutic work. A detailed analysis of the same dreams on both the objective and the subjective plane was made by Von Franz in "Passio Perpetuae", published by Jung in *Aion*, pp. 411–95.

Psychological Types, where he contrasted it with "the sign" and "the allegory". "Every view which interprets the symbolic expression as an analogous or abbreviated expression of a known thing is *semiotic*.[1] A conception which interprets the symbolic expression as the best possible formulation of a relatively unknown thing which cannot conceivably, therefore, be more clearly or characteristically represented is *symbolic*. A view which interprets the symbolic expression as an intentional transcription or transformation of a known thing is *allegoric*."[2] In point of fact we can eliminate the third term. An allegory, after all, is only a particular kind of sign, according to the actual words of the definition. And we must notice that in the passage quoted the phrase "symbolic expression" includes the symbol as well as the sign. This ambiguity dates from the time of the *Psychology of the Unconscious*, when symbol and sign had not been clearly distinguished from each other. In that book, describing the three ways of representing the libido "symbolically", Jung had given three kinds of comparison which are all signs rather than symbols.[3] Later, especially after 1920, he gave these non-genuine symbols the unequivocal name of "sign". In doing so he emphasized the fact that Freud, by setting up the latent content of the dream against its obvious content and regarding the latter as an image-screen, had reduced every oniric construction to the level of a sign. According to Freud the function of the mechanism of "symbolization" was to evoke image-screens so that the representations which the censorship objected to could appear in a different guise. This view of symbolization implied that the dreamer could just as easily have expressed his desire without any camouflage if he had not considered it necessary to hoodwink the censorship. In Freud's view the dream, as a sign, was a deceptive mask. In Jung's view, on the other hand, as a symbol, it was more like an expressive face.

How did Jung arrive at this idea of the symbol? In 1907 he had believed that the precision of the sign and the allegory made them more important than the symbol with its complexity. The

[1] i.e., "having the character of a sign".
[2] *Psychological Types*, p. 601 (1921).
[3] *Psychology of the Unconscious*, p. 57 (1911).

allegory, "an intentional interpretation of a thought—reinforced by emblems" was his favourite. Symbols, on the other hand, "indistinct by associations of a thought, causing more vagueness than perspicuity",[1] found no favour in his eyes. He returns to the same idea twice, quoting Pelletier in full and taking his definition from him. He was thus concerned with the symbol, but in those days could only see its negative side: it lacked clarity, and therefore was "a very inferior form of thought" (Pelletier). To find a Frenchman, a lover of clear ideas, voicing such a judgment is not surprising, but it certainly seems strange that Jung should have followed in his footsteps. With the passage of time, however, he developed a more just appreciation of the light and shade of the symbol. Nearly fifteen years later in *Psychological Types* he pronounced a very different kind of judgment. And thirty years later he summed up his own views in a concentrated passage: "No symbol is simple," he wrote. "Only signs and allegories are simple. For a symbol always covers a complex reality which is so far beyond any verbal equivalent that it can never be expressed all at once."[2]

What characteristics, then, are to be assigned to the symbol—lack of precision and clarity, or richness of meaning and complexity? As Jung progressed he tried increasingly to reconcile these two elements, in this remaining faithful to his habitual practice. With a smile half of amusement, half enigmatic, he says that the richness of meaning is the cause of the lack of clarity. Let us enquire a little more closely into the meaning of this paradox.

I drew attention above to Jung's idea of neurosis as a manifestation of a failure of adaptation or a flagrant lack of psychic equilibrium. I added, anticipating what was to follow, that the psychic function that was supposed to remedy this state of affairs was the symbol. But Jung was unable to discover the part played by the symbol until he had grasped the meaning of its complexity. Whereas the sign is clear (and unequivocal) because it refers directly to what it signifies, the symbol is opaque (and equivocal) for the very good reason that its connection with the nucleus or

[1] *The Psychology of Dementia Praecox*, p. 58 (1906).
[2] "Das Wandlungssymbol in der Messe", p. 130 (1940).

centre it manifests is highly complex. This nucleus is not in fact something unknown because of some repression; it is something unknowable because it comprises, besides elements that were once conscious in the past, unconscious elements that have never come to the surface of consciousness at any time. Jung sees in Mother Church a symbol that facilitates the passage from the mother—the infantile level—to the Church—the adult level. This idea only has any meaning if the known, more or less conscious elements of the infantile attitude are grasped in their essential correlation with the elements of the adult attitude which, though vaguely felt to exist, remain unknown and unconscious because they are still unrealized. The meaning and effectiveness of the symbol are thus not entirely due to a return to an earlier stage, or to an orientation towards a later development. They come from the "symbolic" or "totalizing" character, which while returning to an earlier stage at the same time is aiming at a higher stage of development and in its progress towards the higher stage makes use of the lower one. The symbol is indeed a "sym-bolum" (from *συμ βάλλω*, totalize, unify) of the psychic condition. It understands both conscious and unconscious, past and future, unifying them in an actualized present.

The symbol unifies the conscious and the unconscious. It likewise totalizes the rational and the irrational in man. In Jung's terminology all the psychic elements that are held together by a logical or causal relationship are called "rational": I help some poor fellow because it is my duty to do so, I am upset when a friend lets me down. "Irrational", on the other hand, describes all the psychic elements that make their presence felt by their "factitiousness" or direct evidence: a tree of red roses stands out against a green background, I meet someone and take to him at once. The symbol, which unifies both conscious and unconscious, rational and irrational, is simply the expression of the psychic totality as manifested spontaneously at any particular moment. It is this matter of spontaneity that distinguishes the symbol from the imago. The imago is also the expression of the psychic totality comprising both conscious and unconscious, but in so far as constellated round an object.

Seen from this angle, Jung's definition of the symbol stands out quite clearly. The word "symbol" is the best possible word to signify something relatively unknown in itself but known to be present by its dynamic effect. "The explanation of the Cross as a symbol of Divine Love is semiotic, since Divine Love describes the fact to be expressed better and more aptly than a cross, which can have many other meanings. Whereas that interpretation of the Cross is symbolic which puts it above all imaginable explanations regarding it as an expression of an unknown and as yet incomprehensible fact of a mystical or transcendent, i.e. psychological character, which simply finds its most striking and most appropriate representation in the Cross."[1]

The above remarks show clearly enough how the symbol's richness of meaning leads to its lack of clarity. Since it includes the unconscious and looks towards the future it cannot possibly be fully exhausted by conscious analysis. There is therefore only one suitable attitude to be adopted towards it, that of receptive waiting, so as to enter bit by bit into its full meaning though it impresses itself upon us at once by its mysterious power of attraction.

So far we have been trying to discover an exact definition of the symbol. Let us take a further step forward and examine the consequences of Jung's definition.

We must realize first of all how much more meaning Jung's idea of the unconscious takes on as a result of the above considerations. The unconscious extends far above and beyond the repressed contents and includes as preponderant elements all the psychic possibilities only virtually present but capable of being activated in the future. Consciousness, too, is more closely defined. Instead of being extended, however, its domain is considerably restricted. Again and again it is identified with the "reflective consciousness". This last qualification in the definition of consciousness is one of crucial importance, as we shall see when we come to the matter of the function and significance of individuation. Let us wait until then.

The other consequences, however, can be thoroughly discussed

[1] *Psychological Types*, pp. 601–2 (1921).

now. We shall consider in turn the symbolic value of psychic products, the attitude needed to appreciate their value, and the danger of depriving the symbol of all meaning when it is simply reduced to its elementary data.

Jung's definition of the symbol can be applied to any psychic production—dream, phantasy or spontaneous drawing. Jung takes it to be a fact that these psychic things show what is expected and felt to exist without being immediately apprehended.[1] As soon as a more suitable or satisfactory expression is found to signify what was being sought, awaited and vaguely felt, the symbol is finished. Minus its meaning or symbolic "life", it is now simply a sign. But there is no reason to regret its passing, since it has manfully performed the task assigned to it in the particular psychic development.

Armed with these insights, Jung could complete his definition of the dream. He sees it as a spontaneous representation symbolizing the state of the unconscious at the particular moment in question and running complementary with the conscious.[2] Thus he can escape from Freud's view of the matter, which was altogether too rigid to satisfy him. Whilst accepting the fact that the symbolic expression of the dream may at times coincide with the realization of a desire, he rejects any generalization of this interpretation as illicit and non-proven.

Then again, he is able to explain an even more important point, the question of the symbolic attitude. As consciousness always operates from facts whose content is quite clear, it can never in itself constitute a true symbol. "An expression that stands for a known thing always remains merely a sign and is never a symbol. It is therefore quite impossible to make a living symbol, i.e., one that is pregnant with meaning, from known associations. For what is thus manufactured never contains more than was put into it."[3] This proposition can be reversed: conscious thought, following its own logic, can never in itself succeed in penetrating a

[1] Like the ethnologists Jung has no difficulty in speaking both of representative symbols like myths and religious representations and behaviour symbols like rites and ceremonies. Cf. *Psychological Types*, p. 602 (1921) and *Contributions to Analytical Psychology*, p. 56 (1928).
[2] *Über die Energetik der Seele*, p. 157 (1928).
[3] *Psychological Types*, p. 602 (1921).

symbol. In trying to decide what exactly a symbol means it will turn it into a sign. In some cases this will be intelligible—e.g., the Cross, the sign that distinguishes the Christian—or absurd—an eye in a triangle, a god with the head of a bird.

If then the unaided consciousness is unable either to create symbols or to comprehend them, there must be some other attitude that will do this. Jung gives an example. A Jewish rabbi had been arguing for a long time with a young Jew who had said that he was going to give up his religion. Finally, having tried everything and realizing that he was wasting his time and patience, the rabbi brandished his *shophar*, which is a rather frightening-looking instrument that is sounded before a public excommunication. But when he asked, threateningly: "Do you know what this means?" the only answer he got from the calm young fellow opposite was: "Of course I do; it's a goat-horn." Such a view of the symbol took all the sting out of it. To the older man it was still a living thing full of meaning; to the young man it was quite dead and thus a kind of symbol of his own defection.

Jung maintains that the reductive method, which interprets every symbolic expression as a mere sign of something sexual, misses the true significance of the symbol. He therefore sets up against it—as a complementary method, not one to take its place, as he himself says in so many words—the synthetic or constructive method. This starts by regarding the products of the unconscious as symbolic expressions that show in advance what possibilities there are of any future psychic development. It is therefore not so much a case of discovering real past attitudes towards people and things as of finding out the present subjective attitude towards them. As this is only expressed unconsciously in symbols, their meaning has to be gradually disentangled so as to help towards a new orientation of consciousness in harmony with the unconscious predispositions.

Two examples will help us to get a better idea of Jung's view of these two different ways of proceeding.

In *The Psychology of the Unconscious* he gives in full Catherine Emmerich's description of the way she received the stigmata. After comparing it with incubation by a god, he ends, "One might be tempted to say that these were merely figuratively expressed coitus scenes. But that would be a little too strong and an unjustifiable accentuation of the material at issue."[1] In the revised edition he added a positive explanation of the presence of erotic elements. "These undeniably erotic elements prove only one thing—that the displacement of the libido was not entirely successful. In these circumstances the remains of the earlier attitude are not fully assimilated."[2] For Jung, therefore, the original elements on a lower plane that are taken up into the symbol—in this case simply the bodily union of a man and woman—are not at all decisive. At the very most they are signs of deficiencies in the symbolic expression of an absolutely genuine experience.

There is another passage that stresses even more clearly the insufficiencies of any attempt at reduction. "Plato expresses the whole problem of the theory of cognition in his metaphor of the cave . . . these are genuine and true symbols; namely, attempts to express a thing, for which there exists as yet no adequate verbal concept. If we were to interpret Plato's metaphor in the manner of Freud we should naturally come to the uterus, and we should have proved that even the mind of Plato was deeply stuck in the primeval levels of 'infantile sexuality'. But in doing so we should also remain in total ignorance of what Plato actually created from the primitive antecedents of his philosophical intuition; we should, in fact, carelessly have overlooked his most essential product, merely to discover that he had 'infantile' phantasies like every other mortal. . . . But this would have nothing whatever to do with the meaning of the Platonic parable."[3]

This kind of reduction thus loses all its value when what is involved is some positive work to be done. But it loses none of its importance when it is a case of getting rid of non-genuine psychic constructions. In this case Jung would be the first to make use of it. In the early stages of any analysis it is only too common to come across symbols that lead the libido off into phantasies of an infantile sexual kind: "No experienced psychotherapist can deny

[1] *The Psychology of the Unconscious*, p. 314, n. 27 (1911).
[2] *Symbole der Wandlung*, p. 493 n. (1952).
[3] *Contributions to Analytical Psychology*, p. 232 (1921).

having met with dozens of cases at least which answer in all essentials to Freud's descriptions."[1]

Let us not forget, therefore, that in Jung's own view Freud's method is especially useful for the psychotherapeutic treatment of comparatively young people. This would seem to be for two reasons. In the first place, it is absolutely essential at that age to integrate sexuality with the whole of the psychic life. When there is stagnation or regression it is often due to an unsatisfactory integration of sexuality. In the second place it is certain that at such a time the psychic energy is still in a condition of overflowing vitality. As soon as the particular obstacle—infantile fixation, for instance—has been removed, the energy surges forward of its own accord in the right direction. It is therefore less a case of directing the energy than of removing whatever stands in its way.[2] But Jung is more particularly interested in the treatment of older people. Their "sexual problem" has been, if not solved, at least grown out of. It is too late for them to retrace their steps, even if they have lost their way. Only one solution is possible—to put up as far as possible with the past and look to the future. Rather than try to return to the beginning, now too far away, the only thing is to get back to the right road as quickly as possible, by a cross-road.

In this work of reconstruction Jung's synthetic method uses the same tools as the reductive method. Like the latter it seizes eagerly on any parallels it can draw from mythology, folk-lore, literature, etc. But its general line of interest is quite different. It is concerned with the way the individual is to find his own personal realization in the future. The reductive method, on the other hand, goes backwards from the individual in an endeavour to discover the collective attitudes in his past.

It seems very likely that it was this attitude that led Freud to transplant his Oedipus complex on to the primitive hordes of prehistorical times, whereas it inspired Jung to investigate the dynamism of supra-individual elements, to which he gave the name of archetypes, in the development of the individual. It is

[1] *Modern Man in Search of a Soul,* p. 134.
[2] *The Practice of Psychotherapy*, pp. 38–9.

therefore high time that we moved on and studied these archetypes—fearsome things that have aroused a good deal of enthusiasm but also a good deal more hostile criticism.

To conclude, then. Jung introduces into both the imago and the symbol a complementarity of conscious and unconscious. Both are expressions of the psychic totality as actually constellated. In the former case the constellation centres round an external object, which remains the bearer of the projection for as long as the subject's original contribution remains unconscious. In the latter case the constellation is the result of a spontaneous operation on the part of the subject, an operation that Jung attributes to the activity of the archetypes. The symbol, which comes from the interaction of conscious and unconscious, is a possible prefiguration in symbolic form of the subject's later development. The synthetic method therefore takes the symbol as its starting-point, to help the patient to realize his own totality in his concrete life at the level of both thought and action. The person's totality, however, is not only determined by his own individual past but by the fact of his being a member of the human race. This leads us straight on to the archetypes and the collective unconscious.

III. The Archetypes

THE THEORY OF ARCHETYPES

For Jung himself, the archetypes have always been hypothetical. They remain so to this day.[1] The reason for this is quite a simple one. As they are by definition the deepest part of the unconscious, they are, in a manner of speaking, inaccessible. There is therefore no way of discovering them directly or making them conscious in the full sense of the word. Later on we shall be examining the basis of this assumption in greater detail. The fact that the archetypes are hypothetical, postulated but not apprehended, has done nothing to shake Jung's conviction in the matter. He is sure that his hypothesis is based on solid foundations impervious to criticism. But he is quite ready to grant that description

[1] Cf. *The Practice of Psychotherapy*, p. 170 (1946); *Symbolik des Geistes*, p. 373 (1948); *Aion*, p. 21 (1951).

and analysis of the archetypes is still only in its infancy. It is for this reason that he is determined to carry his investigations into them as deeply as possible; and for the last quarter of a century all his books and all his research have been diverted towards this end. Is it surprising that he has had to review his position more than once in the course of these lengthy investigations? Whilst holding to his initial inspiration with unshaken firmness, he has shown himself capable of great adaptability in the matter of all secondary considerations.

Only a close chronological analysis will take us through the tangled and at first sight inextricable mass of Jung's varying opinions. We shall therefore begin by examining the most fundamental of these. Then we shall try to discover what practical observations and theoretical considerations have led him to his theory of archetypes. After that we shall define the relationship between the three separate elements—archetype, archaic image, and engram. We shall then be in a position to indicate the part played by the archetype as compared with the symbol.

An assiduous reader of Jung's writings who only knew him through his later large-scale works would probably be very surprised to find in a booklet dated 1909 and entitled *Die Bedeutung des Vaters für das Schicksal des Einzelnen*, statements such as the following: "What we see in the development of the world-process, the original source of the changes in the Godhead, we see also in the individual. Parental power guides the child like a higher controlling fate. But when he begins to grow up, there begins also the conflict between the infantile constellation and the individuality, the parental influence dating from the prehistoric (infantile) period is repressed, sinks into the unconscious but is not thereby eliminated; by invisible threads it directs the individual creations of the ripening mind as they appear. Like everything that has passed into the unconscious, the infantile constellation sends up into consciousness dim, foreboding feelings, feelings of mysterious guidance and opposing influences. Here are the roots of the first religious sublimations. In the place of the father, with his constellating virtues and faults, there appears, on the one hand, an altogether sublime deity, on the other the devil . . ."[1]

The pamphlet from which these lines are taken is only about thirty pages long. It is nevertheless a highly significant little work. Does it not for instance seem to suggest that Jung had taken over Freud's theory without making any noticeable changes in it? In the year 1909 both psychoanalysts regarded sexuality as the essential link in the chain of relationships binding the child to its parents. Religion was simply a reactivation of the infantile father-image in the adult. Thus all psychology was explained in terms of the individual and the situations he might find himself in. These situations included some that by their nature were universal in character, for instance the fact that every child has parents. They were therefore bound to have a universal reference. So it was hardly surprising that purely personal reactions should take on a general appearance and assume universal value.

In the third edition of the essay in question, which came out in 1949,[2] the pages from which the above passage is taken have been completely rewritten. The new version brings out what exactly it was that caused Jung to break away from Freud.

"Freud's view is that all ideas of God originate from the father-image. It cannot be denied that they come from it. But what exactly is their connection with this father-image? That is the point that has to be clarified. The parent-imago has extraordinary power. It affects the child's psychic life to such an extent that it raises the question whether quasi-magical power cannot in fact be attributed to mere human beings. That they have such power is undeniable. But the question that has to be faced is, does it belong to them personally? Men possess a number of things that they have not acquired for themselves but inherited from their ancestors. When they are born they are not simply so many *tabulae rasae* but merely unconscious beings."[3]

It would be a mistake to assume from this passage that Jung rejects Freud's views entirely: he condemns them for being

[1] *Collected Papers on Analytical Psychology*, p. 173 (1909) ("The Significance of the Father in the Destiny of the Individual").
[2] The second edition was unaltered.
[3] *Die Bedeutung des Vaters für das Schicksal des Einzelnen*, 3rd ed., p. 28 (1949)

incomplete or one-sided, not for being fundamentally mistaken. What he asks is, does the father-imago owe its magical power of attraction simply to the father's personal ascendancy or in fact to some power that manifests itself through him? This was the thorny problem that Jung was to try to solve.

Jung first began to doubt the purely individual character of the imago in particular and the unconscious in general when in the course of his analyses he came across unconscious products which could not be tracked down to personal infantile situations. He has published the facts about some of these.

In *Die Beziehungen zwischen dem Ich und dem Unbewussten* most of the first chapter is taken up with a detailed description of a course of treatment he applied to a particular case in 1910. Here I can only give a brief résumé of it; to be able to judge it properly it would be necessary to repeat the text in full. The patient, a woman, was suffering from a benign hysterical neurosis that was mainly due to a father-fixation. The usual transference took place. The patient projected her father's qualities—or imago—on to Jung. She soon became aware of the projection but was unable to rid herself of it, as should have taken place in the normal course of treatment. How was an outlet to be found from this impasse? Jung did not want to discontinue the treatment and leave the patient permanently disabled, and so he decided to go on with his dream-analysis. Then, to his great astonishment, he found that the projection, which in her dreams had at first been focused on himself, began before long to seek another object. This took various forms, but they were all concerned with a kind of wise old man. In the end this person took on the appearance of a natural divinity of primitive times, a cosmic, pagan Wotan.

According to Jung there could be no question of any kind of cryptomnesia[1] lying behind these representations. The patient was quite ignorant of the old Nordic mythology. He therefore reasoned as follows: if these representations came out of the unconscious without being put there by the individual—and it was to the individual that Freud attributed the actual creation of

[1] By " cryptomnesia " Jung means the upsurge of a memory whose origin has been completely forgotten, so that it is taken to be a spontaneous production.

the unconscious, simply through personal repression—then they must form part of it quite independently of the individual concerned. Jung came across similar occurrences in other cases: there was a young officer who expressed his being unlucky in love in the form of a snake biting him in the heel and someone else who thought he could see a solar phallus. In both these cases the people concerned had taken their ideas from themes of very great antiquity which in point of fact they knew nothing whatsoever about: the first was producing his own version of the Egyptian Osiris myth, the second a well-known vision in the cult of Mithras.[1]

The fact that these representations came up spontaneously out of the unconscious does not do away with a disturbing question. Did Jung mean that the unconscious was a container of images, symbols, representations, etc., into which we could delve at will? His earliest descriptions lent themselves only too readily to such an explanation; so it is not surprising that strong opposition arose against a theory that seemed in its own way to be reintroducing all the old "innate ideas". The three cases quoted above do not help to settle the question one way or the other. They nevertheless contain the germs of the two methods that were to enable Jung to obtain more precise data. On the one hand he was to use dreams in series to help him in his researches; on the other hand he began to concentrate on a comparative study of the mythical and mythological parallels to oniric themes. As a result of the convergence and interaction of these two methods he obtained cast-iron proofs of what he wanted.

Freud, it is true, had insisted right from the start that dream motifs had very often to be interpreted with the help of other dreams. But Jung was the first to analyse dreams in series, taking them as a whole and treating them as a whole. In the treatment already mentioned he adopted this procedure. As the presentation of such a series must of necessity be a long and complicated business Jung has only published one such series, and even this he shortened considerably.[2] Unfortunately the exact significance

[1] *Seelenprobleme der Gegenwart*, pp. 154–63 (1927).

[2] This series, despite being very much cut down, with the accompanying analysis still takes up 150 pages in the *Eranos-Jahrbuch* for 1934. Some of the

of this particular analysis can hardly be apparent to the layman unacquainted with applied psychotherapy. I have therefore decided to quote another series, presented with admirable conciseness by Boss. It is made up of 823 dreams, extending over a three-year period of treatment, and it follows very closely the sequence of events that finally gave back psychic health to the patient. He was a forty-year-old engineer who had turned to the therapist after giving way under the double burden of a life that had lost all meaning and almost complete sexual impotence.

" For the first six months of the treatment the patient's dreams were entirely taken up with turbines, cyclotrons, motor cars and planes. During the last three weeks of this first period the same dream recurred three times. Each time the patient was trying to cross a bridge over a river frontier in one of these machines, but the bridge blew up and all that remained was a bit of one of the arches sharply outlined against the sky. Then for the first time something living came into the dream: a plant in a plant-pot. During the same week he began to describe trees with thick foliage and very red roses that he had dreamed about. The roots of the roses seemed to be attacked by worms: this clearly affected the flowers and the leaves began to wither. The next dream only came four months later, and now the animals concerned were no longer what had seemed to be worms, but they were still dangerous, harmful insects. These dreams about insects increased: there were a hundred and fifty-five of them in a period of six months, broken from time to time by the old dreams of machines and plants. Then, for about six months, the dreams were full of tortoises, frogs and snakes. Like the machines, these animals were all uniformly greyish in colour, until one fine night came along when a big snake that was entirely red gave the dreamer a great start. The first hot-blooded animal that he saw during the continuation of the treatment was a mouse. He saw it at the last moment, just before it disappeared down a hole. Soon a rabbit followed, to be eaten by a wild boar. After that, for week after

more significant of these dreams are discussed in the last two chapters of *Psychology and Religion.* The whole series was revised, and discussed even more fully, in *Psychology and Alchemy*, pp. 41–213.

week the most important part in his dreams was played by pigs—until the time came when with a certain amount of impatience he asked when all this ' piggery ' was going to end. Gradually the pigs' place was taken by lions and horses. The first person who interested him directly only appeared after the analysis had gone on for two years. It was a gigantic woman draped in a long red gown. Without giving any sign of life she was floating in a pond under a layer of ice that was as clear as glass. He was seized with panic at the sight of her and ran to fetch help. Six months later he was dancing with a woman in a dream and she too was dressed in scarlet but this time she was wide awake and full of life and taking part in a picnic. He fell madly in love with her."[1]

This series is undoubtedly most unusual. It is only rarely that oniric motifs develop so continuously in such a straightforward way. The machines—things that move but have no life in them—were replaced by plants at the very time when the dreamer was succeeding in overcoming his sense of the absurdity of things. When the plants disappeared and gave place to animals, especially lions and horses, there was a distinct improvement in his sexual condition. But it was only when he regained a fully human attitude towards his surroundings that he dreamed of the woman and fell in love with her . . . However, I believe that this continuous development, despite its rather exceptional character, constitutes the real interest of the series. For it seems to show that oniric motifs only reveal their true meaning when the series is regarded as a complete whole. That is why I have given this description by Dr. Boss rather than the one Jung published. Normally, that is to say in most cases, the various motifs mingle and intermingle, disappearing at one moment and then reappearing unexpectedly the next.

The study of dreams in series shows that oniric activity is dominated by " constants ". But are there not grounds for fearing that without realizing it the therapist suggests things to his patients ? Jung foresaw this objection. The series he published with a commentary was noted down without any attempt

[1] M. Boss, *Der Traum und seine Auslegung*, pp. 126–27. In his comments on this series of dreams Dr. Boss criticizes the archetype theory. I shall return to his ideas in the next chapter.

at supervision. The dreamer—a youth who knew nothing about depth psychology—wrote his dreams down day by day without any contact with the psychotherapist whatsoever beyond a single short interview.

I have already mentioned the observations that led Jung to postulate the existence of constants in oniric activity. Empiric observation by itself could do no more. He therefore turned to his theoretical views about myths in an endeavour to penetrate more deeply into the specific nature of these constants.

From his first contacts with oniric motifs which came up from the unconscious when there was no possibility of previous repression Jung had been struck by their similarity to the content of myths in general and mythology in particular. Others had also pointed out this similarity—people like Riklin, Abraham, Maeder and Silberer for instance. Jung had discovered this new vein by chance, but he now began to exploit it thoroughly. He plunged enthusiastically into a comparative study of myths. To this end he analysed the " unconscious " poems that a certain Miss Miller had published under the title of " Some Productions of the Subconscious Creative Imagination ". Around these poems he collected all the data that might by any stretch of the imagination have any connection with them, and this forms the basis of *The Psychology of the Unconscious*, a monumental and highly revealing, if unequal, achievement. Jung tries to prove that both myths, in their original form at least, and " unconscious " poetic creations come from the same source as oniric elements that do not derive from the personal unconscious.

From this point of view Jung regards myths as being of the same order as images. Myths, like images, he says, are made up of subjective material contributed by the psyche as well as by the objective data of the surrounding world which alone seems to be involved in them. Jung had done all he could to discover the child's subjective contribution to the father image; he now endeavoured to find the primitive's subjective contribution to myths about the sun and moon.

In doing this he was going against all the most widely held contemporary opinions. At the beginning of the century mythological circles, known as either " natural " or " astral ", were in the habit of explaining myths in a somewhat simple-minded manner. In their view they were simply a feeble, pseudo-scientific way of explaining natural phenomena or the movement of the heavenly bodies, particularly the sun and moon. In company with the other representatives of the Zürich school named above, Jung rebelled against this one-sided interpretation which only took into account the objective element, and settled down to his new task, carefully examining the interaction of subjective and objective components in *The Psychology of the Unconscious* and *Psychological Types*. In these books he is constantly referring to solar and lunar myths. But his arguments apply equally to all other myths. Is the material contributed by the external world, he asks, sufficient to explain the genesis of myths? The very regularity of the movement of the sun and the phases of the moon, and their ineluctable return, would be sufficient to account for their similarities.

In point of fact, replies Jung, this solution only considers one side of the question. It is quite true that the sun's cycles, both daily and yearly, are objectively given. But the myth never describes them objectively. It is characteristic of the myth that it seizes upon them in order to explain something else. Now this is the essence of the problem that psychology has to solve: how and why does it come about that objective facts like the regular course of the sun and the phases of the moon are used to express something else? How do they come to be transformed into symbols? The fact of having recourse to these objective realities can be explained by the regularity of their appearances; but the meaning of having such recourse to them is a result of the spontaneous activity of the psyche and this constitutes its own subjective, original contribution.

The objector will perhaps be tempted to insist that there would be no solar myth if there was not in fact a real sun: is not this peremptory proof that the external object in itself determines the myth? The objection is not a very solid one, but it is very widespread nevertheless, for it has a certain truth behind it. It is quite true that without the sun there would be no *solar* myth, but it is also true that without the contribution brought by the psyche there would be no solar *myth*. For we must go boldly forward with our reasoning: without the sun there would be no solar myth, true; but without the spontaneous activity of the psyche there would be no chance of any myth whatsoever. There is an ineluctable complementarity.

There can be no doubt whatsoever that similar, not to say identical mythical elements—in particular solar motifs symbolized by the lion that eats up the sun or the hero swallowed by a sea monster—appear amongst peoples separated by distances unbridgeable both in space and time. The resemblance of these to spontaneous representations in dreams or other products of the unconscious cannot be questioned. Jung could see only one way of explaining this. One had to accept the existence of certain dispositions common to all men. These are necessarily unconscious; if not, they would be part of man's conscious life; but they are not the same thing as the personal unconscious, which, according to Freud, only comprises contents repressed by the individual. This is why Jung gives all these unconscious dispositions which direct the psychic life the name of the " collective unconscious ".

Thus Jung based his theory of the dominating tendencies of the collective unconscious or the archetypes on the insufficiency of the personal unconscious, which was unable to account for either the existence of the constants observed in dreams or their resemblance to myth motifs to be found all over the world.

It goes without saying that Jung insisted vigorously on the contribution made by the collective unconscious. But, once again, he made no attempt to minimize the part played by the personal unconscious, which kept its full value in both his psychology and his psychotherapy. This personal unconscious " includes all the contents that have *become* unconscious, either through losing their intensity and so being forgotten or because consciousness has faded from them as the result of some repression. The collective unconscious, on the other hand, comprises all that *is* unconscious, that is to say all the inherited possibilities of representation which are not individual but common to the whole of mankind."[1]

[1] *Seelenprobleme der Gegenwart*, p. 164 (1927). Jung's italics.

Thus the theory of the collective unconscious is not meant to do away with or take the place of the theory of the personal unconscious, but only to supplement it. On this point Jung's ideas have hardly ever changed, and in 1951 he was content to repeat observations made in 1920.[1]

The theory of the collective unconscious and its archetypes enabled Jung to give a clear answer to the original question about the influence of the parent-imago. It is not the individual father who lies behind this but the unconscious forces that are symbolized and totalized by the external object, in this case the person of the father.

The whole matter now becomes a question of discovering what exactly this contribution is. Let us therefore inquire a little more closely into the actual constitution of the collective unconscious.

ARCHETYPE, ARCHAIC IMAGE AND ENGRAM

We have now reached the heart of our problem. Unfortunately Jung's many published works hardly seem to help us in our investigations. If we restrict ourselves to listing the various definitions, or, to be more precise, the series of descriptions of the archetype that Jung has bequeathed to us, it is not hard to find contradictions amongst them. He speaks, in fact, of archetypes as collective representations[2] or " contents " of the collective unconscious,[3] and then a little later goes on to say, sometimes even in the same essay, that these archetypes are only "dominants" of the collective unconscious,[4] or " *a priori* forms " without any representative content.[5]

But why compare these definitions? If we take the trouble to put them in chronological order we find a continuous process of development emerging as Jung proceeds with the interpretation

[1] *Aion*, pp. 27–30 (1951).
[2] *Psychological Types*, " The Relativity of the Symbol", and pp. 555–6 (1921).
[3] *Contributions to Analytical Psychology*, p. 255 (1919) and *Two Essays on Analytical Psychology*, p. 135 (1928).
[4] *Two Essays on Analytical Psychology*, p. 68 (1926) and *Collected Papers on Analytical Psychology*, p. 433 (1917).
[5] *Contributions to Analytical Psychology*, p. 255 (1919) and *Two Essays on Analytical Psychology*, pp. 71–2 (n.) (1928).

of an increasing number of experiments. Whereas in the beginning the archetype is identified with the engram, and, as such, defined as "the psychic expression of an anatomically and physiologically determined disposition",[1] in the end he comes to see that it has three essential sides to it. All his definitions refer either to the archaic image, or to the archetype itself, or to the engram. The archaic image is the symbolic form taken by the archetype when it emerges into consciousness; the archetype itself is the pure unconscious, collective disposition; the engram is the physiological substrate to the archetype.

The archaic image[2] naturally calls for our first attention since it alone can be immediately apprehended by the consciousness. Its psychological function lies, as we have seen, in projecting a psychic force that attaches itself to some real object and transfigures it so that it comes to represent the subjective psychic force just as much as, if not more than, the objective thing. The father is an objective, independent being with whom the child has perfectly real connections. But as an object the father can activate forces present in a latent state. These forces that have been projected on to the father will seem to belong to him, though in fact they come from the subject's own unconscious.

Such projections betray themselves in a special, highly characteristic way. Instead of truly corresponding to their object and so being entirely individual, they all have certain features in common, so that parallel forms of them are to be found in the myths of all peoples and at all times. This forms an infallible standard by which to judge them and it enables us to recognize them unhesitatingly. As soon as any image originating from the unconscious shows affinities with any mythological motif, Jung takes this to be a sign of the activity of the archetypes. He has formulated this rule again and again, and there are no exceptions to it. But the image is not of course the archetype itself: it is, and remains, the emergence of the archetype into consciousness.

[1] *Psychological Types*, p. 556 (1921).

[2] It should be noted that the word "archaic" is a technical term involving no value-judgment, except perhaps in Jung's very earliest works. "Archaic" simply means that the particular representations in question are to be found in the earliest mythical productions.

The difference between the archetype and the archaic image is clearly marked from 1930 onwards. Unfortunately this cannot be said of certain earlier passages in which Jung speaks of "the primordial image (elsewhere also termed the archetype)".[1] At this time Jung was often being accused of reviving in a new form the theory of innate ideas, or rather innate representations. This accusation lost its basis as soon as he introduced the distinction described above.

The archaic image is therefore clearly differentiated from the archetype. But how is the archetype itself to be understood? To understand it properly we have to learn to distinguish it from the image, but without ever separating the two. It is only in the image that it ever appears and that we are able to grasp it.

What then are the characteristics of the archetype? On this point Jung's ideas underwent great development. We have seen that in his early writings he attributed representative value to the archetype itself because at this stage he did not distinguish it from the image. But soon, under the pressure of fierce opposition, he rightly stripped it of any representative characteristics. Thereafter he described the archetype as "potentialities of human representations" or "a disposition to produce over and over again the same, or similar mythical conceptions".[2]

Since then he has never tired of repeating, in face of the obstinate misunderstanding of his opponents, "that it is not a case of inherited representations but of innate dispositions which produce similar representations. It is a case of the psyche having identical universal structures".[3] The archetype is therefore an energic centre of the collective unconscious. As a function of the psyche of any particular person it always manifests itself in an individualized way, but as a function it remains distinct from it—as an active power is distinct from its activation, to use the old classical terminology. For the archetype is not a dormant disposition peacefully awaiting its activation. Far from it: it is a dynamic disposition tending towards its own realization.

[1] *Psychological Types*, p. 555 (1921).
[2] *Two Essays on Analytical Psychology*, pp. 67 and 71 n. (1926).
[3] *Symbole der Wandlung*, p. 260 (1952). Similar statements are to be found in books published in 1928, 1936, 1940, 1946 and 1952.

Jung suddenly rounds upon his opponents: "Critics have contented themselves with asserting that no such archetypes exist. Certainly they do not exist, any more than a botanical system exists in nature! But will anyone deny the existence of natural plant-families on that account? Or will anyone deny the occurrence and continual repetition of certain morphological and functional similarities? It is much the same thing in principle with the typical figures of the unconscious."[1]

A little earlier, in a more reasoned way, he had developed the same argument, not without complaining of the fact that the archetypes were so frequently said to be "unconscious representations"—"a phrase which is in fact meaningless!" Jung comments. He therefore begins by emphasizing that the archetypes can never be regarded as representative contents but only as "forms". "Such an archetype, or 'form' of the archaic images, may be compared in a way with the axial system of crystals. The axial system determines [*praeformiert*], so to speak, the formation of the crystals in their mother-liquor, but has no real existence of its own. The archetype in itself is a purely formal element, a 'facultas praeformandi', a possibility of representations given *a priori* . . . The concretization of the 'form' is also vividly illuminated by comparison with the axial system. The axial system in fact determines the spatial structure but not the concrete shape of each crystal. This latter, whether large or small, can show endless variations due to differences in the relationships between the surfaces and interactions in the constitution of the crystals. The only constant element is the axial system, with its stable geometrical relationships."[2] This analogy helps us to see how the archetype is an energic centre whose significance never varies, even though its concrete appearances depend on numberless factors both inside and outside the subject.

These views were not being put forward for the first time in 1940. They are simply an extension of a remark made in 1920, that innate representations do not exist, but that there are innate possibilities of representations. In fact, "In itself the collective

[1] *Introduction to a Science of Mythology*, p. 219 n. (1940).
[2] *Die Psychologische Aspekten des Mutterarchetypus*, p. 410 (1938).

unconscious cannot be said to exist at all: that is to say, it is nothing but a possibility".[1] We are here concerned with psychic realities as described in the early pages of this book.

An excellent example of the archaic image-archetype relationship is given in *The Integration of Personality*, where Jung mentions, amongst others, representations such as the Syren, the Nymph, the Three Graces, the Erlkönig's Daughters, Helen, Venus, Atlantis. All these are manifestations of the anima, their archetype, at different times and places. In later works there are fuller analyses of the ever-changing, ever-the-same expressions of one single archetype—the child, the girl, the mother, the self.

But, it may be objected at the end of this somewhat lengthy list, we still know absolutely nothing about the real nature of the archetypes. Alas, it is impossible to say any more about them at the moment. The archetypes are the energic "dominants" of the collective unconscious. This brief statement sums up all their characteristics. In less technical terms, we can describe them as follows: the archetypes are structures in themselves unconscious, common to all men, governing all spontaneous psychic energy that is not controlled and regulated by consciousness according to its own laws.

Jung defends the rather feeble abstract nature of this definition of his very brusquely by saying that it is not a matter of inventing some subtle theory but of describing psychic complexes which have so far never been scientifically studied.[2]

Despite the abstract nature of his definition, Jung was unable to resist the temptation to "localize"[3] the archetypes. The temptation was very strong. If the archetypes could be localized, this would silence the opposition to his views. For was he not being accused of trying to introduce into science—science, which aimed to be utterly empirical and positivist!—a certain mystical element? For this reason, unfortunately devoid of any scientific

[1] *Contributions to Analytical Psychology*, p. 246.

[2] In the Preface to the second edition of *Die Beziehungen zwischen dem Ich und dem Unbewussten*, p. 7 (1935).

[3] By "localization" I mean an attempt to give something psychological a place in man's physiological structure.

character, he went on to develop his ideas about engrams, which he borrowed from Semon.

It must be realized from the beginning that these do not fit in with his highly dogmatic assertions about the relationships between the body and the psyche, the physical and the psychical. "I am practically not at all concerned with the classification of psychic energic processes. I am not interested in such classification, because we have at best only the vaguest guesses to work upon and no real point of departure. Although I am certain that psychic energy is in some way or other most intimately connected with physical processes, yet, in order to speak with any authority about this connection, we need far more, and quite other, experience and insight."[1]

Despite such formal statements, Jung did in fact endeavour to discover a physiological substrate with which he could connect the archetypes, hoping in this way to avoid the accusation of inventing "mystical" things. Not that he went in for any anatomical research: he contented himself with a specious line of argument and an unverifiable historical assertion. What he said was that the archetypes are not innate because they are acquired, but not individual, because they are acquired by mankind as a whole. During his history, involving thousands upon thousands of years, man has found himself repeatedly in situations which if not identical at least bear a great resemblance to each other. On each occasion he has had to adapt himself to the inner and outer world. What could be more natural, asks Jung, than that these repeated experiences, to be reckoned not in thousands or millions but in numbers beyond all calculation, should have left almost indelible traces in the human brain? They have not, certainly, supplied us with any ready-made images, but the brain, having had to try at every moment to solve the same problems, has taken certain "creases". These creases or tracks (*Bahnungen*) of ideas have become encrusted in the brain and now direct our unconscious activity. As soon as consciousness relaxes, the unconscious takes up its normal course again and reacts as it has been reacting for century after century. Water that escapes over a

[1] *Contributions to Analytical Psychology*, p. 5 (1928).

dam returns to the bed that the river has hollowed out with endless patience throughout the ages.

This ingenious explanation, which Jung has put forward more than once,[1] has no proof behind it so long as it remains unsupported by anatomical physiology—and Jung has never produced any such proof, and the present state of our knowledge of cerebral cortices hardly seems likely to provide him with it. Jung himself is in fact quite aware of the weakness of his argument, not to say his gratuitous assumption. In *Psychological Types* he states categorically: "The primordial image is a mnemic deposit, an *imprint* ('engramm'—Semon), which has arisen through a condensation of innumerable similar processes." But he is no less categoric in another place in the same book when he says: "The symbol is always derived from archaic residues, or imprints engraven in the very stem of the race, about whose age and origin one can speculate much although nothing definite can be determined."[2]

Five years later he very forcefully announced his attachment to his own theory, though at the same time criticizing it most lucidly. He put the theory forward again without any attempt at mitigation:

"In my view there is no way of explaining the origin of archetypes except by admitting that they are residues [*Niederschläge*] of mankind's repeated experiences." But he at once adds that in fact this theory explains nothing because "it only succeeds in putting the problem back into pre-history, without solving it".[3]

Does it not seem significant in this connection that after the 'thirties Jung made no further mention of engrams? Is not such a silence equivalent to a retraction, especially in view of the fact that he had plenty of opportunities for referring to them, since in his later works he frequently discusses the nature and function

[1] *Collected Papers on Analytical Psychology*, p. 432 (1917); "Über das Unbewusste," pp. 544–5 (1918); *Psychological Types*, "The Relativity of the Symbol" (1921); *Two Essays on Analytical Psychology*, p. 64 (1926); *Seelenprobleme der Gegenwart*, p. 179 (1927); *Two Essays on Analytical Psychology*, pp. 135 and 188 (1928); *Contributions to Analytical Psychology*, p. 378 (1928); "Die Kunst das Menschenleben zu verlängern," p. 535 (1929).

[2] *Psychological Types*, pp. 556 and 295 (1921).

[3] *Two Essays on Analytical Psychology*, "The Unconscious in the Normal and the Pathological Mind," ch. v, note to para. 14 (1926).

of the archetypes? We must therefore make a clear distinction between archetypes and engrams. There is no proof that the latter exist whereas the former are "hypothetical" psychic realities whose existence Jung proves from the resemblances between archaic images and the subjects of myths. We must confess our ignorance of their physiological substrate, as Jung himself admits: "The statement that instincts are always inherited does not explain their origin. It only puts back the problem to our ancestors."[1] An incidental remark in one of his later works fully substantiates my views on this matter: "I have already been asked many times where the archetype comes from, whether it is acquired or not? There is no direct answer to this question . . . From the empirical point of view the archetype is not something that has been created within organic life. It appears at the same time as life itself."[2]

This section on the engrams may appear at first sight a waste of time. It was, however, necessary to reject the engrams categorically in order to obviate a misunderstanding that has led a considerable number of forthright, and unfair, critics of analytical psychology astray.

Whilst, on the one hand, von Gebsattel describes the archetypes with remarkable precision without even mentioning engrams, and Boss quite justifiably attacks the engrams without incriminating the archetypes in any way, Binswanger apparently identifies archetypes with engrams since he treats the collective unconscious as an "anatomico-biological theory".[3] In more popular scientific works the confusion reaches its height. For example, there is a quite important book by Mullahy which gives a just and pertinent appreciation of Jung's contribution to depth-psychology. The author observes, however, that the engrams cannot be accepted, for the very good reason that they are "a product of Jung's imagination". On this point I am in perfect agreement with him. But I cannot agree with him when he goes on to say that this

[1] *Contributions to Analytical Psychology*, p. 273 (1919).
[2] *Symbolik des Geistes*, p. 374 (1948).
[3] V. E. Von Gebsattel, *Christentum und Humanismus*, pp. 27–28; M. Boss, *Der Traum und seine Auslegung*, p. 58; L. Binswanger, *Grundformen und Erkenntnis menschlichen Daseins*, p. 437.

invalidates the archetype theory, "to which the same reasons apply"![1] Mullahy's book is primarily a work of vulgarisation, though copiously documented and quite subtle in its appreciation, but this does not alter the fact that the confusion between engrams and archetypes is a crude error. But—to repeat—it is unfortunately true that many passages in Jung's writings invite this kind of misunderstanding, as the reader will already have seen from the quotations made above. Only scrupulous attention to the actual words and a patient comparison of the various passages can enable us to fathom their exact meaning.

To summarize briefly the conclusions to be drawn from our investigation into the archaic image, the archetype and the engram, we have to distinguish the mythological motif or archaic image that emerges into consciousness, from the archetype or energic centre which lies behind it and combines with the material contributed from outside to create it. These two things are, however, inseparable, like "matter" and "form". The engram, on the other hand, the so-called physiological substrate to the archetype, is non-proven in anatomy and cannot be postulated on psychological grounds. I therefore regard it as something quite separate from the archetype theory with which Jung connected it up for so many years.

THE PART PLAYED BY THE ARCHETYPE PSYCHOLOGICALLY

Having discussed at some length the dominants of the collective unconscious—the archetypes—and their emergence into consciousness as archaic images, it is now time to return to the question from which we started. The problem was to discover the sources from which the symbol and the imago derive their psychic significance.

This can be answered at once: since the symbol and the imago are both archaic images, they are simply manifestations of an archetype in a concrete form, i.e. influenced by external factors. It is therefore quite natural that such symbols or "imaginations" should show a particular tendency to appear whenever conscious-

[1] P. Mullahy, *Oedipus, Myth and Complex*, p. 326.

of violence or prone to apathetic laziness. He is the image of all helpful or harmful elemental powers."[1]

Without realizing it, the father thus concentrates in his own person a considerable number of archetypal features. But from early adolescence onwards the child learns to recognize its father's human reality and objective value. Things previously identified with him personally appear clearly—"the soil of the earth on which the child plays, the fire at which he warms himself, the rain and storms that freeze him"[2]—detached from the father-imago "whose mask they wore". Thus their real nature is revealed and as the child's consciousness develops they develop an individuality of their own. And so the child leaves its undifferentiated family circle and emerges into the adult world of home, country and religion.

For this development to take place, therefore, the father-imago has to be separated from the real father before the adolescent can gain access to the adult world. Naturally, some of the features of the parent imago will be carried on into the subsequent development, but these do not condemn the realizations achieved in maturity as mere ersatz achievements or secondary consequences. On the contrary, through these realizations the adult gains a more acute consciousness of the objective values that he had in the first place projected on to the person of his father. For a full development of the conscious attitude, this process of "detachment" has to be pushed as far as possible. With this aim in view Jung made it his main purpose to help his patients to integrate the archetypes into their individual lives. It is not surprising that this process, the crowning achievement of Jung's method, should have been given the name "individuation".

The above theoretical and practical considerations should have revealed the fundamental relationship between the archetype and the symbol. At the bottom of every symbol is an archetype which is its "form" or "possible prefiguration", and every symbol is

[1] *Contributions to Analytical Psychology*, pp. 124–5 (1927).

[2] Ibid., p. 125. These concrete instances are only given as examples. They are not an exhaustive list, or even the most important examples. They all relate to the father because to make things clearer I have kept to a single example. Similar if not identical features could be mentioned with regard to the mother. Cf. ibid., p. 124.

the expression of an archetype in a concrete collective or individual situation. Through this concrete expression the symbol manifests the archetype to a greater or less degree: it will be more densely packed and more significant and have more universal validity the more truly and perfectly it reflects the archetype. Indeed its actual concrete form is as much a matter of limitation as expression.

The interaction of psychic realities thus appears in all activity, both normal and abnormal. In Jung's view the pathological element as such is to be found not in the activity but in the fact that the consciousness is not in a fit state to integrate the unconscious contribution made by the symbol. Neurosis arises when there is some conflict, either unconscious or repressed, between the two complementary parts of the psyche. In studying the process of individuation, therefore, we shall have to examine closely this complementarity of unconscious and conscious—a complementarity that culminates in the full flowering of human potentialities.

IV. Individuation

If a man wants to be happy he cannot live at odds with himself. Through his psychological views Jung has given this old truth a new meaning. If a man's being is to attain its full expansion he must be in a position to develop all the potentialities latent within himself into a harmonious unity. Now in Jung's view it is the archetypes that make up man's "authentic nature"—"by 'nature' I mean what in fact is given and present, and no more" (*das schlechthin Gegebene und Vorhandene*).[1] How can such a united personality be achieved unless an attempt is made to work in harmony with this nature, which manifests itself in symbolical productions, at the same time avoiding doing it any violence? Any inner conflict, whether deliberate or not, will inevitably end in neurosis. It is therefore absolutely essential for any psychotherapy worthy of the name to do all it can to facilitate this full expansion which the patient has previously found it impossible to attain and to encourage it in every possible way. The essential

[1] "Der Geist der Psychologie," p. 455 (1946).

aim of analytical psychology is unquestionably the psychical process of individuation or the individual's expansion into personal totality. At the beginning of a course of treatment Jung is often satisfied with a purely reductive operation to get rid of the false construction. Frequently, especially in the treatment of very young patients, he regards this reduction as quite sufficient to meet the case. He will then describe it as a cure of symptoms, for in his view the term "psychotherapy" has no meaning unless individuation is directly intended.

Let us not forget, however, that individuation, or "'coming to selfhood' or 'self-realization' ",[1] is not simply a result of unconscious activity. In point of fact it only begins when man consciously allows his aptitudes to develop unhindered. On the other hand it is not to be attributed purely to the consciousness. The consciousness is only too ready to ignore the depths of the unconscious and to distort it as it feels inclined. Individuation is only possible on two conditions. First, credence has to be given to the signs that reveal the real nature of unconscious dispositions. Secondly, these dispositions have to be incorporated into the conscious attitude. Individuation as such means above all things a confrontation—Jung likes to use the untranslatable word *Auseinandersetzung*—between consciousness and the unconscious.

To discover the meaning of this confrontation and thus breathe a bit of life into the abstract statements made so far, we shall now proceed in three stages. First we shall try to find out what exactly Jung means by consciousness. Then we shall enquire into the compensating part played by the unconscious that leads to the confrontation of the two psychic factors. Finally, we shall suggest the "dialectical" methods that can help to stimulate this confrontation. The new light shed at each of these three stages should then enable us to take a further bird's eye view of individuation—the psychic process which is rightly regarded as the key to analytical psychology since it binds all Jung's discoveries and ideas into a whole.

In psychology consciousness is simply a psychic function,

[1] *Two Essays on Analytical Psychology*, p. 171 (1928) and "Bewusstsein, Unbewusstes und Individuation," p. 257 (1939).

never on any account to be identified with any philosophical views that may, rightly or wrongly, be held about it. Jung himself insists that "the essence of consciousness is a riddle the solution of which is beyond me."[1] From the psychological point of view, consciousness is to be described as "the relatedness of psychic contents to the ego . . . in so far as they are sensed as such by the ego."[2] We must not ignore the limitation involved in the second term of this definition, for it is of capital importance. Jung refuses to use "consciousness" in the strict sense of the word unless he is concerned with contents which the subject relates consciously and explicitly to his own ego. In his own words, therefore, consciousness equals reflective consciousness.

This definition of consciousness needs to be strongly emphasized, otherwise it is impossible to grasp the reasons for Jung's repeated statements about the "unconscious" state of children and primitives. These statements do not at all mean that children and primitives are incapable of any autonomous psychic life, but only that they are unable to lead a reflective psychic life or to take up a "conscious" attitude towards the inner or outer world. They lead human lives, certainly; they think and love, suffer and rejoice, doubtlessly; but they do not know all this "consciously". In a very generalized way Jung sums up his position as follows: "Psychic processes and psychic functions came into existence long before the dawn of consciousness. Men had ideas long before some particular man thought of saying: 'I am conscious that I am thinking.' "[3]

Seen from this point of view, primitives are not to be dismissed as inferior, stupid or immoral creatures, as Preuss and Freud would have it, any more than children are. For this latter pair the distinctive mark of the primitive was an *Urdummheit* or a *polymorph perverse Anlage*. Increasing ethnological research has played havoc with this simple-minded—and unfair—criticism. The primitive is unquestionably both an intelligent and a moral being. After his own fashion he is even something of a philosopher, expressing his philosophy, through various projections, in his

[1] *Contributions to Analytical Psychology*, p. 81 (1926).
[2] *Psychological Types*, p. 535 (1921).
[3] " Bewusstsein, Unbewusstes und Individuation," p. 262 (1929).

myths. He shows every sign of possessing wisdom and prudence, goodness and moral worth; he can also, of course, reveal the fact that he is stupid and perverse. But all these qualities and defects have nothing to do with the question whether or not he has any consciousness, or is only slightly conscious. Consciousness is a quality that has been acquired over the last five thousand years, and it is still far from general. The primitive in point of fact lives on in us all, and the dominant feature of the psychic life of great numbers of Westerners remains, even in the twentieth century, the "primitive unconsciousness".[1] In the light of this it is easy to see how Jung could produce the following statement: "Consciousness comes from an unconscious psyche that is anterior to consciousness and still goes on working either with the consciousness or in spite of it."[2]

Before passing on to the second half of this statement we must inquire a little more closely into the characteristics of the conscious attitude. The distinctive mark of consciousness is undoubtedly the fact that it works towards a particular end. As a conscious being man is in search of an end which, if he deliberately adheres to it, will unify his life. This unification can be achieved in different ways because it is governed by two opposed groups of qualities. The whole of Jung's book on typology is devoted to a study of these qualities. He divides them into one group of two parts and another of four parts. The first includes the two attitudes that can be adopted towards the external world—extraversion and introversion. The second is made up of the four "functions" or irreducible activities in which psychic energy manifests itself in a regular, coherent way—i.e. thought and feeling, sensation and intuition. Here there is no space for any detailed discussion of this typology, which has only an incidental interest so far as our present subject is concerned. I shall therefore do no more than give a brief description of the two opposing

[1] In this connection the following point is not without interest. From 1915 onwards Jung opposed Freud, who in his *Three Essays* had defined the child as a "polymorphous pervert". In Jung's view the child is "polyvalent". Cf. *The Development of Personality*, pp. 4–5. R. Dalbiez was later to draw a similar distinction when he described the child as "pervertible" (in his *Psychoanalytical method and the Doctrine of Freud*, vol. ii, pp. 164 ff.)
[2] "Bewusstsein, Unbewusstes und Individuation," p. 262 (1939).

groups, putting special emphasis on the aspects that have a direct connection with the matter in hand.

Jung speaks of a person being extraverted "when he gives his fundamental interest to the outer or objective world, and attributes an all-important and essential value to it". There is introversion, on the other hand, "when the objective world suffers a sort of depreciation, or want of consideration, for the sake of the exaltation of the individual himself, who then monopolising all the interest, grows to believe no one but himself worthy of consideration".[1] The introversion-extraversion duo is characterized by the fact that its parts are complementary to each other. The two components are always present in an inverse degree: the more one is in the ascendant, the more the other declines.

The second group of opposites is composed of four parts, in two pairs of two—thought and feeling, sensation and intuition. Thought as a function predominates in the man who acts according to reason; feeling, on the other hand, in the person whose attitude is decided by the "values" (pleasant or unpleasant, good or bad, etc.) he attributes to objects. In these two cases the activity is based on reasons, either intellectual or "sentimental", and Jung therefore calls these two functions "rational". Sensation, still as a function, is found in the person whose attitude is in accordance with a direct perception of things as they appear to him at first sight; intuition, on the other hand, in the person who acts according to a direct perception of the hidden relationships that are suspected to exist between things. In these two cases the "factitiousness", grasped without any mediation of a logical or sentimental kind, is the important thing, and so Jung calls them "irrational". This does not by any means mean that he regards them as anti-rational, or absurd.

In this second group of opposites the law of complementarity still holds. But the mutual relationships are necessarily more complicated than in the binomial of extraversion and introversion. As a general rule, there is a higher or dominant function—e.g.

[1] *Collected Papers on Analytical Psychology*, p. 288, " A Contribution to the Study of Psychological Types " (1913). In this article, originally published in French, Jung summarises the views put forward in *Psychological Types*, pp. 542–3 and p. 567.

thought. The function opposed to it—in this case, feeling—is thus the lower one. The other two functions—sensation and intuition—stand half-way between. One of them will be more in evidence and influence the higher function, whereas the other will be more in the background and contaminate the lower function. Thus a great number of combinations, all very clearly defined and showing endless variety, will be realized according to concrete circumstances.[1]

This bare-bones account of Jung's very lengthy book on typology should nevertheless help us towards a better understanding of the structure of conscious life. As a general rule only one function emerges fully into consciousness. It thereby achieves its full development. Unfortunately, this causes a one-sided movement that means that the other functions are ignored, and they are therefore kept under as soon as they threaten to invade the consciousness. Their activity is relegated to the sphere of the unconscious. But this does not mean that they are condemned to inactivity, just because they are beyond the control of consciousness. Unconscious productions offer them a sure outlet. In itself this unconscious activity may seem quite inoffensive, nevertheless behind it lurks a real danger. The man, in fact, who only concerns himself with his conscious function, flatters himself that he is free from the others, with the result that he plans far too narrow a scheme of life for himself and fails to realize that he is doing violence to his real dispositions. He adopts an attitude that satisfies him in a way and sacrifices everything else to it. Alas, he is forgetting that he is quite unable to escape from the complexity of his own being. It is possible that by forcing himself to play this particular part he can manage to hide his limitations from himself. He may even succeed in deceiving those around him too. It is nevertheless still a borrowed part that he is playing. This process of personal alienation can be seen in a great number of people. Because of its frequency Jung gave it a special name—*persona*, a Latin word meaning a mask or a borrowed part. For most of the time the falsity of the persona goes unnoticed for the simple reason that it corresponds to the predominant conscious

[1] Cf. *Psychological Types*, in particular pp. 412–517.

attitude. But as this persona arises from the fact that the being as a whole is being identified with one of its partial aspects, it sooner or later produces an unbearable psychic tension. The repressed psychic components simply change their field of activity. Being banished from the sphere of consciousness, they lay siege to it, making sudden unexpected sallies that become all the fiercer the more they are withstood. The conflict between consciousness and the unconscious usually leads to a sudden release of the stifled psychic forces in neurosis, preceded by manifestations of varying violence in dreams.

The ravages caused by the neglected unconscious contents can only be repaired by accepting and recognizing them. When a partial attitude has been the cause of a breakdown, only an attitude that respects the person as a whole can act as a remedy. But as the consciousness is imprisoned by a one-sided attitude that has been developing over a long period, there is only the unconscious left in which the neglected or repressed components can manifest themselves.

The appeal to the unconscious in the belief that it would bring effective help was not simply an expedient. On the contrary, it only came after repeated experiments. Every time Jung was confronted with a case that seemed insoluble, it turned out to be effective. Above we mentioned the case of the woman neurotic who was aware of her projection but unable to rid herself of it. Jung, having tried everything else, decided to go on with his dream analysis. The dreams themselves brought the solution.[1] Another patient, again a woman, who, without being asked to, brought spontaneous drawings and so "invented" the active imagination method, had the same experience. In the light of a great number of such observations Jung felt driven to accord the unconscious some kind of compensating activity.

The compensating activity of the unconscious is not to be equated with the complementarity of the groups of opposites discussed above. Complementarity involves a stable relationship:

[1] This case is described by Jung in the opening chapter of "The Relation of the Ego to the Unconscious", in *Two Essays on Analytical Psychology*, the second in "A Study in the Process of Individuation", in *The Integration of Personality*.

any change in the first part of the equation leads by an inevitable reaction to a change in the second. This stable relationship, which Jung is perfectly prepared to attribute to the other pairs of opposites, is in his view too rigid and mechanical to explain the often highly disconcerting behaviour of the unconscious with regard to the conscious. He therefore speaks of compensation, to suggest that there is a real interaction between the point of view of the consciousness and that of the unconscious—an interaction that is destined to establish a closer connection or rectification.

The compensating character of the unconscious does nothing to explain its real nature, if one can speak of it as having one. Jung knows no more about this than he does of the nature of consciousness. But because he has observed in most dreams an effective correction of the conscious attitude he feels driven to conclude that the unconscious has a compensating function.[1] But he at once warns us against jumping to any premature conclusions. He has never discovered any real unity or perfectly autonomous line of development in the unconscious. Every reification of the unconscious, therefore, no matter in what disguise it may appear, lacks a real basis: "The unconscious is neither a pure instinct nor a metaphysical reality. Still less is it the ultimate explanation of the world. Like consciousness, it is simply a psychic phenomenon."[2]

This last remark shows clearly that Jung is very careful to avoid saying anything too precise. Despite its vagueness, however, his theory of compensation is highly important, because it is diametrically opposed to the idea of repression. According to the latter theory, at least if it is taken to be self-sufficient, unconscious contents are by definition opposed to conscious contents. If not, they would not be rejected by the consciousness. They are therefore complementary, i.e., in inverse opposition to the conscious attitude. In Jung's view, however, the unconscious contents enjoy greater freedom than this. They may be opposed to the conscious contents, but they may just as easily coincide with

[1] *Contributions to Analytical Psychology*, p. 309 (1925).
[2] "Über das Unbewusste", p. 550 (1918).

them when the conscious attitude finds its optimum vital equilibrium. The heterogeneity between the conscious and the unconscious is not by any means absolute, since assimilation, i.e., the mutual interaction of conscious and unconscious contents, goes on unimpeded.[1]

Jung has described a number of cases in which this complementarity was clearly revealed in dreams. By way of example I shall here mention only one. One day he was visited by a very arrogant type of patient, who was in charge of some business enterprise jointly with his brother. In spite of the need for collaboration—or perhaps because of it—there was a complete lack of understanding between the two. The continual tension that resulted from this was one of the main causes of the patient's neurotic symptoms. In his dreams his brother played a leading part: he became Bismarck, Napoleon, Julius Caesar, and his house would look like the Vatican. In all these ways the patient's unconscious kept bringing the brother to the forefront unceasingly, according him an importance that he was very careful not to grant him in his conscious life. As the parts assumed by the brother had other features of a valid universal kind, it seemed probable that his contempt was unjustified not only with regard to the brother but with regard to people in general. The course of the cure fully confirmed this. As soon as the patient was able to recognize his own arrogance his condition improved rapidly.[2]

This is a very simple case. Jung has observed much richer and more complicated ones in the processes of individuation. Some of these he has described in, amongst other works, *Gestaltungen des Unbewussten* ("Zur Empirie des Individuationsprozesses") and *Psychology and Alchemy* ("Dream-Symbols of the Process of Individuation") but, though highly interesting, there is no room to go into them here, and all I can do is to point out the two methods that Jung chooses to use during treatment to explore the compensating part played by the unconscious. Instead of free association he uses amplification of oniric motifs, and in

[1] "Über das Unbewusste", p. 548 (1918) and *Psychological Types*, p. 525 (1921).

[2] *Two Essays on Analytical Psychology*, p. 177 (1928).

addition to dream analysis he exploits to the full the possibilities offered by the active imagination.

Freud had made use of free associations to ferret out the latent content of the manifest oniric image. Jung continued to use the same method for many years, even after his break with Freud. This method is based on the assumption that the latent content can be directly apprehended and that it is only necessary to catch the censor out to unmask the manifest images. Jung on the other hand believes that the symbol is not a mask but the manifestation of an unknown, indeed unknowable, reality, which no amount of artifice can therefore succeed in uncovering. Furthermore, he is quite certain that every symbol is related to a definite archetype and that a considerable number of symbols express the same archetype. In his endeavour to track down and isolate one of these centres of energy he collects the symbols that show an identical structure and compares them together. The patient himself can do this by comparing the different oniric images: in this way he can throw light on the archetype from different angles and discover the many different sides to it. But the psychotherapist, being acquainted with myths, folk-lore, religious symbolism, alchemy and gnosis, can also uncover parallels in which the same archetypes have come to light as in the patient's own representations.

Let us take the following dream. The patient finds himself in front of a large rectangular stretch of water, on which a piece of wood is floating. Suddenly it stands up on the water, then falls down again with a great splash. The dreamer finds to his surprise that there are people sitting in this "boat" and thinks to himself what a highly original fairground attraction this is. After zigzagging for some time the piece of wood that is also a pleasure boat heads for the middle of the lake, and the deck opens at the front so that it looks like a crocodile's upper jaw. The sharp white teeth can be seen quite plainly. Gently the piece of wood that is also a crocodile moves whistling up to the bank looking like a fairground dragon and all the people get out in a state of happy excitement. The dreamer, who would have liked to get on board and go for a trip, goes off feeling an anguish that he cannot understand. . . .

Even in cases when the patient is short of associations the Jungian therapist can be of real help to him. He can tell him of the initiation rites that take place amongst certain primitive peoples in a hut whose roof has been made to look like a crocodile's upper jaw. The youths who are to become men through the initiation come out from under this roof to enter into adult life. Again, he can quote myths in which a dragon is the guardian of priceless treasure or the elixir of life. There was also Jonas, who was thrown up on the seashore by a sea-monster so that he could go and do what he had to do—not forgetting that Jonas himself was regarded as a prefiguration of Christ, who, after being imprisoned for three days in the bowels of the earth, was freed to begin his life of glory. Collecting all these converging signs, it seems reasonable to interpret the dream in question as a manifestation of the reticences of the patient who is afraid of embarking upon a course of treatment even though it is to lead him to a new life . . .

Clearly, a single dream is not sufficient to corroborate an interpretation. Other dreams will provide new elements and these will affect the original interpretation to some extent or other. But by collecting all these symbols together and comparing them with the myths and rites common to the whole of mankind and then with his own conscious attitude, the patient can make contact with the unknown and unknowable archetypal centre. The different points of view and unexpected manifestations will render him increasingly familiar with the significance of the archetype, as he gradually approaches it by a circular, centripetal movement. Finally, he will be able to assimilate its essence into his conscious attitude. Thus this amplification is an excellent way of encouraging the confrontation of consciousness and the unconscious.

Even more than on amplification of oniric motifs Jung relies on the active imagination method. He asks the patient to draw and paint and follow his own inspiration without making any attempt at supervision. The artistic value of the result is of no importance: all the patient is asked to do is to take note of how he achieves his "work". Why does he choose a certain colour? Why does he adopt a certain form? What are his reactions while he is working? What does he think of the result afterwards?

This kind of work may go on for several weeks, or months, or years, so that the evolution of the sequence of drawings becomes just as revealing as the series of dreams discussed above. Any attempt to illustrate this method by giving practical examples would involve a considerable amount of space, and I can therefore do no more here than refer the reader to the series that appeared under the title "A Study in the Process of Individuation".[1] This is the only series out of his extensive collection that Jung has published.

The active imagination method has the advantage of associating the consciousness with the productions of the unconscious. The inevitable result is a "dialectical" confrontation. It goes without saying that the psychotherapist, like the patient, must take care not to make any arbitrary intervention that may disturb the spontaneity of this confrontation.

These digressions about the two methods of amplification and active imagination are not without their value from the theoretical point of view, since they bring out so clearly the exact significance of the consciousness and its positive function in this confrontation. As Jung lays such great emphasis on the compensating part played by the unconscious, it has been tempting to conclude that he regards the unconscious as playing a preponderant part in psychic life. Again and again he has been accused of supporting an absolutely irrational attitude that ignores the rights of consciousness. He has never had any such intention. He has never grown tired of repeating that the psychotherapeutic process begins with consciousness and ultimately aims at consciousness. The ideal thing, without any question, would be for consciousness never to allow any of the kind of conflicts that end in neurosis. As Jung admits that individuation takes place in the normal course of affairs in every approach towards maturity, he acknowledges that consciousness can lead this delicate process to a successful conclusion, but when consciousness has usurped its rights to the point of hampering the harmonious development of the individual—as is all too often the case in the over-rationalistic world

[1] This first appeared in the *Eranos-Jahrbuch* for 1934 and is completely rewritten in *Gestaltungen des Unbewussten* (1950).

we live in today—there is only one remedy left: to turn to the unconscious. In doing this we cannot afford to give the unconscious free rein and entrust ourselves to its good pleasure, but it is essential to achieve some kind of release that will give new life to the potentialities latent at the centre of interest. The aim is in fact to give back to consciousness the fullness of a balanced direction instead of the tyranny of a one-sided despotism.

Jung sees in the activity of the unconscious which compensates for faults made by the consciousness a striking illustration of the unity "of the two dissimilar parts of the psyche".[1] This unity enables us to speak of the auto-regulation of the psyche, which by its own nature tends towards the complete unfolding of all its potentialities.

This auto-regulation of the psyche is the *sine qua non* of any kind of individuation and it imposes a more or less fixed form of development upon it by the successive activation of the various archetypes. Individuation, in fact, generally begins with a confrontation of the "shadow", i.e., the characteristic features that have been ignored. It then passes through a stage in which the anima or animus emerges, i.e., the predominating attitude towards the qualities of the opposite sex. And it culminates in submission to the "sage" or "magna mater", i.e., the qualities that transcend personal consciousness. It would take more than a few lines to analyse these different stages and describe the hazards to be overcome and the dangers to be avoided; so let me simply note that Jung himself has devoted a whole essay to this matter—"The Relation of the Ego to the Unconscious". The final phase in the process of individuation requires, however, a word of explanation. Jung noticed that in all the analyses in which individuation reached a satisfactory conclusion the patients, as a result of their continuous contact with the symbols surging up from the unconscious, came to realize the inevitable actuality or inalienable nature (*das schlechthin Gegebene und Vorhandene*) of their own being, whose dominant tendencies were made up of the archetypes. They knew without being told that consciousness was not an independent entity but the master-key and crown of a higher totality including both itself and the unconscious.

[1] "Bewusstsein, Unbewusstes und Individuation", p. 268 (1939).

This totality, which is composed of " the two dissimilar parts of the psyche ", was given the name of the self. The self is the actual whole of all the psychic factors, without any exceptions. It is thus both at the basis of consciousness, as the nourishing soil from which it arises, and at its end, as the full expansion that it is to achieve. As long as the totality of the self remains hidden from the eyes of that inveterate rationalist, Western man, he goes on basking in the illusion that he can be a complete autocrat. Only the emergence into consciousness of this totality can bring him out of this dream state. If he does not allow it to emerge, the neglected psychic components go on tyrannizing over him as projections; a clear acceptance of it, however, leads to submission to the self and this in turn leads to a harmonious integration of all the psychic potentialities. And then, individuation, or the confrontation of consciousness and the unconscious, reaches its culmination. The victory thus gained does not mean the end of human effort. The collaboration needs to be carried on in the future; if not, after flying towards the heights there will be a descent back into the narrow confines of the persona. Nevertheless the ideal conditions will have been realized for a life developing all the psychic components to the highest degree.

In analytical psychology, the process of individuation is the psychic process par excellence through which the patient recovers psychic health and, what is more, develops his individuality to the full. As a general rule, the psychotherapist only intervenes when the neurosis is fairly acute. This occurs when the consciousness has adopted such a narrow attitude that it ignores man's fundamental dispositions and thereby releases neurotic manifestations, sent out as compensating signals by the unconscious.

To re-establish the whole system of psychic values these compensating signs need to be attended to and inquired into. By the judicial application of amplification, dreams will reveal the character of unconscious contents and tendencies. But it is even more important to integrate these tendencies into conscious life. By giving free rein to the active imagination, with cautious control and prudent collaboration from the consciousness, the latter's attention will naturally turn to the latent dispositions.

The influence of the unconscious, which in neurosis becomes an absolute tyranny, is reduced to its proper proportions and assimilated as far as possible by the consciousness. In this way a higher regenerated personality develops thanks to submission to the self, i.e., all the genuinely psychic dispositions. Henceforward it can try to live in harmony with it; whereupon the compensating hostility of the unconscious against the consciousness gives place to happy collaboration no longer threatened by sudden psychic outbursts.

IV

SYNTHESIS OR COMPROMISE

THE two preceding chapters have both been concerned with a single point, namely, that of discovering the specifically Jungian significance of Jung's most important views on psychotherapeutic method. This has been done by consulting his theoretical statements and then turning to the way he has applied his theories in practice. The detailed inquiries to which this has led were absolutely essential in the circumstances, for the fact is that anyone who is not intimately acquainted with depth psychology is apt to get lost in the maze of Jung's ideas, intermingled as they are in the most unexpected fashion, unless he is given a thread to hold on to; while at the same time the specialist who is hoping to pass an informed judgement on Jung's work finds himself obliged to discover the precise meaning of his ideas.

But all this scrutiny of detail can only be really fruitful if one further step is taken, and we must now go on to examine the fundamental attitude which lies behind all the views analysed so far. This should enable us to grasp the close connection between the various views, and we shall then be in a position to give some backing to our subsequent criticisms.

I. THE COMPLEMENTARITY OF OPPOSITES

Anyone who studies the exact meaning of the fundamental ideas of analytical psychology at all closely—ideas like psychic energy, imago, symbol, archetype, individuation, the self—will gradually see the salient features of Jung's whole conception emerging in firmer outline. Both his actual practice and his theoretical ideas are marked by a strong desire for synthesis. Is there not for instance something striking in the fact that, while putting forward his own views and defending them at times with some asperity, he has always tried not to reject *in toto* whatever position he was attacking? He always used to say about Freud and Adler that what was wrong with their positions was not so much that they were false as that they were incomplete. All opposition became in this way a matter of complementarity in which two elements were necessarily involved. It was indeed possible that in the heat of battle or discussion one particular element could come so much into the foreground that its complement would be lost sight of, but a little later Jung would be the first to redress the balance. Even in 1906, in his work on the *dementia praecox*, he chose as his motto Erasmus's words, " Unumquemque move lapidem; omnia experire, nihil intentatum relinque ".[1]

It was in this spirit that Jung began to wage pitiless war on any idea that showed a tendency to use the word *nur* (" only ", " merely "), which he considered an unpleasant word because it was so narrowing. He rejected it whenever he came across it, whether it was applied to religion and art regarded as " mere " sublimations of sexuality or compensations for a feeling of inferiority, or as relating in any way to the psyche considered as " only " an epiphenomenon or a resultant of physical reality. Every time Jung came up against some dichotomy (*entweder . . . oder*) he knew no rest or peace until he had managed to synthesize the two parts into a group or a pair of opposites (*ebenso . . . als auch*).

There is no lack of examples of this kind of complementarity. His energic theory did nothing to detract from the value of the causal approach; but it brought out the aspect of finality, which had been far too much neglected. His study of the subject's contribution to the imago did not do away with the part played by objective factors, since the imago was made up of regularly recurring external images everywhere present, as well as the psyche's own structure. His interpretation of dreams on the subjective plane, which he was the first to introduce, did not mean ignoring the objective plane. Even when the reductive method was

[1] *The Psychology of Dementia Praecox*, p. iv (1906).

condemned for its insufficiencies in being, unlike the constructive method, incapable of leading to the patient's full development, its efficacy in helping to get rid of non-genuine psychic constructions was never called in question. The part played by the energic centres of the collective unconscious was strongly emphasized, but this did not minimize the influence or lessen the activity of repressed complexes in the personal unconscious.

A similar "complementary" view lies behind most of the oppositions that have not been explicitly mentioned in the course of this investigation—the progression-regression, projection-introjection, evolution-involution duos . . . but there is no need to extend the list any further: the names already given show clearly that this kind of complementary opposition or complementarity of opposites is a fundamental thought-category in Jung's psychology.[1] And they all seem to be rooted in the opposition between introversion and extraversion.[2] This duo governs the whole structure of Jung's most popular book, *Psychological Types*. It has also, undeniably, had a considerable influence: despite their systematic hostility, several implacable opponents of analytic psychology have borrowed this opposition from him.[3]

Jung has frequently described the mechanism and characteristics of this pair of opposites in other works. He has done so in detail in *Die Psychologie der Unbewussten Prozesse* (1917)[4],

[1] Walder defines this kind of "union of opposites" as a *Polarität*. By this he means that we are not concerned here with a contradiction in logic (*logischer Gegensatz*), one of whose terms excludes the other, but with an oppositional reality (*realer Gegensatz*), whose parts are opposed to each other but at the same time inter-dependent, thus forming a duality within the actual unity and a unity of the two opposites. Cf. P. Walder, *Mensch und Welt bei C. G. Jung*, p. 11.

[2] My own position is very different from that adopted by Walder, who regards the masculine-feminine duo as being the fundamental opposition (*Urgegensatz*). This is taken from Chinese philosophy and is made up of the masculine principle *Yang* (light) and the feminine principle *Yin* (night). Jung refers to this incidentally, to illustrate his extraversion-introversion opposition. But it seems a mistake to give it the importance that Walder gives it. Cf. *Psychological Types*, p. 271.

[3] Some have been content to borrow the words and then tacked a new meaning on to them. Rorschach, for instance, says so in so many words. Cf. H. Rorschach, *Psychodiagnostik*, pp. 76–8.

[4] "The Psychology of the Unconscious Processes", in *Collected Papers on Analytical Psychology*, 1922.

Das Unbewusste im normalen und kranken Seelenleben (1926)[1] and lastly in *Über die Psychologie des Unbewussten* (1942).

I have already, in discussing the groups of opposites in the conscious attitude, quoted Jung's concise description of the extraversion-introversion duo. I shall now repeat it for the light it sheds on our present point: "We say that he is extroverted when he gives his fundamental interest to the outer or objective world, and attributes an all-important and essential value to it: he is introverted, on the contrary, when the objective world suffers a sort of depreciation, or want of consideration, for the sake of the exaltation of the individual himself, who then monopolising all the interest, grows to believe no one but himself worthy of consideration."[2]

Jung himself suggests that he came to this view through comparing the opposing systems of Freud and Adler. The first of these "is essentially reductive, pluralist, causal and sensualist; this is Freud's standpoint. This theory limits itself rigidly to empirical facts, and traces back complexes to their antecedents and their elemental factors. It regards the psychological life as being only an effect". It therefore concentrates entirely on the object and its influence. "On the other side we have the diametrically opposed theory of Adler which is an entirely philosophical and finalistic one. In it phenomena are not reducible to earlier and very primitive factors, but are conceived as 'arrangements', the outcome of intentions and of ends of an extremely complex nature." In this case only the subject and his individual reactions are concerned. Jung concludes: "The difficult task of elaborating a psychology which should pay equal attention to the two types of mentality belongs to the future."[3] In these lines Jung sets out the programme that he himself was to follow.

II. Compromise, an Attempt at Synthesis

Nevertheless, it seems to me that in thus deriving the opposing systems of Freud and Adler from their implicit "psychological

[1] "The Unconscious in the Normal and the Pathological Mind", in *Two Essays on Analytical Psychology* (1928).
[2] *Collected Papers on Analytical Psychology*, p. 288 (1913).
[3] Ibid., pp. 297–8.

types" Jung was coming to an end rather than making a beginning. The beginning is to be found fifteen years earlier, in his first published works, *Zur Psychologie und Pathologie sog. occulter Phänomene* (1902) and *Über die Psychologie der Dementia Praecox* (1906). These were written before he had even met Freud; nevertheless, in them he openly announced his acceptance of Freud's psychoanalytical views, though with reservations: "Fairness to Freud does not, however, signify, as many fear, a conditionless surrender to a dogma."[1]

Three main points can be gathered from these works. Jung is emphatic about the part played by subjective dispositions, which under influences from outside release psychic manifestations and pathological disturbances. He also fiercely defends the inner cohesion (*der ganzheitliche Charakter*) of the psyche against any kind of psychology that tries to split it up into elements. Lastly, even in these two works he manages to combine the two preceding views. First he explains subjective dispositions as complexes that are more or less autonomous with regard to the ego, and then he brings these complexes back into the psyche, regarding them as an integrating part of the unconscious.

Adler's was the first dissentient voice to make itself heard in the newly formed group of psychoanalysts. His ideas were diametrically opposed to Freud's. In his cries of protest Jung undoubtedly heard an echo of his own objections, but as he had never surrendered unconditionally to "the master" he felt no need to abjure him in order to assert his own personality. He hoped to be able to preserve both Freud's discoveries and the complementary ideas held by Adler: all that was needed was to find some kind of bridge between those two banks of the psychic stream, sexuality and the will to power. Jung imagined that he could do this through his theory of psychic energy. If this energy was able to take the two different forms of sexuality and the will to power it could not have any specific character of its own: it would have to be something radically undifferentiated and hence capable of manifesting itself at any level. In Jung's view such a fundamental lack of differentiation was fully in line with the

[1] *The Psychology of the Dementia Praecox*, p. iii (1906).

character of physical energy as postulated by the natural sciences. In the event the harmony between his own views and those of the natural sciences—which have always fascinated him—was to do more than anything else to convince him of the basic truth of his hypothesis.[1]

So far, everything seemed to indicate that Jung's only concern was to discover how to unify all the new knowledge gained by psychoanalysis. To do this, all he seemed to need was a single postulate flanked by two hypotheses. In point of fact the hypothesis regarding the complementary attitudes of the psyche proceeded not only from scientific considerations but from a more fundamental attitude still. Jung has never realized this, explicitly. What could be more natural indeed for a man of science than to present his hypothesis as a distillation of his psychological experiences drawn from empirical observations? Nevertheless we shall see that the hypothesis in question was only possible because of a more or less conscious search for a universally valid attitude which gradually crystallized and became the central axis of Jung's thought.

The assumptions—in point of fact they form a philosophic sub-structure—behind the psychological theory of extraversion and introversion come out clearly in the few pages in *Psychological Types* that deal with the problem of universals. Even to this problem, which is as old as philosophy itself, Jung believed that he could bring a radical solution full of enlightenment. Casting all subtleties aside, he sets up the two opposing camps firmly against each other. On the one hand there are those who, following Plato, support a realist point of view, i.e., "that the universal concepts have existence in themselves". The others are for nominalism, i.e., "that the so-called universalia . . . are nothing but nomina (names) or words derisively called 'flatus vocis'."[2] Jung ends this argument with one brief and final sentence: "For here again the question at issue is the typical opposition between the abstract standpoint—in which the decisive value lies in the

[1] A. C. Meier in the *Jung-Festschrift, Die Kulturelle Bedeutung der Komplexen Psychologie,* like a true disciple compares analytical psychology as a whole to atomic physics, even making the similarities between them standards of truth.

[2] *Psychological Types,* p. 37 (1921).

thought process itself—and the specific thinking and feeling upon which, whether consciously or unconsciously, the objective orientation is based."[1] The realists believe that the idea of any object exists in itself before being realized in concrete objects (*universale ante rem*), whereas the nominalists maintain that the idea is deduced, wrongly, from the existence of concrete objects and does not exist in fact (*universale post rem*).

Jung was familiar with the strictly philosophical solution of this problem provided by Aristotle and St. Thomas Aquinas, who support the *universale in re*, i.e., the idea that exists as the universal "form" of the concrete objects, but for some mysterious reason he only mentions it in passing, not even bothering to refute it but simply putting Aristotle and St. Thomas in their place and twitting them for their "primitive concretism". He then goes on to give his own solution of the problem.

The conflict between those who defend the objective validity of the idea and those who maintain that it is a pure illusion is fruitless. And therefore, says Jung fatalistically, there will be no end to it. But the two opposing parties should be able to agree that the objective idea appears in the mind of every individual. The idea of objectivity is thus subjectively realized and is therefore psychically and subjectively true. Jung goes on to argue as follows: Kant has shown conclusively that the object in itself can never be known by the human reason, which only reaches phenomena through its own *a priori* categories. As philosophers have nevertheless gone on arguing about this matter for centuries, this can only have been due to their own psychological attitudes: those who are clearly extraverted have postulated the reality of the object as something radically autonomous with regard to the subject, which simply has to give way to it; those on the other hand who are clearly introverted have only valued the object for its relationship to the subject, to which it has to submit. In either case, whether the object triumphs over the subject or vice versa, the object, though it remains essentially unknowable, has an undeniable value inasmuch as it enters into communion with the

[1] *Psychological Types*, p. 50. Cf. " Spirit and Life ", § 22–24, in *Contributions to Analytical Psychology*, pp. 86–8.

subject it influences. With a single magnanimous—and rash—gesture Jung cheerfully throws away absolute truth and knowledge of the object in itself, consoling himself with the—in his eyes—highly comforting thought that the object is at any rate psychically real and true in so far as its union with the subject is concerned.

Jung thus imagines that with a turn of the hand he can solve one of the thorniest problems in the whole of philosophy. It takes him less than fifty pages to do so. Unfortunately he does not see that his solution misses the point. The fact that the object is related in some way with the subject—or, to use Jung's language, is psychically real and true—has never been questioned by philosophers. The question has always been whether any non-subjective value is to be attributed to this psychically real and true object. The solution that Jung offers as a synthesis of the two opposing views in fact misrepresents both of them. It simply replaces the two extremes by their highest common denominator. Instead of an antagonism between absolute object and absolute subject we have a correlation of them—not, however, on the ontological level, but on the psychic level.

By adopting the same procedure Jung hoped to harmonize the views of Freud and Adler. These were both looking for the instinct that lay behind all the unconscious manifestations of psychic life in an endeavour to provide a firm foundation for their different systems. Jung groups sexuality and the will to power together under the heading of undifferentiated energy. But this energy is not an instinctive thing: it is to be found on the abstract level of psychic realities.

All Jung's attempts at harmonizing conflicting views give proof of a legitimate ambition to do justice to all the components in the different pairs of opposites: this is the great and incontestable merit of his attitude; but unfortunately the result is always rather unsatisfactory, for it unifies the components only by reducing them to a common denominator which does not exist at the level of the dispute. This is the weak point in his attitude.

The principle of unifying opposites by turning them into relative matters governs all Jung's theoretical work. We shall investigate, first, the advantages and disadvantages of this principle as compared with the attitude adopted by Freud; then we shall go on to inquire more closely into the fundamental views of analytical psychology and so try to discover what exactly these advantages and disadvantages are.

The wealth of new material that Jung brought to orthodox Freudianism is obvious. It should be noted that Freud himself kept his system within a far narrower compass than his most important discoveries and best insights might have led him to do.[1] Jung never tired of stressing the subjective elements as well as the objective factors in psychic life. He took care not to bring down the higher levels of human activity—morals, art and religion—to a lower plane. He strove incessantly to integrate the reduction of non-genuine psychic constructions into the development of the patient's personality as a whole. All these endeavours, which were by no means fruitless, should not be forgotten. It is possible, and indeed highly probable, that Freud glimpsed all these things and mentioned them in passing in his own writings. In this connection Boss has given a number of very valuable pointers;[2] but it seems unfair to use Freud to depreciate Jung. Boss seems to forget that he himself has made a somewhat unbalanced attack on Freud's exclusive, one-sided ideas, which he describes as being "absolutely saturated by the physical and technical sciences", and which "reduce everything to a play of forces that can be calculated in advance".[3] I am not suggesting that Freud may not have given more than one hint in the right direction; but this does not alter the fact that Jung was the first to develop the constructive method and dream analysis on the subjective plane systematically.

It should be realized, however, that the passages in which

[1] Let me repeat that in this book Freud's theories are discussed only in so far as they are relevant to Jung's work. They help by contrast to bring out Jung's own position. This does not mean that I am in agreement with the interpretations given, either as a whole or in detail. A detailed study of the exact significance of Freud's fundamental views is shortly to be brought out by Dr. J. Schotte, who has been kind enough to acquaint me in advance, to my own great benefit, with his leading ideas. Cf. the interim report *Remarques sur la connaissance d'autrui dans la situation psychothérapeutique*.

[2] M. Boss, *Der Traum und seine Auslegung*, pp. 41 and 49.

[3] Id., ibid., p. 37.

Jung praises the psychological value of religion, or criticises the exaggerated claims made for logical and scientific thought, or exalts the value of respect for the patient's personality, seem most impressive to people who have no psychological background. No scientist should be put off by a layman's enthusiasm at finding respect kindling in the piercing eyes of the psychotherapist. He should be indulgent enough to be able to understand the excitement behind J. B. Priestley's exclamation: "Perhaps Jung's greatest achievement is this—that using the instrument of modern Western man, the scientific intellect, he has cleared a way through dark jungles into blue mountain air."[1] Nevertheless, it is quite easy to understand that any seeker after truth who is enamoured of the exact sciences will not be satisfied with reasons of a sentimental kind, and such enthusiasm will naturally arouse his suspicions and put his critical faculties on the alert. Edward Glover makes no attempt to hide his contempt when he quotes this exclamation of Priestley's, and his bad temper makes him launch into a violent criticism of Jung. Giving full vent to his sarcasm, he hurls vituperation against "the immense lather of verbosity in which Jung's concepts are smothered".[2] Unfortunately biting remarks like this only weaken the value of his otherwise fair criticism, which contrasts Freud's strict brevity with Jung's confused long-windedness.

I have already given the reasons which in my view lie behind the differences between Freud and Jung. The compromise of a pure and simple psychic energy at once enabled the views of Freud and Adler to be unified, but this basic concept meant inevitably that all Jung's other particular postulates were abstract in character. In saying this I am thinking particularly of the archetypes and the self. Psychic energy is simply the undifferentiated intensity that manifests itself in all psychic processes. The archetypes are simply "potentialities" of representations. The Selbst is simply a "limiting concept" (*Grenzbegriff*), of whose content and objective value we are utterly ignorant. The long digressions on the symbols in which the archetypes and the self manifest themselves do nothing towards giving any content to

[1] E. Glover, *Freud or Jung*, p. 17. [2] E. Glover, *Freud or Jung*, p. 31.

these absolute abstractions. The impression of vagueness left by the great amount of material amassed by Jung is only emphasized when compared with the subtle precision and close logic of Freud's *Three Essays*, which describe in detail the constitution, development, activity and deviations of the sexual instinct.

In my view, all Jung's highly meritorious endeavours to neglect no single aspect of the psyche have been handicapped by his inability to achieve a genuine synthesis. The natural result of this is that his unifying effort has been found most impressive by people whose contact with analytical psychology is of a somewhat superficial kind. But it diminishes its value in the eyes of those who are seeking a properly articulated system. They would be prepared to accept the fact that such a system was slightly exclusive if it could provide them with a proven, effective instrument adapted to the demands of psychological practice.

So far I have been considering the advantages and disadvantages of analytical psychology as compared with psychoanalysis. I must now go on to examine the main things discovered by Jung, to back up my judgment.

Jung's new ideas seemed likely to be most fruitful in connection with the imago, the symbol and the myth. There can be no doubt that on all these points Jung anticipated discoveries soon to be confirmed by the phenomenologists and ethnologists. In Jean-Paul Sartre's book on the imagination, the idea that the image is a "photographic copy of an external object, lodged somewhere in the brain" is rejected, for instance.[1] Like Jung, Sartre was beginning to wage war against associationalism and trying to rehabilitate the image as a state of consciousness unifying object and subject. Mircea Eliade's definition of the symbol as something opposed to the sign is perfectly in line with Jung's position. Eliade in point of fact describes the function of the symbol as being to reveal "a reality . . . that no other 'manifestation' is in a position to reveal".[2] Myths and ritual, which Jung had interpreted as symbols of representation and behaviour,[3] are similarly explained

[1] J.-P. Sartre, *L'Imagination, passim.*
[2] M. Eliade, *Traité de l'Histoire des Religions*, p. 381.
[3] "On Psychical Energy", in *Contributions to Analytical Psychology*, pp. 55–6 (1928).

in the religious phenomenology of G. van der Leeuw, and the phenomenological ethnology of A. Jensen.[1]

These parallels are real, but they must not be allowed to mislead us, for there are also significant differences. Sartre followed up his historico-critical book with an article entitled "La Structure intentionelle de l'image" in which he tried to sketch a phenomenology of the image. A little later he revised this article and published the result as a book called *L'Imaginaire*. In both these publications Sartre states his own theory most emphatically. The image, he says, as "consciousness", is to be considered for its own sake and not for any fictitious relationship with an object. Now Jung is constantly referring from the image to the object. He states it as a principle that the image only partly coincides with the object—except when, in pathological cases, it gets away from it completely. This means that, though firmly upholding Kant's denial of any possibility of real objective knowledge, Jung has to postulate an object that not only exists in itself but, moreover, must be known as such. Surely there is some inconsistency here?

Mircea Eliade's definition of the symbol also reveals a rather different viewpoint from Jung's. According to Eliade the reality revealed in the symbol could not be manifested in any other way, but it is really revealed by the symbol. In other words the symbol is the reality itself in so far as it is made manifest. Jung, on the other hand, is never tired of repeating that the reality manifested in the symbol is in itself unknowable. But, in that case, by what right can he speak of a manifestation? Is it not inconsistent to refer to a manifestation of something in itself unknowable?

We therefore find an object which Jung states emphatically to be utterly unknowable and inaccessible popping up every other minute as a criterion of the objective value of the symbol and the subjective character of the imago. Jung, it is true, tries to account for this by saying that the actual facts drive him to this illogical position and that facts are more important than the subtlest forms of reasoning; but may there not be grounds for fearing that Jung

[1] G. van der Leeuw, *Religion in Essence and Manifestation*, pp. 413 ff.; A. Jensen, *Mythus und Kult bei den Naturvölkern*, *passim*.

is unaware of the part played by his own assumptions in establishing what purport to be facts of experience? There are many passages throughout his writings to confirm such fears. Rather than make brief references to them all, I shall limit myself to one such passage and analyse it thoroughly. It is taken from an article called "Das Grundproblem der gegenwärtigen Psychologie" in which he attempted to prove for once and for all the irreducible reality of the psyche. As usual, he takes as his starting-point a group of opposites, in this case the *Physis-Geist* duo, rejecting any solution that only takes into account either the physical or the spiritual side of the psychic being. He goes on: "The conflict of the material and spiritual aspects of life only shows that the psychic is in the last resort an incomprehensible something. Without a doubt psychic happenings constitute our only immediate experience. All that I experience is psychic. Even physical pain is a psychic event that belongs to my experience. My sense-impressions—for all that they force upon me a world of impenetrable objects occupying space—are psychic images, and these alone are my immediate experience, for they alone are the immediate objects of my consciousness. My own psyche even transforms and falsifies reality, and it does this to such a degree that I must resort to artificial means to determine what things are like apart from myself. Then I discover that a tone is a vibration of the air of such and such a frequency, or that a colour is a wave-length of light of such and such a length. We are in all truth so enclosed by psychic images that we cannot penetrate to the essence of things external to ourselves. All our knowledge is conditioned by the psyche which, because it alone is immediate, is superlatively real."[1]

A passage like this proves beyond any shadow of doubt that Jung looks upon physical pain, sounds and colours—to repeat his own examples—as objects existing outside us. In his view we only perceive the psychic representations of these things, and to these he denies any objective value. This raises an important question: where does he get his certainty about the existence of the objective outer world from? Either he knows it psychically,

[1] *Modern Man in Search of a Soul*, pp. 219–20 (1931).

in which case there is no need to describe objects as being beyond our grasp; or he knows nothing of it—and then he has no right to speak of it as something he can postulate or use as a criterion. Jung's attitude is the result of two different beliefs, behind which lies a real contradiction. On the one hand he maintains—not that he supplies any proof of it—that the objective world is quite separate from the subjective or psychic world. On the other hand he also says that the objective world cannot possibly be known through the subjective world. This latter view should naturally lead him to a radical subjectivism—if only he did not go on to say, making a further assumption, that psychic reality is real being. And this, he says, we know directly, after having insisted a little earlier that it is ultimately unknowable!

This same kind of oscillation between two extreme—almost contradictory—points of view enables Jung to chop and change about in a way that rouses his opponents to fury. First he volatilizes his archetypes and presents them as pure "possibilities" of representations, or significant centres with no content of their own, then he concretizes them to the extent of making them "the motive forces behind oniric activity" and "sources and regulators of unconscious activity".[1] First he describes the self as a pure limiting concept, then he stuffs it with the whole of psychic life as the supreme reality, directly apprehended.

All the complaints and objections that have been made against his "many inconsistencies and occasional evasions", against the fact that he hypostasizes psychic realities that only a little while before he had presented as mere possibilities, against his inability "to call a spade a spade and keep on calling it a spade",[2] in a word, against his psychologism, which he presents as though it was experience, are aimed without exception at the most fundamental of Jung's attitudes, which superimposes upon a realistic view of the subjective and objective worlds as two independent realities mutually influencing each other the Kantian belief that we are unable to know anything about the objective world whatsoever.

[1] "Der Geist der Psychologie", p. 447 (1946).
[2] E. Glover, *Freud or Jung*, p. 31.

To the realist and the positivist Jung peremptorily points out the reality of the psychic subject as the only thing that can be directly perceived. Then he rounds upon the idealist to remind him of the reality of an objective world with its own existence and takes this as the standard by which to judge the by no means trustworthy psychic representations we have of it. And then he immediately calls upon the realist again and assures him that this objective world is unknowable!

I am convinced that Jung is unaware of the ambiguity lurking behind his efforts to create a unifying synthesis. Again and again he complains that the opponents he is trying to reconcile are too narrow-minded to appreciate the importance of his solution: when he says that everything is " at least " psychic, they come back at him and say that he is saying that everything is " only " psychic. Their failure to agree with him is however perfectly understandable. The opposing parties are in no doubt whatsoever as to the truth of what Jung positively asserts: they are quite ready to accept this in fact without any help from him at all. What really interests them and gives them something to argue about is the next step to be taken, and as Jung absolutely refuses to take this step they both reject his compromise, no matter how invitingly he holds it before their eyes.

If Jung really wants to achieve a harmony between the various opposing view-points that he has enumerated he should go back either to Aristotle or to phenomenology. He refers to the categories of " matter " and " form " in several of his explanations. He has also mentioned the views of phenomenology on the interaction and correlation of subject and object. Whichever solution he adopted, he would have to sacrifice either his view of the objective world as an absolute reality external to the subject, or his belief that the objective world is essentially unknowable.

It is not surprising that Jung should find it impossible to achieve such a mental revolution. No one can put forward the same ideas for nearly half a century without getting attached to them. The regrettable thing is that other investigators, determined in their turn to unify Freud's position and Jung's, have not understood this compulsion. Their well-intentioned efforts have been bound to fail because they have all tried to insert Jung's grandiose abstractions, such as the archetypes and the self, into Freud's quite differently orientated system.

H. Schultz-Hencke has suggested that Jung's archetypes should be regarded in the same way as the relationships between parents and child, and vice versa—" the father and son, son and father, mother and daughter relationship, and vice versa, brother and brother, brother and sister, husband and mother-in-law, wife and father-in-law, and so on ".[1] He regards them either from the man's point of view, or the woman's. This suggested solution is however misleading and brings us no real light, for in point of fact it fails to take into account either the abstract character of Jung's theory of archetypes or the concrete character of Freud's theory of instincts. Schultze-Hencke makes no attempt to hide the fact that he is on Freud's side rather than Jung's, and it seems to me therefore that his conclusion is less arbitrary, or rather less ambiguous, than the solution put forward by Charles Baudouin. Baudouin tries to reconcile Freud and Jung by taking odd pieces from their two systems and soldering them together. In his *Précis de Psychologie analytique* he juggles with Freud's three psychic instances—id, ego and super-ego—and with three of Jung's archetypes—the persona, shadow and self—and throws in a seventh instance, the automaton, which is his own personal discovery. This gives the following sevenfold system—automaton, id, persona, ego, shadow, super-ego and self, in an ascending triangular order of interlinked circles.[2] This, it must be confessed, is a highly ingenious achievement, but unfortunately it is highly dubious too. Nowhere is it explained to us how or why Freud's instances can be linked without more ado with Jung's archetypes. Nowhere are we shown why only three of the archetypes have a right to this special treatment. Nowhere is it explained why the number seven makes up a coherent and self-sufficing whole. Baudouin contents himself with an asser-

[1] H. Schultz-Hencke, *Über die Archetypen*, p. 38. Professor Carp has adopted this interpretation without qualifying it, as Schultz-Hencke does in his final paragraph. Cf. E. A. Carp, *De Analytisch-psychologische behandelingswijze volgens Jung*, pp. 53–4.

[2] Cf. the drawings of this sevenfold system in C. Baudouin, *De l'Instinct à l'Esprit*, p. 224.

tion of the practical usefulness of his achievement and with pointing out its similarity to other " psychic " systems such as the seven chakras in Kundalini Yoga and the seven mansions in Theresa of Avila's " Interior Castle ".[1]

This kind of electicism may be useful from the practical point of view, and what value it may possess it derives from this. Unfortunately, it also only serves to heighten the confusion of language that was so rife in the camp of the depth psychologists from the beginning, for it takes certain terms and applies them to ideas quite remote from each other, without any respect for their specific content.

I have laid much—perhaps too much—emphasis on the weak point in Jung's fundamental position. I have also been equally uncompromising about the solutions that have been suggested, which try to solve the problem by manufacturing further compromises. It was necessary for me to go boldly forward and do this if my criticism was not to degenerate into an incidental rejection of secondary elements for inessential reasons. This is not the only advantage of the method that I have adopted, of going to the very heart of the problem. It also enables me to concentrate, just as impartially, on all the valuable new material that Jung has provided. I shall now go on to this in the third part of this chapter, and discuss what Jung has called the phenomenological character of his psychology. We have seen that an effort at synthesis does not necessarily mean a coherent philosophy. But it is equally true that inconsistent philosophical views do not inevitably lead to faulty practice. In both cases the same condition holds good: all that is necessary is a fault in logic. And Jung has never been accused of being over-logical.

III. A Phenomenological Psychology

The terms " phenomenology " and " phenomenological " have only come into Jung's vocabulary quite recently. They are not to be found in any of his writings before 1925 at the earliest.

[1] Cf. also H. C. Rümke, *Aantekeningen over het instinct, de archetypus, de existentiaal.*

After that they crop up occasionally, but never, except perhaps in *Psychology and Religion*, with sufficient frequency to allow one to speak of a systematic use of them. In all Jung's voluminous work there are at the very most ten passages devoted to a description of their exact meaning. Nevertheless the two terms have such an importance in analytical psychology that we are obliged to take a closer look at them; moreover, they are becoming so fashionable in contemporary philosophical and scientific writing that it is essential to try to tie down their meaning if ambiguities and blatant contradictions are to be avoided.

Jung has always used these two particular terms for two features of his science for which he has a particular fondness. Phenomenological psychology, or psychological phenomenology, is the opposite of clinical symptomatology, which is only concerned to establish the external features or symptoms of psychic phenomena. The former, on the other hand, tries to discover the actual meaning of these phenomena: " A descriptive study of the psyche . . . enables us to formulate certain theories about its structure. From the empirical application of these theories there is finally developed a conception of psychological types."[1]

Such a phenomenology aims to grasp the actual structure of phenomena. To do this, instead of using definitions taken from any other branch of knowledge it tries to discover the meaning behind the " manifestations ". It starts in fact from the assumption that phenomena, i.e., the things that appear, contain their own meaning. The thing that has to be done, then, is to find this hidden meaning. It is not impossible that the same meaning may be found in a number of different phenomena, in which case one can speak of a similarity of meaningful structures. If we then come upon a number of structures that have certain features in common it will be legitimate to group them under the higher unity of meaningful types. Thus a careful attention to the phenomena and their insertion into life as a whole gives us a deeper insight into their actual meaning. Now and again Jung

[1] *Modern Man in Search of a Soul*, p. 89 (1928). Jung's definition undoubtedly brings him very close to Dilthey's ideas. G. van der Leeuw has also used it as a basis for his phenomenological method in the sphere of religious knowledge. Cf. G. Van der Leeuw, *Religion in Essence and Manifestation*, pp. 682 ff.

even speaks of a penetration into their nature or essence. This is rather unfortunate. The founder of phenomenology, Husserl, does indeed say that its ultimate aim is *Wesensschau*, i.e., an understanding of the ontological reality of phenomena, but Jung will have absolutely nothing to do with this, and he erects *epoché*—i.e., abstention from all judgments involving value or ontological reality, which Husserl had put forward as a methodological stage that had to be transcended—into an absolute final principle. He does this so insistently that it becomes the predominating aspect of his use of the term. In 1927 he stated his position as follows: " The conception of soul that I am now using is to be compared with the primitive conception . . . rather than with the Christian idea of the soul, which is an attempt at an inclusive philosophical idea of a metaphysical individual substance. My conception of the soul has nothing to do with this, since I use it in a merely phenomenological sense."[1] And in the introduction to a French edition of some of his writings he said again, in 1938: " Psychology cannot—and does not wish to—establish any *metaphysical* truths: all it is concerned with is *psychological phenomenology*."[2]

Phenomenology is therefore to be regarded as a method of discovering the actual meaning of the phenomenon as it appears to the person studying it and investigating it without making any attempt to pass judgment on its ontological value. This was in perfect accord with Jung's views and in line with his dearest wishes. He too wanted to be able to study psychic phenomena without having to bother about any philosophy that lay down the law about them from the outside and judged them from the outside, either as a deductive idealism or as an inductive positivism. He had already come up against these two tendencies which governed the current of ideas at the end of the nineteenth century, and he could accept neither. The phenomenologists' rallying-cry, *Zu den Sachen selbst*, suited him down to the ground, for he wished above all things to get to grips, in a spirit perfectly

[1] *Contributions to Analytical Psychology*, p. 132 (1927).
[2] *Phénomènes occultes*, p. v. (1938). Jung's italics. Cf. also *Psychology and Religion*, ch. i, § 2a (1937); *The Practice of Psychotherapy*, pp. 310–11 (1946); *Symbolik des Geistes*, p. 3 (1948).

free from bias, with what he called *Tatsachen*—empirical facts. Later he found that the phenomenological method had a second advantage. His original loyalty to Kant's theoretical agnosticism had been an object of attack from a number of hostile critics, and the phenomenologists' *epoche* enabled him to present his attitude more elastically. Instead of saying that the object was unknowable, he began to speak of a " self-limitation in psychology that is both free and inevitable "[1]: as an autonomous science, psychology was unconcerned with any metaphysical position. I shall be returning to this watering-down of Jung's view in this matter.

This was the attitude that Jung described as " phenomenological ", for the very good reason that it concerns itself exclusively with phenomena and ignores all the problems deriving from ontology and the criticism of knowledge; from it has come all the new material that has been amassed as a result of Jung's continuous endeavour to take all the factors of psychic life into account.

Respect for phenomena enabled Jung to overcome his mistrust of symbolic language. At first he dismissed this as " an inferior form of thought ", but gradually his careful observation of the way symbols were present and active in dreams and the way they developed in them, and his study of spontaneous drawings, convinced him that symbols could lead into unsuspected worlds that would always lie beyond the scope of logical scientific thought. In his study of them he came across the psychic components that lay behind their appearance. He was able to recognize their particular characteristics in a way that meant that he could no longer " reduce " them or put them down to purely external influences. Furthermore, he was enabled to appreciate the interaction and correlation of subject and object at their true value. Boss quite rightly says that this is the first step on the way to a philosophico-phenomenological view of things. The fact that the imago has two sides to it enabled him to shed vivid light on the activity, the sometimes disconcerting activity, of projection and introjection, and to bring out the undeniable value of oniric analysis on the subjective plane. Lastly, this led him to develop an

[1] *Symbolik des Geistes*, p. 3 (1948).

absolutely new way of looking at such matters as gnosis, alchemy and the various religions, whose representations all seemed more or less absurd in the eyes of purely causal scientific thought. By renouncing any pretentions to absolute value judgments he was able to focus all his attention on their structure and their particular meaning. He thus succeeded in creating a science around phenomena hitherto, either through inadvertence or disdain, ignored. By the metaphysicians these phenomena had been rejected as faulty or false; by the religious they had been condemned as blasphemous or diabolic; whilst the scientist has dismissed them as illusory or merely pseudo-scientific. The establishment of a comparative science of the phenomena and representations of mythology, gnosis, alchemy and the most widely separate religions, is without doubt Jung's most original contribution during the second half of his long scientific career.

The word "phenomenology", in the sense outlined here, covers Jung's constant endeavour to ignore no single element. This effort was vitiated in several points by assumptions almost totally lacking substantiation, as I have tried to point out in the second part of this chapter. It nevertheless bore fruit in discoveries of lasting value, as has been pointed out above.

So far I have been discussing the benefits and insufficiencies of analytical psychology without any mention of the religious problem involved. This has been intentional. It would in fact be unfair and unsound to isolate Jung's ideas about religion and religious feeling from the context in which they were conceived. One can hardly be in a position to appreciate either the reasons that have inspired Jung with his respect for religion or his critical attitude towards it until one has grasped the exact meaning of his fundamental ideas and the assumptions on which they are based. Before passing on to the second part of this book I shall end by summarizing the conclusions to which the foregoing critical analysis seems to lead.

The longing for synthesis that governs all Jung's empirical psychology appears at once in the complementarity principle. An ever-increasing sequence of pairs of opposites impresses this principle even on the most superficial reader. But this complementarity, recurring again and again in ever-new forms, is not a mere surface phenomenon. It is firmly anchored in Jung's fundamental attitude.

Though less suspicious of philosophy than Freud, Jung has never really made a thorough investigation of his own assumptions. They are borrowed for the most part from "common sense", with a thin veneer taken from Kant, Schopenhauer and Nietzsche. This has meant that his longing for synthesis has degenerated all too easily into a search for a compromise that simply reduces the opposites to their highest common denominator. Despite his unflagging determination to follow the way of pure empiricism, all the solutions he has put forward have ended up with abstract realities like psychic energy, the imago, the symbol, the archetype and the self. The emphasis on the psychic reality of these abstractions does nothing to diminish their abstractness.[1]

From time to time Jung becomes perfectly aware of the nature of his psychology. He has described it for instance as "today's myth": "Psychology . . . operates with ideas which in their turn are derived from archetypal structures and thus generate a somewhat more abstract kind of myth [than that of primitives and the ancients]. Psychology therefore translates the archaic speech of myth into a modern mythologem—not yet, of course, recognized as such—which constitutes one element of the myth 'science'. This 'hopeless' activity is a *living and lived myth*, satisfying to persons of a corresponding temperament."[2] Jung's procedure is not, in itself, a thing to be rejected. Unfortunately, all too often he succumbs to the temptation to turn these abstract realities into concrete "entities" or "essences". Then the archetypes become "personalities", or at least "motivators" and "regulators", and the symbols become "transformers of

[1] "Abstract" does not mean non-existent or unreal! Abstract realities can be not only psychologically real, as Jung rightly maintains, but ontologically true too. "Abstract realities" means realities which in both psychology and philosophy are postulated from a general observation of the phenomena or put forward as explanatory hypotheses.

[2] *Introduction to a Science of Mythology*, p. 136 (1941).

energy ". And the psyche becomes the same thing as man himself.[1]

Jung has always defended this pendulum movement, which takes him from the most rarefied abstractions to the crudest concretizations and from absolute subjectivism to pure objectivity, generally by referring to the undeniable unity of opposites and the conceptual limitations of the human mind. These two latter points are supposed, according to Jung, to result from an impartial scrutiny of the empirical facts. In point of fact they derive from philosophical assumptions that are never made clear. These assumptions combine a realistic " common-sense " philosophy, which regards the objective and subjective worlds as existing in two separate watertight compartments, with a theoretical agnosticism borrowed from Kant, who said that it was impossible for the subjective world to lead to the objective world.

This illogicality sunders subject and object irremediably. But Jung had emphasized their interdependence. In his interpretation of dreams he—not unsuccessfully—drew attention to analysis on the subjective plane. But he could not succeed in unifying it with analysis on the objective plane. The same illogicality deprived the symbol, which Jung had distinguished most admirably from the sign, of all ontological content and objective value. This same illogicality again enlarged the archetypes and the self out of all proportion, to the point of emptying these " pure potentialities " and " limiting concepts " of all content. Psychic energy, which was supposed to be all things to all things, was no longer in itself anything at all.

Jung had sense enough not to grow hidebound in this illogicality. By softening his attitude in the matter of method, describing it now as " phenomenological ", he was able to develop the new material that had resulted from his longing for synthesis. The real, undeniable interaction between subject and object, the true significance of the symbol as an avenue into worlds previously

[1] H. Trüb, a former disciple of Jung's who broke away from him, accuses him of missing the element of human " meeting " out of his treatment. This complaint, which incidentally Trüb does not make at all clear, seems to me to refer to this identification of concrete man with the abstract psyche. Cf. H. Trüb, *Heilung aus der Begegnung*, pp. 30–4 and 78–82.

closed to technical and scientific thought, and the proper meaning of the representations of gnosis, alchemy and the most varied types of religion—all these things have been fully revealed by his researches.

This makes it all the more regrettable that Jung has not seen fit to reconsider the shaky philosophical assumptions on which his fundamental position rests. He could have done this either through an Aristotelian hylomorphism or by way of metaphysical phenomenology, to which he is certainly no stranger.

It is equally regrettable that none of the critics who have tried to go at all deeply into his work has so far pursued this course, with the possible exception, in one or two respects, of Boss. In view of the particular aim of this book I must limit myself to Jung's results, both positive and negative, especially in the matter of the practical and theoretical problems raised by religion. To these the whole of the second part of the book will be devoted.

PART II

V

THE PSYCHOLOGY OF RELIGION

It is highly exceptional for a psychologist to regard religion as a thing of outstanding importance, as Jung does. I have already (in Chapter I) remarked in passing on the " religious " character of analytical psychology. Now that we have looked a little more deeply into Jung's fundamental ideas and made a closer criticism of his assumptions, we can devote the whole of our attention to the religious problems he raises.

These problems are already evident in Jung's earliest writings, but gradually they invaded the entire field of his investigations; so that it is not surprising that a number of writers, Catholic as well as Protestant, have tried to determine their exact significance. The most important of these writers are, on the one side, Von Gebsattel, Goldbrunner, Frei and Victor White, and on the other Frischknecht, Schaer and Sierksma. Also to be mentioned are Tuinstra, Buber and Edward Glover.

Unfortunately the judgments passed by these writers are somewhat conflicting, not to say contradictory. Jung himself, in a tone of resignation not entirely free from malice, says that he has been saddled with some delightful names—" not only gnostic and agnostic but also theist and atheist, mystic and materialist."[1] He maintains that such conflicting judgments and contradictory condemnations give him the right to plead not guilty to them all. It would however be unfair to ascribe these undeniable differences of opinion to the purely subjective prejudices of the critics concerned—who all in fact manage to draw up an imposing list of quotations from Jung's own works to support their views.

[1] "Religion und Psychologie," p. 468 (1953).

The real causes of their conflicting interpretations must be sought elsewhere. Either they content themselves with analysing a single book out of the whole of Jung's voluminous production, or they take a single period, or they try to sketch the whole development of his thought in a brief article or a single brief chapter. In each case they are obliged to stress only those elements which accord with their own views, and they inevitably find it impossible to give us a bird's-eye view of Jung's development as a whole.

Sierksma and Schaer concentrate entirely on the new material that has been provided by psychological phenomenalism and make no reference to the agnosticism manifest in Jung's earliest writings and its inevitable repercussions in the later works. Frischknecht, on the other hand, despite the wide documentation his work shows, concerns himself entirely with the agnostic passages. White has made a close study of a number of problems intimately bound up with the question of religion, but he makes no attempt to analyse Jung's thought chronologically. Goldbrunner in the final edition of his *Individuation* mitigates considerably the charge of psychologism brought against Jung in the partial, interim edition of his book published in 1940, but there is still no discussion of any of the works that Jung has produced since 1944: as important a work as *Psychology and Alchemy* is mentioned in the bibliography, but it plays no part whatsoever in the actual text. Von Gebsattel's study, admirable as it is in the subtlety of its appreciation, is devoted entirely to the three lectures that Jung published under the title *Psychology and Religion*. Tuinstra's book appeared in 1933 and so could only treat of a small fraction of Jung's work. Buber and Glover each give Jung no more than a dozen pages, and though in certain respects they do much to correct the balance they can hardly be said to exhaust the subject. Finally, Frei has published some extremely interesting extracts from letters received from Jung, concerning his religious conceptions; but these of course simply reflect Jung's ideas at the time of writings (1944–8) and need to be compared with the writings of the earlier periods.

It is my aim to avoid above all things the danger inherent in analysing simply one aspect of Jung's views or a single moment in his slow and lengthy evolution. I shall therefore stick to the well-tried chronological method, made necessary by the fact that Jung's works stretch back through over half a century of scientific endeavour. This will enable us to form a proper opinion of Jung's own views, and the opinions passed on them at the time, and to bring the two together without doing violence to either. In the course of this inquiry I shall once again omit all the criticisms that might be made—quite justifiably—from any particular religious or dogmatic point of view, and concentrate entirely on the curve of Jung's development. This should enable us to see how Jung himself has done all he can to include every element that has come within his ken in the course of his researches and observations. Jung takes pride in being a man of science who never misses out any of the facts of experience. Let us therefore follow in his footsteps, not only so that we can find out when and why he has gone off the rails—if indeed he has—but still more so that we can follow him into the various new fields for whose discovery we are indebted to him alone.

For the sake of clarity I shall divide his development into three separate periods. The first will include the articles that appeared between 1905 and 1912, all of which show unmistakable signs of Freud's influence. This period culminates in the appearance of his first large-scale work, *Wandlungen und Symbole der Libido*, which heralds period two. Period two means essentially the shorter books in which Jung put forward his views on psychology. In these are already to be seen signs of his concern with religion. The third period includes the large post-war works in which he published the results of his inquiries into all kinds of symbolism and in particular religious symbolism. The series of lectures given at Yale University in 1937, published under the title *Psychology and Religion*, provided the link between the two latter periods.

I. An Unorthodox Starting-Point for Psycho-analysis

Jung has never been indifferent to religion. From his earliest days he was fascinated by the mystery of things. A childhood memory described in one of his books sheds a vivid light on his state of mind in this matter.

His father was a Protestant pastor and he prepared his son for confirmation personally by way of the catechism. The boy was bored to death by these lessons. One day, when he was looking through the little booklet in search of something really interesting, he came across the pages in which the Trinity was explained. Puzzled but intrigued, he waited impatiently for the time to come when this subject should come up for discussion. "But when the longed-for lesson had arrived, my father said, 'We will skip this section; I cannot make anything out of it myself'. With that my last hope was laid in the grave."[1] This tiny incident left its mark for a long time: another fifty years were to pass before Jung could find the confidence to risk embarking upon his own personal study of the Trinity. In the meantime a process of psychological, if not religious, revaluation had taken place—for the fact cannot be denied: Jung's first written words on the subject of religion are out-and-out Freudianism. And if he found it so easy to adopt Freud's views, the reason can only have been that they chimed in so very closely with his own.

One has only to turn to the final section of the little book mentioned above,[2] "The Significance of the Father in the Destiny of the Individual", to see all the essential elements of a ruthless psycho-analytical reduction of all things to one basic fact. Following Freud absolutely, Jung describes religion as a "sublimation" of infantile sexuality. This sexuality centres upon the parents, particularly the father. As the child gets older, the activity of the censor opposes any open manifestation of it. Forced to find some way of masking itself, the father fixation takes the form of a tendency towards God, and subservience to Him. It is therefore not surprising that analysis should reveal an image of the father in this God. The so-called "objectivity" of the idea of God is therefore a mistake and an illusion, to be found not only in individuals but throughout the whole history of mankind.

This perfect agreement with Freud did not last long. As

[1] *The Integration of Personality*, p. 64 (1934).
[2] Cf. p. 49.

soon as Jung put forward his theory of the energic libido as something devoid of any qualities whatsoever, including sexuality, it was impossible for him to regard religion as "simply inadmissible sexual desires first repressed and then sublimated. . . . This kind of argument is like saying in physics, for instance, that since electricity comes through a waterfall being trapped and led off through pipes into turbines, it is really only a waterfall atrophied artificially. It is an argument that is all very well in an appeal for the preservation of natural beauty, but there is no scientific logic behind it."[1]

The slow but steady evolution of Jung's views on religion was a result of his real determination to omit none of the facts of experience. He found that religions had helped to create Western culture not only intellectually but morally. Christianity had produced a higher form of morality and after the disintegration of the Roman Empire had for many centuries been the bulwark of civilization. "It is going against the whole principle of scientific method to reject these results of religion as the phenomena of auto-suggestion."[2]

Following Reinach, Jung regarded Christianity as one of the sects that grew up out of the Graeco-Roman world's passion for mystery religions. These religions owed their success to the fact that they reacted violently against the general decadence and immorality. "The meaning of those cults—I speak of Christianity and Mithraism—is clear; it is a moral restraint of animal impulses. The dynamic appearance of both religions betrays something of that enormous feeling of redemption which animated the first disciples . . . for we can hardly realize in this day the whirlwinds of the unchained libido which roared through the ancient Rome of the Caesars . . . So for us the necessities which brought forth Christianity have actually been lost, since we no longer understand their meaning . . . In the past two thousand years Christianity has done its work and has erected barriers of repression, which protect us from the sight of our own 'sinfulness'. The elementary emotions of the libido have come to be unknown to us, for they

[1] "Über das Unbewusste", p. 543 (1918).
[2] *Wandlungen und Symbole der Libido*, p. 69 (1911).

are carried on in the unconscious; therefore, the belief which combats them has become hollow and empty . . . With this disbelief in the crudeness of human nature is bound up the disbelief in the power of religion . . . Whoever, on the other hand, to his conscious sin just as consciously places religion in opposition, does something the greatness of which cannot be denied. This can be verified by a backward glance over history. Such a procedure is sound religion. *The unconscious recasting of the erotic into something religious lays itself open to the reproach of a sentimental and ethically worthless pose.*"[1]

In the last few lines of this passage Jung accepts religion as a psychological value and clearly distinguishes it from sublimation. If today religion has become superfluous as a result of the education of Western feeling during close on two thousand years, that is no reason for despising it. But the modern ideal is nevertheless stated quite clearly: religion is more admirable the more it manages to make itself unnecessary. "This would be the course of moral autonomy, of perfect freedom, when man could without compulsion wish that which he must do, and this from knowledge, without delusion through belief in the religious symbols. It is a positive creed which keeps us infantile and, therefore, ethically inferior. Although of the greatest significance from the cultural point of view and of imperishable beauty from the aesthetic standpoint, this delusion can no longer ethically suffice humanity striving after moral autonomy. The infantile and moral danger lies in belief in the symbol because through that we guide the libido to an imaginary reality. The simple negation of the symbol changes nothing, for the entire mental disposition remains the same; we merely remove the dangerous object. But the object is not dangerous; the danger is our own infantile mental state . . . I think belief should be replaced by understanding; then we would keep the beauty of the symbol, but still remain free from the depressing results of submission to belief. This would be the psycho-analytic cure for belief and disbelief."[2]

Notwithstanding slight changes of emphasis that occurred

[1] *The Psychology of the Unconscious*, pp. 42–4 (1911).
[2] Ibid., pp. 145–6 (1911).

later, the muffled tones of this cry from the heart can be heard in a number of Jung's books. It expresses a wish that even Jung himself seems to have felt was well-nigh impossible. And so he warns us against rushing forward too quickly. There is a certain apprehensiveness as he looks forward to man's liberation: "He who is repelled by the historical and philosophical weakness of the Christian dogmatism and the religious emptiness of an historical Jesus, of whose person we know nothing and whose religious value is partly Talmudic, partly Hellenic wisdom, and discards Christianity, and therewith Christian morality, is certainly confronted with the ancient problem of licentiousness. Today the individual still feels himself restrained by the public hypocritical opinion, and, therefore, prefers to lead a secret, separate life, but publicly to represent morality. It might be different if men in general all at once found the moral mask too dull, and if they realized how dangerously their beasts lie in wait for each other, and then truly a frenzy of demoralization might sweep over humanity . . ."[1]

In perusing the above passages the reader should not take too much notice of the frequent statements with regard to the religious and historical personality of Christ. Jung took these from current Protestant theology, and in point of fact they obscure his own views, which are all we are concerned with here. He makes a real effort to appreciate the positive part played by religion in human life. It is true that this part is essentially a transitory one in his eyes and only makes sense if it ends in moral autonomy; nevertheless, religion is no longer condemned as a mere sign of neurosis. That is one step forward, at least. As a conscientious investigator into empiric fact, Jung finds that religion has had a beneficial effect on mankind. In the past it domesticated the life of the instincts. Today it can still do the same. And he even wonders whether the pursuit of moral autonomy put forward as the fully adult man's ideal in *The Psychology of the Unconscious* would not be fatal to the masses, whose intellectual and moral faculties have not yet reached their full development. May not one therefore have to suggest a "sublimation" for them that will

[1] *The Psychology of the Unconscious*, pp. 142–3.

gradually transform erotic tension into an elevated poetic, religious feeling? His answer is forthright: "One is wrong to storm against this conception from the radical standpoint of fanaticism for truth."[1]

Are we then to accept Jung's ambiguous compliment with delight: "The Christian religion seems to have fulfilled its great biological purpose, in so far as we are able to judge"?[2] It seems necessary, rather, to point out that there is a flagrant contradiction at the very root of this idea; for is it not in fact ridiculous to claim that a religious error lies behind the whole of Western thought and that a religious illusion has fashioned its elevated moral code?

Jung anticipated this objection, and he is quite prepared to admit that error cannot lead to truth or illusion give life to reality. What he says is that positive error—in the matter of religion, for instance, as regards the historical existence of the God-Man and the objective existence of God—can conceal within itself a core of psychological truth. In this particular case the truth is simply man's tendency to transcend the instinctive stage of the unconscious. The fact that this tendency is projected on to the symbols Christ and God means that the objective error contains a subjective reality. Anyone who imagines that he is following Christ and submitting to God is, by a happy error, simply developing his latent potentialities. "The religious myth meets us here as one of the greatest and most significant human institutions which, despite misleading symbols, nevertheless gives man assurance and strength, so that he may not be overwhelmed by the monsters of the universe. The symbol, considered from the standpoint of actual truth, is misleading, indeed, but it is *psychologically true*, because it was and is the bridge to all the greatest achievements of humanity."[3] And Jung adds in a note that one has to adopt the point of view laid down once and for all by Kant in his theory of knowledge—and not only in the matter of theory but, even more importantly, in the matter of practice too.

In these latter quotations we come up against the Kantian assumptions already referred to in the previous chapter. Jung's

[1] *The Psychology of the Unconscious*, p. 39 (1911).
[2] Ibid., p. 45.
[3] Ibid., p. 144 (1911).

empirical approach to the phenomena of religion had enabled him to make a new evaluation of the part played by religion in history. But this did not mean that he had escaped from Kant's clutches. On the contrary, he pushed to extremes Kant's contrast between the transcendent reality of the object inaccessible to reason and the phenomenon directly perceptible by reason. Where Kant had posited the object as a postulate of the practical reason, Jung tried to do away with any kind of transcendence whatsoever. This position of his, which goes beyond the province of psychology proper in all directions, appears more or less clearly according to circumstances. Here I shall simply give a few of the most characteristic passages. "The idea of the masculine creative deity is a derivation, analytically and historically psychologic, of the 'Father-Imago', and aims, above all, to replace the discarded infantile father transference in such a way that for the individual the passing from the narrow circle of the family into the wider circle of human society may be simpler or made easier."[1] "Since, psychologically understood, the divinity is nothing else than a projected complex of representation which is accentuated in feeling according to the degree of religiousness of the individual, so God is to be considered as the representative of a certain sum of energy (libido). This energy, therefore, appears projected (metaphysically) because it works from the unconscious outwards, when it is dislodged from there as psychoanalysis shows."[2]

Since in these two passages Jung takes the trouble to state his position from the analytic-psychological point of view, we may be tempted to assume that he refrains from making any incursions into the field of ontology. But elsewhere he says that the analytic-psychological point of view is the only pertinent one. He denies categorically that Christ has any objective reality as a divine person. "What is divine in the mystery of Christ is what is universally human. Every god . . . is impersonal and universally valid. Christ is a 'spirit', as is shown quite clearly by the original Christian tradition."[3] In these words and others of a like kind Jung's real ideas come out quite clearly. The "divine" simply

[1] *The Psychology of the Unconscious*, p. 29 (1911).
[2] Ibid., p. 38 (1911).
[3] *Wandlungen und Symbole der Libido*, pp. 324–5 (1911).

covers whatever is not individual. It represents whatever is valid universally, which is the same thing as saying, universally human. God is everything in man that transcends the ego. As Jung can only see this kind of immanence, the divine can only be a universal or "collective" psychic reality.

To what conclusions are we led, then, by a study of Jung's leading ideas about religion as developed in *The Psychology of the Unconscious*?

On the one hand he tries to show the positive part that has been played in history by mystery religions in general and Christianity in particular; on the other, he refuses to grant these religions any absolute or objective value. These two conclusions are the result of a great effort to gain a clearer idea of the true function of religion, a function which he believed to be misrepresented by the psycho-analytical theory of sublimation.

Jung's aim was to take Freud's opinions and correct and complete them in accordance with his realization that the merits of religion, both past and present, were beyond question: this was an irrefutable empiric fact that was all too often ignored. But to this he added a philosophical principle taken from Kant: he asserted Kant's theoretical agnosticism—which divorced the phenomenon as something directly perceived from the ontological reality of the object itself—against Freud's realism, which seemed to regard energy and sexuality as the same thing. The agnosticism that Jung took from Kant was attenuated in its turn as a result of his experience as a psychologist. He knew only too well that to explain any psychic phenomenon—and still more, to get rid of it—it was not sufficient to show that it was unreal or an illusion. Any psychological phenomenon that appeared regularly and generally must have a psychological meaning. It was therefore psychologically true at least. Even when Jung says that the divinity is only a projection of unconscious contents he produces a valid psychological reason to explain the meaning of this projection. Anything that appears always and everywhere is the manifestation of an inner necessity. Jung lays this down as a rule at the beginning of the book: "When an idea is so old, and also generally believed, it is probably true in some way, and, indeed, as is mostly the case, is not literally true, but is true psychologically."[1]

Two main assumptions underlie Jung's empirical observations—on the one hand, as a philosophical principle, there is the most unmitigated agnosticism, and on the other, as a psychological principle, there is an absolute certainty about the psychological truth of any generalized phenomenon. These two assumptions determine the meaning of religion for Jung and decide the part played by it in the synthesis developed during his first period and formulated in *The Psychology of the Unconscious.*

There is nothing to be said against the psychological principle that Jung introduced. But the philosophical principle, which he puts forward as though it was a fact of his empirical science, needs further discussion. Jung does indeed seem to have regarded this principle as a matter of genuine scientific certainty. The postulate of the unknowability of the object in itself appeared to him to be confirmed by empirical study of the imago, symbol and myth, which seemed to distort the objective world through the subjective contributions they brought to it. It had the further advantage of freeing his investigations from any sort of supervision by philosophy or theology. Was there not reason to fear, indeed, that these two branches of knowledge might impose standards that were foreign to his own science? And so he did not content himself with saying that the psychologist could and must speak only of what he discovered through his own method, and must abstain from any sort of absolute judgments about the ontological reality of his object;[2] he went one stage further and maintained that any knowledge of the object itself is absolutely (*überhaupt*) unthinkable. In doing so he went right outside the field of psychology and plunged head foremost into the error committed by so many

[1] *The Psychology of the Unconscious*, p. 41 (1911). G. Bachelard takes this principle from Jung and expresses it in an even more forthright manner: "Opinions objectively so absurd must have some profound psychological cause" (*La psychanalyse du feu*, p. 66).

[2] This is a principle which Jung always maintained, and it can hardly be questioned. Of course the psychologist can only speak about what he has observed and in so far as he has observed it. The classical way of putting this is to say that the formal object of psychology is man as a psychic being. In this case the ontological aspect forms part of the material object but being what it is it is outside the psychologist's range and he must be careful not to say anything about it.

scientists: dazzled by the effectiveness of their empirical method within their own science, they have no eyes for any methods of an ontological kind.

Such a denial of the rights of philosophy and theology is, however, very disconcerting. Jung realized very early on the specific, irreducible nature of the religious function. In 1917 he spoke of it as a genuine psychic instance. In 1921 he said this again.[1] Lastly, in 1924, he gave his views on this matter in a blunt answer to his own questions: "Can science be so sure that there is no such thing as a 'religious instinct'? Can we really suppose that the religious phenomenon is nothing but a secondary function based on the repression of sex? Can anyone show us those 'normal' peoples or races who are free from such silly repressions? But if no one can point to any race, or even a tribe, which is quite free from religious phenomena, then I really do not see how one can justify the argument that religious phenomena are not genuine and are merely repressions of sex."[2] A remark as straightforward as this at once gives rise to a second question: how is it possible to regard religion as an irreducible function if it does not bear any relation to any objective reality? This question will form the topic of the next section of this book.

Although Jung started from a purely psycho-analytical position he soon, under the influence of his own observations, realized that Christianity has played a positive part in human history. But he wanted it to be a part that came to an end, because he thought it was a source of error. He demanded, or rather desired, that the age of symbolic illusion should give place to an age of moral autonomy. Let us therefore look a little more closely into his conception of the psychological part played by religious symbols.

II. The Psychological Significance of Religion

In 1920 Jung found himself driven by his investigations in the religious field to face an apparently insoluble problem. On the

[1] "The Psychology of the Unconscious Processes", (1917) in *Collected Papers on Analytical Psychology: Psychological Types*, Part VIII (1921).

[2] *The Development of Personality*, p. 83 (1924).

one hand he could no longer regard religion as a pure epiphenomenon or sublimation, on the other he could not admit that religion bore any relation to an objective personal God.

As one might expect, he set off in search of some middle way. His resulting "synthesis" presents religion as an irreducible psychological function but one which should lead to moral autonomy. Following his usual line, he claims that this synthesis can unify the two opposing points of view by affirming them both on the psychological level. It is hardly surprising that the supporters of the two hostile positions joined forces against him. And so during all this second period he was doing his best to justify his psychological theory and all its many implications.

If we are to get a true idea of the successive stages of Jung's thought we must not forget the viewpoint which he had adopted in *The Psychology of the Unconscious*.[1] That book is inspired by Frobenius's studies of the myths centring round the sun-god. According to Jung these myths are disguised forms of the regression and progression of the essential dynamism of psychic energy.

Frobenius[2] had reduced all the solar myths to a very simple scheme. The god, like the sun rising in the east, moves forward towards the culminating point in his career. But this ascending movement inevitably changes and comes down again, and the god, like the sun, is devoured by the sea monster in the west. After he has been devoured he struggles desperately to overcome the monster until he touches one of its vital organs. Meanwhile the "night voyage" (*Nachtmeerfahrt*) brings him back to the east. The god is thrown up by the monster, comes back to life with the sun and again starts on his journey towards the zenith.

Jung seized upon all this with avidity. But, still faithful to his own conception—described above—as to how symbols and myths had been formed, he took the solar myths as figurative expressions of a subjective or psychic reality which had been inspired by an objective fact, the course of the sun. The sun-god

[1] It should be said in passing that all the topics that Jung investigated in the later part of his career are already to be found explicitly mentioned in this book, which, despite the chaotic way it is constructed and its deficiencies from the point of view of method, is still Jung's most important work.
[2] L. Frobenius, *Das Zeitalter des Sonnengottes*.

is simply a symbol of the dynamism possessed by the libido. This dynamism has a dual rhythm. As long as the energy can pour forth unhindered, its flow adapting itself without difficulty to concrete circumstance, there is progression. But when, as frequently happens, this adaptation to the surrounding world comes up against hindrances, the person himself doing his best to oppose it or unforeseen circumstances preventing it from taking place, then the libido is no longer able to find its normal mode of exit and is forced to build up in the unconscious. Then there is regression. Consciousness having blocked up all the outlets, the libido that has accumulated in the unconscious attaches itself to some psychic structure or other. These structures or complexes manifest archaic or infantile features because they belong to the unconscious. It is not surprising, therefore, that the symbols in which regression expresses itself show symptoms of decadence or degeneration. In point of fact the appearance is deceptive. The symbols that come up from the unconscious are all driven by the energy towards further development, and archaic features inherent in the symbols do not prevent the process as a whole from being an enrichment leading to further development.

In Jung's view, the sun-god myths are simply objectivating descriptions, i.e., descriptions, in the form of projections, of the dual rhythm of psychic energy. The journey in the sun-chariot is an expression of progression, the night voyage, on the other hand, an expression of regression. The energy that loses interest in the external world is symbolized by the god's being swallowed by the dragon or sea-monster. The night journey with its various wanderings represents all the efforts to achieve some sort of adaptation to the unconscious psychic world into which the libido has withdrawn. The god succeeds in cutting off one of the vital organs, i.e., the energy that has been activating the unconscious. This brings him victory over the monster and he can emerge from it, generally with all the other people whom the monster of the unconscious has swallowed, and come back to the light and consciousness.[1]

[1] "The Psychology of the Unconscious Processes" (1917) in *Collected Papers on Analytical Psychology*, pp. 436–7.

According to Jung, a comparative study of mythological parallels sheds a great deal of light on the person of Christ, who is supposed to represent the same sun-god as Mithras in a different guise. Like Mithras, Christ symbolizes the libido, which engenders life beyond death. Because he concretizes psychic energy in a particularly striking way, Christian believers look to him as a personal example that they themselves can follow. Without realizing it, they recognize him as the ideal projection of the psychic energy that is at work in the depths of their own being. They submit to him as a person—believing him to be an objective reality—because he is in fact simply the most precious part of themselves.[1]

Regression, as I said above, does not in Jung's view signify any sort of degeneration. It is a form of development resulting from an incursion into the unconscious. It is obliged to disguise itself in an archaic or infantile garb because the stage that it is to lead to is still not fully realized. It only reveals its objective meaning to the person who can discern the symbolic clothing in which the projection is wrapped. It goes without saying that "religious symbolism erected into a system"—such is Jung's definition of the higher religions—is simply one stage on the way to the moral autonomy that is to be achieved through scientific psychology. This evolution from the religious symbol to moral autonomy is realized both in the history of mankind and in the individual, who recapitulates the whole of human history in his own personal evolution.

To make his ideas quite clear, and give them a scientific basis, Jung makes use of the distinction between archetypes and instincts. These both form part of the human being, but instincts are right at the opposite end of the scale from archetypes. Instincts are an expression of the biological side of man's nature, archetypes of the "spiritual" side. As the two sides together make up the whole

[1] It is impossible in a few lines to give any idea of the immense amount of material that Jung has amassed in support of this. Moreover, it would need to be subjected to a most rigorous criticism. I shall simply mention by way of example two points that play a major part in this comparative study. Christ dies, spends three days in hell, and then comes back to life. For this reason the liturgy and the writings of the Fathers praise him as the "invincible sun"—*sol invictus*.

range of man's dispositions, they create a state of conflict which is simply "the expression, and perhaps also the foundation, of the tension which we term psychic energy."[1] If things are to proceed properly, this state of conflict must give place to careful control over the biological instincts by the spiritual archetypes. This, dressed in a new scientific terminology, is a re-statement of the ideas to be found in *The Psychology of the Unconscious* on the subject of religion. (Jung values religion for the way it develops the moral sense.) We have seen in our discussion of the archetypes why Jung finds it impossible to attribute the genesis of the archetypes to education alone. But as the archetypes are active in the unconscious, they are inevitably projected. The archetypes which were first projected on to the parents soon give birth to a being that has always been known as "God". "Science calls this 'being' energy."[2]

By thus distinguishing archetype and instinct, which oppose and thereby complement each other, Jung can answer the question, Can one accept the fact that the religious phenomenon is always a derivative function? with a No. (Religion, that is to say, submission to God—who is only a projection of the archetypes in the unconscious—is an irreducible function and has nothing to do with instinct) whether sublimated or not.

Jung therefore accepts the existence of a "religious function,"[3] orientated towards a reality whose projection has been known from time immemorial as God. In point of fact, he says, this reality is the psychic reality of the archetypes, on which man feels himself to be dependent. It follows that religion is mistaken about the reality of what it imagines to be its object; but it also follows that religion is psychologically true, inasmuch as it expresses man's most fundamental dispositions. Religious symbols are a help to people who through lack of proper moral development and personal greatness of soul remain bound in by their own projections. "They make it possible for many people to bring a certain amount of useful activity into their lives." But

[1] *Contributions to Analytical Psychology*, p. 60 (1928).
[2] Ibid., p. 63.
[3] I have intentionally avoided using the unfortunate phrase, "religious instinct", which Jung often uses as a synonym for "religious function".

these people will never attain to " a primitive religion, a religion of a very individual kind which is altogether different from the regnant dogmatic religion of the community."[1]

After this general introduction we must go on to consider in detail how Jung's revaluation of the religious function is developed in three particular respects. First we shall examine his views on the historical origins of the idea of God. Then we shall find out by what psychic processes religion is rooted in the individual person. Finally I shall give an account of the " collective " forms that the higher dogmatic religions impose upon the religious life of their practitioners.

THE HISTORICAL ORIGINS OF THE IDEA OF GOD

We must never forget that Jung's direct observations, comparative studies and most significant ideas are concerned entirely with " modern " man, i.e., the kind of man who has lived his life in the higher cultures of Europe and Asia during the last three thousand years.

Jung has however spent considerable periods, on three different occasions, amongst primitive peoples. His idea was to inquire more closely on the spot into their psychic dispositions, customs and habits and their moral and intellectual ideas. As touchstones for his own opinions about modern man these contacts have no doubt been quite fruitful; but it would be absurd to try to base any consistent theory on the handful of articles and lectures—comprising in all no more than a hundred pages—that he has bequeathed to us from his sojourns in Africa and America.

The study of primitive psychology has done very little to help solve the religious problems of analytical psychology. It has affected only two points. In the first place Jung believes that the various pre-animistic conceptions confirm the existence of a world-wide diffusion of the energic or dynamic conception of the psyche, and his belief that the idea of God is simply a projection of psychic energy operating in the unconscious. Secondly, he quotes primitive beliefs in " spirits " and " souls " as a striking

[1] *Contributions to Analytical Psychology*, p. 67 (1928).

example of the projection of individual and collective complexes on to immaterial beings.

In a special chapter of his *Contributions to Analytical Psychology* Jung gives a list of the many different words used by primitive peoples in different continents—*wakanda* (Dakotas), *oki* (Iroquois), *manitou* (Algonquins), *wong* (Gold Coast), *chirunga* (North Australia), *mana* (Melanesia) etc.—to signify a force that manifests itself in both living creatures and inanimate objects. Lacking any specific characteristics, this force appears in everything that is "active". Jung therefore refuses to follow Tylor in personifying this force and turning it into a "soul". He says that the fundamental idea of the pre-animistic stage—"mana"—should be rendered by the modern word "energy". This almost world-wide diffusion "of the tension which we term psychic energy"[1] is supposed to prove that views on the dynamism of psychic phenomena are corroborated by observations made by man from the earliest times. In the beginning this energy was directly perceived as an undifferentiated force. Only later was this direct perception replaced by symbolic signs that gave birth to souls and spirits. These signs were the result of an abstraction, whereby the energy was separated from the objects that carried it, the souls and spirits the result of a projection whereby the energy was separated from the subjects from which it proceeded.

Jung says in so many words that none of the ideas of "mana" has any religious connotations. He believes, however, that through their gradual evolution towards the ideas of souls and spirits, the same energy does indeed lie behind present-day ideas of God, "if not as the one and only condition, at least as an essential determining condition."[2] Souls and spirits were born in the mind of the primitive from "the seeing of apparitions, the phenomenon of the dream, and the pathological disorders of the psyche."[3] These three kinds of experience drove the primitive to accept the existence of immaterial beings that guided and governed his life and were beyond his control. As psychology has traced back dreams, hallucinations and dementia to the activity of unconscious

[1] *Contributions to Analytical Psychology*, p. 60 (1928).
[2] *Über die Energetik der Seele*, pp. 110–11 (1928).
[3] *Contributions to Analytical Psychology*, p. 255 (1919).

complexes that have been split off from consciousness, only one conclusion is possible: souls and spirits must be the projected expressions of psychic complexes of an individual or collective kind.

From this account, short and sketchy though it is, it should nevertheless be clear that Jung only turned to "historical" investigation into the origin of the idea of God for interested reasons, using it in so far as it helped directly or indirectly to back up his own psychological views. To this end he made particular use of Tylor's theories, which he filled out with pre-animistic data. Hence my criticisms of the two points in the account above are aimed not so much at Jung himself as at the ethnologists on whose theories and facts Jung based his ideas.

One looks in vain in Jung's account of his ideas for any sort of classification of all the many tribes and peoples which he lumps together indiscriminately under the heading of "primitives". Today all ethnologists recognize that the old cultures had a far subtler idea of God than was thought by the animists and pre-animists, and no one can hope to discuss the origin, development and changes in their ideas without first making some sort of classification, based on scientific standards of a trustworthy kind, of the various types of primitive.[1]

Lacking this classification, animistic and pre-animistic theories have had to fall back upon an assumption in their attempts to classify the meagre data about mana-forces, ancestors, souls and spirits. This assumption is simply that of a development from the simple to the complex. There is no need to point out, of course, that every science is built up on assumptions, and as long as these do not conflict with the facts or method of the particular science concerned there can be no grounds for complaint. Unfortunately the contemporary development of ethnology has played havoc with the assumption of a gradual development from the simple to the complex. In point of fact the ethnologist, in so far as he is still able to approach the past through those primitives who still survive—should not one rather say, who are still in process of

[1] It is impossible here to give any idea how such a classification could be made, and all I can do is to refer those interested to the great number of publications for and against the cultural-historical school in ethnology.

disappearing?—comes up against highly complex religious practices and ideas, all of which give a flat denial to any suggestion of primitive "simplicity". But the assumption is not only untenable in practice; it is just as unsatisfactory theoretically. How can one discover what is "simple" without some historical proof or some *a priori* assumption? What right has one to assert that "mana", which is a highly complex conception of primitive magic, is simpler than the one God of monotheism, which, no one can deny, has a far less complex and intricate structure than any polytheistic pantheon?

This criticism applies primarily to the ethnologists' animistic and pre-animistic theories. But it is also valid in connection with the way Jung applies their facts. We must not forget that in the first place Jung is a psychologist, and that his interest in ethnological problems is therefore that of an amateur: what he really hopes to get from ethnology is confirmation for his own psychological views. Such an attitude, alas, hardly favours the kind of objective impartiality which is essential for any proper approach to the uncertain data and arduous problems that face the ethnologist. A psychologist should avoid any incursion into the field of ethnology unless he is prepared to be constantly on his guard. Even then he can never take the ethnologist's place. No opinions about the primitive peoples of any cultural group at any stage of their evolution can have any real value for the psychologist unless they are the result of a deep study not only of primitive behaviour but of the mind of the primitive. Theoretically this is not impossible. But so far no branch of depth psychology has faced such a Herculean task, which would need a rare knowledge of two of the most enormous fields in modern science.

In short, our excursion has brought us little that is rewarding. So let us return to the subject of more interest to analytical psychology—modern man. Here too we can easily underestimate the difficulties. For the development and evolution of the idea of God in the individual is a most complex process, and it is not easy to present its various stages without some sort of falsification. The higher cultures bring a considerable number of new elements into the picture, consciously introducing them through education or having them unconsciously imposed by the surroundings, and these, far from encouraging spontaneous development, often hinder or distort it.

THE EVOLUTION OF THE IDEA OF GOD IN THE INDIVIDUAL

Jung remains faithful to Freud's views in so far as he regards the child's emotional and affective life as centring primarily round the parents. In its moderate form this assertion is hardly debatable. We are quite prepared to agree with commonsense psychology that the bonds that unite a child to its parents are of a different kind from those that unite it to its brothers and sisters, and, even more, those that are to unite it to the vast society which it will enter upon leaving the bosom of its family.

Freud maintained that these bonds were sexual, Jung says that they are affective; and although both agree that they lead to a projection, all their subsequent explanations differ because of this initial difference of opinion. Jung does not feel that there is sufficient justification for saddling the real mother and father with the whole of the imago that the child forms of them. I have already tried to show in detail how he attributes the main part in the formation of parent-images to the archetypes. So long as the lie is not given to the imago by concrete experience it is by no means easy to discern the part the archetypes play. As the child grows up he inevitably has to leave his childish world—it might not unfairly be described as his parent-world—behind, and follow the normal course of development towards independent adult life. It is then at this stage that the archetypal elements which have previously been projected on to the parents present him with a difficult problem. On the one hand the projected elements belong to him personally, so that he cannot easily reject them; on the other hand they have previously been projected on to others, so that he cannot see how he can regard them as his own.

The mechanism that controls the detachment of the archetypal elements from their first object can be clearly seen in the reabsorption of the transference during treatment. To go beyond the transference a patient who has returned to an infantile attitude or never advanced beyond it has to free himself from his parent-fixation, reactivated through his attachment to the doctor as a result of his projecting his parent-imago upon him.

The first thing the patient has to do is to become aware of his projection. Until he does this he cannot be in a position to realize that he is saddling the doctor with a personality created by his unconscious. But as soon as he does do so he can adopt a real attitude towards his doctor. But now a new danger arises, the danger of "inflation". In point of fact the discovery that the imago has been created by the unconscious leads almost invariably by a process of reaction to an introjection of the imago: the patient regards all the qualities which he had focused first upon his parents, then upon his doctor, as his own property. In his own eyes he rises up as a superman and a prophet.[1]

The alternative between projection on to another person or introjection on to the ego also faces the adolescent when he is freeing himself from his bonds with his parents. Usually however it is avoided by a compromise: the unconscious archetypal components of the parent-imago are projected outside the world of human beings altogether. This compromise, which is a universal phenomenon, Jung sees as "the psychological reason why men must always have demons and cannot live without gods". And so he insists most emphatically that "the concept of god is simply a necessary psychological function of an irrational character which has nothing to do with the question of the existence of god".[2]

In practice the psychotherapist has to remember the need felt by a great number of people to project archetypal elements on to metaphysical entities. There need be no difficulty in this, at least if he realizes their real nature and hidden significance. On the one hand he must say that "the gods cannot and must not die".[3] On the other hand he must realize that any affirmation of their objective existence is and always will be meaningless. In this way he will be able to appreciate the precise part played

[1] If the fixation on the father or mother was negative in character, the introjection will have a similar result but in the opposite direction, and the patient will then attribute the negative qualities to himself and regard himself as an evildoer or a lost soul.

[2] *Two Essays on Analytical Psychology*, pp. 72–3 (1926).

[3] Ibid., p. 74 (1926).

by unconscious archetypes without either repressing them or projecting them on to the absolute. The man who really absorbs this psychological truth is as far from the trusting faith of childhood as he is from the pretentious incredulity of the people who have failed to reach proper maturity. He has gone beyond both projection and introjection and reached the kind of fullness that submits consciously to unconscious realities.

Jung has no hesitation in accepting this psychological meaning of the idea of God. This is in perfect conformity with his passionate desire to defend the psychological value of religion. It also, in fact, introduces a new factor which gradually absorbed all his attention. This factor is the self.

What exactly the self represents, and what its nature is, Jung in the last analysis is unable to say. He is most emphatic in proclaiming that he has absolutely no intention of going beyond observed fact, but these observed facts nevertheless tell him that the self includes things on both the hither and the thither side of consciousness. The ego is clearly not the centre of the self, because it "has neither a hand in producing such experiences [arising from the unconscious], nor the necessary intelligence to understand them. It can only be their victim—or the receiver of divine grace".[1] Although the self sometimes appears in forms that seem to refer to "a consciousness that is not our own", it is hardly possible for us to know much about its nature. "As long as we have no other means of ascertaining the existence of a transcendental consciousness we have to admit our uncertainty."[2] The self is therefore a necessary psychic reality, but unknowable. "The problem thus seems to border on the extra-human realm which has always been known by a divine name."[3]

All this shows that Jung's original views did not undergo any essential change, even though his growing number of observations led him to express his ideas more precisely. The idea of God remains a projection, inevitable at the infantile or primitive stage of development, transforming the archetypal elements into metaphysical entities. There is only one decent attitude for a

[1] *The Integration of the Personality*, p. 16 (1939).
[2] Ibid., p. 16.
[3] *The Development of Personality*, p. 182 (1932).

man to adopt when he reaches maturity: he must see through this projection and come to realize that it proceeds from the collective unconscious, whose nature is something essentially unfathomable. These unfathomable depths of the unconscious Jung calls the self to make it quite clear that he is not being duped by any God: "Our intellect has long known that one cannot think god, much less conceive in what fashion he really exists, if indeed at all."[1]

Jung's work is studded with passages like this. Here is a particularly fierce one: "A mind that is still childish either thinks of the gods as so-called metaphysical entia, existing in themselves, or it regards them as playful or superstitious inventions. . . . But the mind is exceeding its limits when it asserts the metaphysical existence of the gods. Such a statement is just as presumptuous as the opinion that they could be invented, for undoubtedly they are personifications of psychic forces."[2] In another place he lets off the passing shot: "Whether energy is God, or God is energy, concerns me very little, for how, in any case, can I know such things."[3]

It has not so far been made clear, however, why Jung, who quite rightly distinguishes the idea of God from his objective existence, denies the latter so categorically.

In a lecture on "Analytical Psychology and Poetry" published in *Contributions to Analytical Psychology*, he gives an excellent statement of method. Discussing the work of art, he says most emphatically that psychological analysis can never penetrate to the essence of art; at most it can uncover the inner and outer influences that determine the way in which it appears. He goes on: "A like distinction must also be made in the realm of religion; there also a psychological consideration is permissible only in respect of the emotional and symbolical phenomena of a religion, where the essential nature of religion is in no way involved, as indeed it cannot be. For were this possible, not religion alone, but art also could be treated as a mere sub-division of psychology."[4]

[1] *Two Essays on Analytical Psychology*, p. 73 (1926).
[2] *Essays on Contemporary Events*, p. 7 (1936).
[3] *Modern Man in Search of a Soul*, p. 218 (1931).
[4] *Contributions to Analytical Psychology*, p. 225 (1921).

This passage, despite its conciseness, its remarkable clarity and precision, can hardly arouse a great deal of enthusiasm. The lucidity shown in such words does not prevent Jung from going on shortly afterwards to make a categoric denial of the existence of God which is not only not justified on psychological grounds but trespasses upon the field of philosophy. This sort of mixture of genuine psychological wisdom and methodological insight on the one hand and unimaginable metaphysical confusion on the other sometimes takes a disconcerting form, as for instance in the following passage: "The concept of god is simply a necessary psychological function of an irrational character which has nothing to do with the question of the existence of god. The human intellect can never answer this question, and still less can it give any proof of god. Furthermore, such proof is altogether superfluous, for the idea of an all-powerful divine being is present everywhere, if not consciously recognized, then unconsciously accepted, because it is an archetype. Something or other in our souls is of superior power, and if it is not consciously a god, it is at least the 'belly', as St. Paul says. Therefore I consider it wiser to recognize the idea of god consciously; otherwise, something else becomes god, as a rule something quite inappropriate and stupid, such as only an 'enlightened' consciousness can devise. Our intellect has long known that one cannot think god, much less conceive in what fashion he really exists, if indeed at all."[1]

Why is Jung so determined to deny God's objective existence? To this question there seems to be only one possible answer: his intransigence is a result of his determination to remain absolutely faithful to the proven methods of his own science. In our discussion of the works of his first period we have already seen how he made use of Kant's theoretical agnosticism, and extended it to include the practical reason to keep his "empirical" conclusions free from any taint of philosophy or theology. In the purely psychological books of the second period Kant is barely mentioned, but the agnosticism that he had taken from him is still there, sometimes, indeed, emerging in the form of

[1] *Two Essays on Analytical Psychology*, p. 73 (1926).

vehement diatribes. This is particularly the case when he is taking up the cudgels against some real or imaginary opponent who wants to minimize or destroy the results achieved by analytical psychology and uses metaphysics or theology to do so.

In this connection some remarks on the "psychological basis for the belief in spirits" seem to me to be not without interest. Is it not surprising, for instance, that Jung does not reject the existence of spirits out and out? "I have confined myself to the limits of science and have purposely avoided the question whether spirits are real or concrete objects . . . not because I regard it as futile, but because I am not competent to discuss it from a scientific standpoint, having no evidence in my possession."[1] His observations in the matter of pathology have provided him with endless cases in which the spirits existed only in the morbid psyche of his patients, and it is quite understandable that under the influence of all these observations Jung should have a horror of making any objective judgement about them.

In the essay from which the above quotation is taken Jung describes the psychological process of the conversion of Paul of Tarsus. He ends with these words: "Science does not, in a way that satisfies our intellectual conscience, allow us to explain the case of St. Paul on supernatural grounds." (What Jung means by this is that St. Paul's case cannot be taken out of the field of psychology and presented as a "miracle" going against or outside the bounds set by the normal laws of psychic life.) "We should be compelled to do the same with many similar cases within our medical experience, which would lead to conclusions antagonistic both to our reason and our feeling."[2] This passage seems to me to show quite clearly that Jung, tortured by a fear that one might almost call instinctive, is determined to prevent philosophy and theology from interfering in any way with psychology. He seems to be afraid that the slightest infiltration from these other fields will swell into a rushing torrent and sweep away his psychology. Jung ends the book with a sigh of resignation. "Science must, I think, confine itself to the limits

[1] *Contributions to Analytical Psychology*, p. 268 (1919).
[2] Ibid., p. 258 (1919).

of cognition, for science is essentially intellect; it means the application of one undoubted psychological function, namely thought. But intellect is only one among several psychological functions, and therefore does not suffice to give a complete picture of the world . . . But when we make use of the intellect, as in science, we have to adapt ourselves to the demands of intellectual criticism, and we must limit ourselves to the scientific hypothesis so long as there is no reliable evidence against its validity."[1]

This passage is revealing: what makes Jung have such excessive confidence in empirical observation is his mistrust of the fallible human intelligence. This kind of attitude—which is a very common thing in the world of empirical science—makes it clear why the psychologist, armed with his exact science, has defended his metaphysical excesses with such passionate intensity.

During the whole of his second period, then, Jung never for one moment forsook his agnosticism. He nevertheless says that religion is "psychologically true" because it is "a vital link with psychic processes independent of and beyond consciousness, in the dark hinterland of the psyche. Many of these unconscious processes may be indirectly occasioned by consciousness, but never by conscious choice. Others appear to arise spontaneously, that is to say, from no discernible or demonstrable conscious cause."[2] Collective religions, too, in so far as they are the expression of these unconscious activities, play a positive part in the psychology of the individual.

THE PSYCHOLOGICAL PART PLAYED BY THE DOGMATIC RELIGIONS

In Jung's view the various "creeds"—this is the word he prefers to use to describe the higher religions, because of the importance they attach to their professions of faith—are "codified and dogmatized forms of original religious experience".[3] Dogmas are particular forms of "symbol". Dogmatic symbols express an intensely lived psychic reality for the people who first make use

[1] *Contributions to Analytical Psychology*, pp. 268–9 (1919).
[2] *Introduction to a Science of Mythology*, p. 102 (1940).
[3] *Psychology and Religion*, p. 6 (1937).

of them. Whenever a man of religious genius succeeds in discovering an especially appropriate symbol that is full of meaning, he immediately finds disciples. For he is giving them a highly developed idea of God, with its own appropriate rites, in a ready-made dogmatic form. He is helping them to direct their psychic energy along channels already prepared. He is giving them a chance to transpose, effortlessly, safely, their own particular parent-projection. All they have to do is to adopt his rites and representations and then they avoid any risk of coming into direct contact with the activity of the archetypes. "The dogmatic symbol protects a person from a direct experience of God."[1]

The particular kind of symbol that is known as a dogma has a twofold positive value. On the one hand it is a substitute for being confronted with the unconscious without any intermediary —and experience proves that such a confrontation overtaxes most people's psychic strength and is always fraught with peril. On the other hand it does justice to the unconscious components of psychic life, even though it does so in the form of a projection.

Jung believed that he had discovered a striking example of the dual role played by the symbol in the life of Nicholas of Flue, the Swiss "peacemaker" who was canonized in 1947. Brother Nicholas, a "confederate" and peasant farmer, the father of ten children, a member of the local council, a peace-time judge and a war-time general, left his wife and children at the age of fifty so that he could spend the rest of his life in contemplation as a hermit (*Waldbruder*). His retired life did not, however, prevent him from exerting a considerable influence in political matters: his advice was sought by the great ones of the world, both inside and outside the confines of his own country.

After the new hermit left home frightening visions descended upon him. He tried to fathom their meaning: he "made researches into the nature of his vision with the aid of the illustrated booklet of a German mystic, and struggled to get his original experience into tangible form . . . This is what I call the 'treatment' of the symbol. Reflection upon the symbol led necessarily to the

[1] *The Integration of the Personality*, p. 59 (1934). In Jung's terminology a direct experience of God simply means being confronted directly with the unconscious, not in a " collective " but in a purely individual manner.

conclusion that he must have gazed upon the holy threefoldness itself." But the original experience had been very different. In his ecstasy he had seen a face ravaged by terrible anger, and the sight had been so terrifying that it had distorted his features to such an extent that everyone who looked at him had been overcome by fear too.

This terrifying vision "which had burst like a volcano upon his harmless religious outlook without any introduction on the part of dogma and with no exegetical commentary—this vision must have required a long labour of adaptation before it was changed into a vision of threefoldness. . . . the dogma at that time was as firm as a rock. . . . And the dogma showed its power of assimilation in this, that, with a saving grace, it transformed something fearfully alive into the lovely clarity of the idea of the Trinity ". What would have happened if Brother Nicholas had kept entirely to the sinister reality of his vision in his attempt to discover its significance? Would he have developed a new idea of God? Or would he have collapsed into madness under the weight of a revelation beyond his strength to bear? Jung's answer is evasive, but not free from bitterness: Brother Nicholas would not, in any case, have got away with it: "He would then have become not a saint but a heretic and would perhaps have ended his life at the stake."[1]

The dogmatic symbol thus acts as a kind of protection while some genuine religious experience is being assimilated. But though it guarantees real security it exacts a hard price. The acceptance of ready-made religious representations goes hand in hand with a progressive decline in genuine religious experience. The dogma's content diminishes as the experience fades away into the past. In Jung's view the weakening of religions is always due to this kind of disintegration. The symbols that bring peace of mind to generation after generation of believers slowly lose their content until in the end—sometimes after centuries, even millennia—people are terrified to discover that they have lost their meaning altogether. For they have never been questioned, any

[1] *The Integration of the Personality*, pp. 58–9 (1934). Cf. " Bruder Klaus ", *passim.*

more than one questions the habit of decorating Christmas trees or hiding Easter eggs. "The fact is that archetypical images are so significant in themselves that people never think of asking what they mean. That the gods die from time to time is due to man's discovery that they do not mean anything, that they are good-for-nothings made by human hands, fashioned out of wood and stone. In reality, man has thus discovered only this: that up till then he had not achieved one thought concerning these images."[1]

According to Jung dogmatic religions derive their value from the fact that they originate in a genuine, immediate experience, which they then express in the form of projections. For this reason he repudiates the absurd pretensions of the age of enlightenment, which imagined that "religions had been invented by the cunning human reason. As though one fine day had come along when someone had suddenly taken it into his head to create a god and other dogmas so that he could use this phantasy, the realization of so many desires, to take in the whole human race".[2] Nevertheless this symbolic-dogmatic representation only has any meaning in so far as it enables psychic realities to express themselves. Jung's criticism of "the great philosophical systems of the East" therefore applies to "all the dogmatic religions of the West." "To understand metaphysically is impossible; it can only be done psychologically. I therefore strip things of their metaphysical wrappings in order to make them objects of psychology. In this way I can at least get something comprehensible out of them and can avail myself of it. Moreover, I learn psychological conditions and processes which before were veiled in symbols and out of reach of my understanding . . . my admiration for the great Eastern philosophers is as great as my attitude towards them is irreverent. I suspect them of being symbolic psychologists to whom no greater wrong could be done than to take them literally."[3]

Jung is thus quite certain about the psychological part played by creeds and dogmatic religions. This gives him a wise respect for them in the course of actual treatment. We have seen how at the very beginning of his career he doubted whether "fana-

[1] *The Integration of the Personality*, pp. 60–1 (1934).
[2] *Wirklichkeit der Seele*, pp. 219–20 (1934).
[3] *The Secret of the Golden Flower*, p. 129 (1929).

ticism for truth" might always be the right thing. Later, he was to state it as a principle that the psychotherapist should lead any patient who asks for help along the path of his own religious convictions. The exact significance of this rule will be investigated in more detail in the next chapter, when we come to discuss the connection between psychotherapy and pastoral theology.

All the writings discussed so far reveal a fairly consistent attitude. The qualifications on a number of finer points are not without interest but they do not involve any essential change in Jung's position.

In Jung's eyes religion has always had a positive psychological value, if only as a useful, even desirable, makeshift. The taming of human instincts and the development of a conscious culture are two of the benefits which it has brought to generation after generation and we are still enjoying them today. But though these may evoke our respect, they must not make us lose our critical clear-sightedness, and if the only reason for the existence of religions lies in their psychological significance it is only natural that we should prefer a lucid adult attitude towards them. For we cannot allow ourselves to be led astray by childish toys—even though we may retain a sentimental affection for the Meccano sets that first started us on our way towards becoming engineers, or the copying books that woke us into being artists.

Again, Jung is quite clear about the limits of his psychological science. It cannot say anything definite either way about the objective truth of religion or the existence of God: he rightly restricts his investigations to ideas about God. But for some reason which he has never made clear, but which seems to be a fear of having philosophy and theology intrude into his own empirical science, he has never tired of saying that it is impossible to know anything about the existence or nature of God. At first he justified his position by calling in Kant, extending Kant's theoretical scepticism to include the practical realm too, and so ending up in an absolute agnosticism in no wise justified by his scientific data.

Consequently, with regard to the critics who have dealt only with Jung's pre-1940 work it may be said that their charge of agnosticism is thoroughly substantiated. For the first two periods I am ready to accept Goldbrunner's view of Jung as an agnostic positivist.[1] Jung is a positivist because he will only accept empirical methods modelled almost entirely on those of the natural sciences. He is an agnostic because he rejects any method but the psychological one and so turns metaphysics into an inevitable but illegitimate projection of psychic realities.

On the other hand I know that there are other critics, who have no use for any positive revaluation of religion in the field of pure psychology and see quite clearly that Jung's agnosticism is a purely arbitrary affair, who have considered it best to unmask him as an "unconscious believer" who whilst claiming to be no more than a psychologist has tried to do again what the gnostics tried to do so presumptuously in the past. It seems to me that these two views of Jung are not incompatible: one judges him from a materialistic and atheistic point of view, the other considers him from the viewpoint of a theist and a believer.

My own conclusion is that however much we may and must sympathize with Jung's attempts to achieve a revaluation of religion from the psychological point of view, we must nevertheless insist most strongly upon the unmitigated and uncalled-for agnosticism that appeared in all his writings until the years 1935–40.

III. Beyond Agnosticism

Throughout his life Jung has been concerned with the problems raised by religion, but though they can be sensed in all his books there is only one in which he has discussed them officially. This is *Psychology and Religion*, which contains three lectures, slightly revised and amplified, given at Yale University in 1937, and they sum up all his earlier views. There is no need for us to consider again the psychological significance of religion and the difference between the idea of God and God's objective existence. Fortunately *Psychology and Religion* is not simply an attempt to present Jung's past ideas in a rather more systematic form. It

[1] Cf. J. Goldbrunner, *Individuation*, pp. 161 ff.

opens out on to the next stage in his development. In this book for the first time he analyses the characteristics of the religious function itself.

THE NUMINOUS

Jung talks a great deal about psychic realities, but he has been very sparing in his definitions of them.[1] So far he has only given us one definition of religion. In his view it is "a vital link with psychic processes independent of and beyond consciousness, in the dark hinterland of the psyche".[2] This is hardly worth calling a definition, for after all it is no more than a vague approximation. What exactly, in this context, is the "vital connection", and what unconscious processes are involved? On both these points a certain amount of enlightenment is to be found in *Psychology and Religion*, and we shall begin by examining the empirical basis of what Jung says there.

Like every other therapist Jung has been struck by the way some dreams and oniric images leave an extraordinary impression behind them, a mysterious kind of fascination that continues even into the dreamer's waking life. Sometimes only one motif may have this power, more often a whole episode is intensely lived or a voice will address the dreamer in tones of harsh reproach or solemn warning or noble exhortation. Dreams like this that leave such a strong impression behind them are often dismissed as unimportant by the critical consciousness, which rebels against their content because it seems so trivial or absurd. Boss describes a dream of this kind.[3] A thirty-six-year-old woman dreams that she is visited by a well-known professor of physics. He is an old man and so stiff in the joints that he has great difficulty in walking, but his mind is as clear and penetrating as ever. While he is lecturing he happens to repeat the following extraordinary sentence: "If this place had a door I would go out into the open

[1] In his *Psychological Types* he gives his definitions once and for all. There are about three score of them and they take up more than a hundred pages, the shortest of them occupying half a page, the longest no less than ten. Jung was careful to add to the title of this section on definitions an appropriate sub-title, "*Begriffliche Umschreibungen.*"

[2] *Introduction to a Science of Mythology*, p. 102 (1940).

[3] M. Boss, *Der Traum und seine Auslegung*, pp. 153–4.

air." While the woman is dreaming this sentence seems to take on a shattering significance, but when she wakes up the more she thinks about it the more trivial it seems to her to be.

If we want to uncover the real meaning of this kind of oniric motif we have to do more than study the one isolated fragment; we have to consider it in the context of the dreamer's whole life. Thus the professor's "trivial" sentence takes on its full meaning as soon as we find that the woman who dreamed about him is herself an academic type who is proud of her intelligence and technical knowledge and who throughout her whole life has regarded things entirely from the scientific point of view. Is it not a matter of the utmost importance for someone leading such a "stiff" intellectual life to find some way out of the narrow confines of her existence and get "out into the open air"?

The first thing that struck Jung was the fact that dreams could make such a strong impression. Soon he noticed during long courses of treatment that these significant dreams crystallized round certain affective centres or archetypes. In the matter of spontaneous drawings even more than in dreams it was significant how fascinated his patients were by all the variations and contrasts in bright colours that they made on subjects particularly charged with meaning for them. At the same time Jung found that certain symbolic expressions usually developed according to fixed rules. He always tried as far as possible not to influence his patients, contenting himself with trying to discover the significance of the particular symbols later.[1] Sooner or later, either during analysis or outside it, a dream or drawing would come up which to the astonishment of the person concerned would express a synthesis of all his tendencies in a most impressive general way. Often the result coincided with a period of stable equilibrium in his psychic development. The unconscious production signified a period of marking time. Even when not conclusive it was like

[1] *Psychology and Alchemy*, p. 43 (1944). In 1926 Jung had said in "The Relation of the Ego to the Unconscious": "I must therefore expressly emphasize that my method of treatment does not consist in causing my patients to indulge in strange fantasies. . . . I merely put it on record that there are certain cases where such a development occurs, not because I force anyone to it, but because it springs from inner necessity" (*Two Essays on Analytical Psychology*, pp. 221–2).

a landmark on a long journey, or a nice shady spot half way up a very steep slope.

In *Psychology and Religion* Jung described a dream of this kind in detail and added a mass of material to support his interpretation of it.[1] But many years before, he had described other dreams of the same kind when discussing the matter of individuation. He had related amongst other things the experience of a woman patient of his who had had a "visual phantasy or vision" which she had described as follows: "I climbed the mountain and came to a place where I saw seven red stones in front of me, seven on either side, and seven behind me. I stood in the middle of this quadrangle. The stones were flat like steps. I tried to lift the four stones nearest me. In doing so I discovered that these stones were the pedestals of four statues of gods buried upside down in the earth. I dug them up and arranged them about me so that I was standing in the middle of them. Suddenly they leaned towards one another until their heads touched, forming something like a tent over me. I myself fell to the ground and said, 'Fall upon me if you must! I am tired!' Then I saw that beyond, encircling the four gods, a ring of flame had formed. After a time I got up from the ground and overthrew the statues of the gods. Where they fell, four trees shot up. At that blue flames leapt up from the ring of fire and began to burn the foliage of the trees. Seeing this, I said, 'This must stop. I must go into the fire myself so that the leaves shall not be burned.' Then I stepped into the fire. The trees vanished and the fiery ring drew together to one blue flame that carried me up from the earth."[2]

All the dreams with this strange fascinating quality have one characteristic in common. Having no logical coherence or apparent meaning, they make no appeal to the intellect; nevertheless their mysterious symbolism and felt significance fully satisfy the person concerned, who feels instinctively that in them he is drawing near to some mystery, something stronger than

[1] *Psychology and Religion*, pp. 78–93 (1937). This dream and the whole series of which it forms a part are commented on by Jung in the essay entitled "Dream-symbols of the Process of Individuation" in *The Integration of Personality*, first published in the *Eranos Jahrbuch* for 1935. There is a fuller commentary in *Psychology and Alchemy* (1944).

[2] *Two Essays on Analytical Psychology*, pp. 220–1 (1926).

himself to which he must submit if he is to find real peace of mind, even though its first appearance in the sphere of consciousness may have been terrifying and overwhelming.

All the characteristics analysed above were observed by Jung in the psychic development of a large number of patients. With the passage of time he was able to collect data about people who had not been analysed for a long time or had never been treated but had nevertheless undergone similar experiences. He could see only one way of accounting for all the converging evidence: the psychic development of individuation which he had followed from day to day in his patients must be a phenomenon common to the whole of mankind: through dreams and the activity of the imagination the unconscious must combine with consciousness to lead man towards the complete unfolding of his psychic life. All the parallels in works of literature and historical documents confirmed him in this belief, for they too described the same symbolic psychic processes. The distinctive mark of all these experiences was always the same: they always overwhelmed the people concerned with an irresistible power of attraction and a sense of mystery.

The activity of the archetypes in individuation thus appeared, in all the cases which Jung observed, as possessing the same characteristics as Otto had described as numinous "moments" in his book on the phenomenology of the sacred. What was involved was in fact a sense of dependence, majesty, energy, mystery, fascination . . .[1] Jung regards the agreement between the psychological data drawn from experience and Otto's descriptions as irrefutable proof that the religious function can be identified with a "vital connection with the archetypes". Starting from his own observations, then, as the empirical basis, he uses Otto's descriptions to help him formulate a clearer and more compact definition of the religious function.

The religious is an irreducible function inasmuch as it is "a

[1] Cf. R. Otto, *The Idea of the Holy*, pp. 5–49. Nowhere does Jung say how far he agrees with Otto's phenomenological descriptions. To judge by his account in *Psychology and Religion* his agreement is simply of a general kind. He seems for example to soft-pedal the "feeling of creatureliness" (*das Kreaturgefühl*), despite Otto's express words, to the point of equating it with Schleiermacher's feeling of dependence.

spontaneous expression of a certain predominant psychological condition".[1] Religious experience therefore does not derive essentially from any objective content, which in fact varies endlessly, but from a subjective value-judgment that sees the content as the mediator or symbol of the supreme value that the person concerned must aim at.[2] Naturally this kind of value-judgment takes the form of a personal experience. No mere arbitrary decree, or any attempt to establish by logical deduction or scientific induction—it matters little which—that some particular content represents the highest value, can *ipso facto* achieve a religious attitude. The numinous is not posited, it imposes itself. Consciousness does not so much prompt it as submit to it. The numinous as such subjugates man independently of his will.[3]

For this reason, both according to religious teaching and in the general opinion of mankind, the activity of the numinous has its source in a region beyond the individual. Jung, as a scientist who has no wish to extrapolate his observations in the psychic field, does not feel justified in adopting this view, and so he gives this force a new name, the self, and, vigorously excluding everything that lies outside the field of psychology, describes it as a psychic totality which, though it utterly transcends and overflows beyond the conscious ego, at the same time includes it and stands behind it as an impenetrable background. Hence he can define religion as "the attitude peculiar to a consciousness which has been altered by the experience of the numinosum",[4] or, in other words, the attitude of a consciousness that has submitted to the psychic totality in so far as this totality manifests itself as man's highest value.

The numinous, which by its very nature can only appear in personal experience, is regarded by Jung, as by Otto, as something irrational. The validity of such an experience can never be proved by logical argument. Religion is only proved on the

[1] *Psychology and Religion*, p. 108 (1937).
[2] Ibid., pp. 75–6 (1937).
[3] Jung does not mean by this that man cannot adopt any attitude towards the numinous, but only that the numinous is not at his disposal. This in fact is what causes the feeling of dependence.
[4] *Psychology and Religion*, p. 76 (1937).

pulses: "Religious experience is absolute. It is indisputable. You can only say that you have never had such an experience, and your opponent will say: 'Sorry, I have.' And there your discussion will come to an end."[1]

This irrationality was not displeasing to Jung. It fitted in very well with his empiricism. Had he not seen with his own eyes how many patients went through an experience of the numinous which he himself had done nothing to encourage? Had he not seen how the experience gave meaning and beauty to their lives? And so he was prepared to make quite magnanimous concessions: "No matter what the world thinks about religious experience, the one who has it possesses the great treasure of a thing that has provided him with a source of life, meaning and beauty and that has given a new splendour to the world and to mankind . . . And if such experience helps to make your life healthier, more beautiful, more complete and more satisfactory to yourself and to those who love you, you may safely say: 'This was the grace of God.'"[2] For this reason Jung has always paid a great deal of attention during actual treatment to the symbols that rise up from the unconscious in the form of dreams, phantasies, drawings, etc., firmly convinced that sooner or later light will issue from the darkness.

The symbols that come up from the unconscious charged with a strictly personal affective tonality are not to be confused with dogmas. Dogmas arise when the experience itself is followed by faith in it as a genuine direct experience of the numinous: "The practice and the reproduction of the original experience have become a ritual and an unchangeable institution."[3] The undeniable value of the resulting dogma thus comes from the experience that lies behind it, and in psychotherapy this gives it a value far transcending that of any scientific theory, in so far as giving a meaning to life is concerned. Every dogma, in fact, "owes its existence . . . to so-called 'revealed' immediate experiences, such as the God-Man, the Cross, the Virgin Birth, the Immaculate Conception, the Trinity and so on", each expressing

[1] *Psychology and Religion*, p. 113 (1937).
[2] Ibid., pp. 113–14 (1937).
[3] Ibid., p. 6, and also p. 52 (1937).

an "irrational entity",[1] or, as we might say, a mystery inaccessible to the human reason. A symbol is far more satisfactory than any scientific theory in explaining life, and no scientific theory will ever succeed in dethroning religious creeds or supplanting religious dogmas. For such theories, however penetrating they may be, are by their nature strictly rational. The whole reason for their existence lies in their elimination of any irrational element. They can thus never do more than express consciousness by means of abstract concepts. A dogma, on the other hand, describes, so to say, the vital process of the unconscious far more appropriately in, for example, "the form of the drama of repentance, sacrifice and redemption".[2]

In the final paragraph of *Psychology and Religion* Jung is not afraid to call experience of the numinous a "grace of God". Dogma too is presented as something with living value "attacked by the imprudent and the foolish but not by people who care for the human soul".[3]

It is difficult to catch in the tender tones of this conclusion any echo of the fierce dogmatic denials handed out in *The Psychology of the Unconscious*, and as it is the notes that make the music quite a number of critics, especially amongst psychologists, have been led into believing that in saying this Jung was restoring religion, and indeed dogma, to its old place of honour. In this they were not entirely wrong, for if these particular notes went on modulating for long enough they could indeed transform the whole song. There is no denying, indeed, that Jung's original hostility was slowly but surely undergoing a change: after accepting the fact that religion had played an important part in history he had gone on to recognise that it had a genuine psychological value too. Finally the numinous character of individuation had raised the religious function into the highest realms of the self. Was not such a spectacular ascent enough to justify the wildest hopes?

Theologians, on the other hand, Protestant as well as Catholic, not content with concessions affecting points of only secondary

[1] *Psychology and Religion*, p. 56 (1937).
[2] Ibid., p. 57 (1937). Cf. also *Symbolik des Geistes*, p. 364 (1948).
[3] Ibid., p. 190 (1937).

importance as regards the matters in which they were themselves directly concerned, reacted violently against this "breviary" of Jung's religious ideas. And without forgetting the change of emotional tone in what Jung says, I feel obliged to agree that so far none of his essential tenets had changed. It is quite true that he says again and again that he is only discussing the idea of God; but it is also true that he says that we have no way of knowing anything about final causes. He stresses, not without a certain nostalgia, the importance of creeds and dogma, but then he describes them as consequences of immediate or "personal" religious experiences.

Jung had nevertheless taken a decisive step forward in this book. Previously, religion had only been a stage in the development of an individual or group, something to be got beyond as quickly as possible so that there could be a full flowering of moral autonomy. But now, as a genuine experience of the numinous, religion was not only a necessary stage in human development but indeed the culmination of this perfect unfolding. And inasmuch as the codified forms of dogma and ritual gave man an indirect experience, they helped him to participate in the numinous without being exposed to danger or obliged to make greater efforts than he was capable of.

The revaluation of religion clearly apparent in *Psychology and Religion* truly heralds a new period. But the agnosticism persists. We must therefore try to find out why Jung devoted his attention to religious symbolism in his great post-war books.

SYMBOLISM IN RELIGION AND ALCHEMY

Since 1935 Jung has been engrossed in the study of religious symbolism. Before that he had already agreed to write commentaries from the psychological point of view on ancient texts such as the *Bardo-Thodol*, Tibetan meditations on death and reincarnation, and the *I Ching*, a Taoist book about Chinese Yoga. But he had undertaken those comparative studies at the request of other scholars and the texts he thus dealt with, coming as they did from countries in the Far East, had no direct connection with the religious psychology of the West. Since then his own personal interest has focused on Christian and more particularly Catholic symbolism. The ritual prayers of the Mass, the various creeds about the Trinity, the fish—ἰχθῦς—as the symbol of Christ, the revolt and submission of Job, the terrors of the Apocalypse, have formed the object of his patient comparative researches.[1]

What was Jung's aim in embarking upon this study of religious symbolism? Was he really attracted by the religious side of the matter, or was he fascinated by the symbolism itself, rich and varied as it is and promising to be so full of enlightenment? I have no doubt myself that the latter was the true reason, and this seems all the more likely from the fact that only a little while before Jung had chosen the symbolism used in alchemy as the special object of his investigations.

Jung hesitated a good deal before embarking on this new course. Silberer's book[2] had not succeeded in convincing him of the psychological significance of the esoteric expressions used in alchemy, a subject of which he was in practice quite ignorant. Nearly fifteen years later, personal observations, described in an article written for the *Eranos-Tagung* of 1933 under the title of "Zur Empirie des Individuationsprozesses," caused him to modify his views. The symbolic sketches in which one of his woman patients who knew nothing about alchemy expressed her psychic process bore an unmistakable resemblance to the typical illustrations accompanying descriptions of supposedly chemical processes in the old books on alchemy.[3] Jung determined to get to the bottom of the matter and began to study this abstruse branch of knowledge. As he gradually became more familiar with the ideas behind this pre-scientific chemistry, the more he advanced the more convinced he became of the similarity between the descriptions of the old experiments and the various stages in the process of individuation.

[1] I have already pointed out above that all these subjects had been touched on in *The Psychology of the Unconscious*.

[2] H. Silberer, *Probleme der Mystik und ihrer Symbolik* (1914).

[3] This series of drawings was republished in *Gestaltungen des Unbewussten* (1950), where the commentary is considerably expanded.

In most of the old books the starting-point is primal matter at the "nigredo" stage: this is an apt symbol for the unconscious, which includes all the various potentialities in a chaotic, undifferentiated state. As the alchemic process develops it goes from disintegration (*putrefactio*, *mortificatio*, *calcinatio*) to the production of the white substance known as "albedo" by way of the unification of opposites (*coniunctio* or *matrimonium*). This is a metaphorical way of expressing confrontation with the various archetypes—the shadow, the anima or animus, etc.—that are to be integrated by the conscious attitude. The final result of the process is described by the old authors as a carbuncle or a rose—both of which express the "rubedo" stage—or a homunculus—a winged hermaphroditic creature with a body, soul and spirit—or again as the philosophers' stone which can change any metal, even the basest, into gold.

All these symbols apply very well to the qualities possessed by the unified psyche. Jung therefore believes that the alchemists' "opus" is to be regarded as a series not of chemical experiments but of "psychic processes expressed in pseudo-chemical language".[1] This language interests him because it "filled up the abysses of ignorance about chemical processes with a great heap of mythological motifs and found compensation for the unknown in mythical projections".[2]

It is easy to understand the importance that Jung attached to this discovery of the supposed psychological significance of the alchemists' symbolism. It provided him with a highly developed symbolic language, amply described and copiously illustrated, of the process of individuation. Alchemy, from this point of view, was primarily a rich source of comparative material. Secondly, it gave him a kind of independent check on his own psychological views. And thirdly, it testified to the universality of the psychic processes that he was trying to establish scientifically. For these three reasons he embarked upon a careful study of these old books, which at first sight seem quite incomprehensible and indeed, with their fantastic illustrations, rather absurd.

[1] *Psychology and Alchemy*, p. 231 (1944).
[2] *De Sulphure*, p. 27.

Jung's interest in the old alchemists' symbolism is therefore fundamentally psychological, and the same must be said of his interest in religious symbolism. All the references to alchemy in his studies of the Trinity, the Mass, Christ, etc., show this beyond all doubt. It is therefore impossible to speak of Jung as having any genuine interest in religion for its own sake. At the most it may be said that he values religion because it provides an unfailing source of symbols.

We have to realize that the psychological aspect is cardinal if not absolutely determining for Jung. But is there not another fact to be remembered, namely that religion represents a far higher value than alchemy? Both provide an abundance of highly original symbols charged with meaning; but is not religion the expression of an irreducible function, as stated above, and alchemy simply a matter of symbolism and nothing more?

This distinction between alchemy and religion is a valid one, but we must be careful not to make too much of it. For it hides an ambiguity which Jung does not take sufficiently into account. Religion as an irreducible function, i.e., as an experience of the numinous character of the archetypes and the self, exists at quite a different level from alchemy. On the other hand, religion as a matter of creeds and dogma, projecting psychic contents on to collective symbols, is on the same level. Readers of Jung have always to be remembering that his use of the word "religion" is equivocal. The religious symbol which as a dogma constitutes the very essence of a creed is in point of fact simply something that comes after a direct personal experience. The genuine religious experience, on the other hand, is simply a direct awareness of the numinous character of the self. It follows that religious symbolism is an expression of the numinous, differing not at all in value from the symbolism of the alchemists, both being made up of projections of the same order. Dogmatic religion and alchemy are not essentially different; they differ only in the specific form of their symbols.

FAITH IN GOD

So far we have simply been discussing Jung's empirical discoveries in the field of religion.

Jung was not at all surprised to find that these discoveries were unacceptable to the champions of materialism, who regarded religion as an epiphenomenon or a mere sublimation of an instinct, but he was taken aback when he found that he was being just as fiercely criticized by Christian believers. "When I point out that the soul possesses by nature a religious function (Tertullian: anima naturaliter christiana) . . . then it is precisely the theologian who seizes me by the arm and accuses me of 'psychologism',"[1] he exclaims, not without bitterness, turning his back on those critics, both Protestant and Catholic, who had attacked the views expounded in *Psychology and Religion*.

We have already studied in detail the various "syntheses" suggested by Jung to reconcile the opponents on the neutral ground of psychology; unfortunately the only result of this manoeuvre was to upset both sides, each of which felt equally misrepresented. In the same way, Jung's attempt at a revaluation of religion from the psychological point of view came up against opposition both from believers and from unbelievers. Both sides objected to his subjective religious feeling, regarding it as either insufficiently objective or exaggeratedly subjective. Once again Jung found himself caught between two fires.

In this highly uncomfortable situation Jung fought back with energy. He not only protested against the charges of atheism, psychologism and gnosticism brought against him by Frischknecht, von Gebsattel and Buber, but, what is more, tried to clarify his own position a little further. The result of all this was that he managed to clear up a number of ambiguities, and in stating his own final position was able to justify his own scientific attitude towards religion and at the same time accept the validity of the religious believer's point of view. A full and detailed account of this important step is contained in an essay that forms part of *Psychology and Alchemy*: being a declaration of principle, it is

[1] *Psychology and Alchemy*, p. 12 (1944).

placed at the beginning of this, the first of the main works that have followed one another since 1944. It has the significant title, "Einleitung in die Religionspsychologische Problematik der Alchimie" ("Introduction to the Psycho-religious Problems of Alchemy").

In an effort to discover alchemy's rightful place in religious psychology Jung quite properly begins by outlining his own psychological attitude towards religion. Again he insists that he only claims to be a psychologist, i.e., an observer of empirical facts. He repeats that his science is only concerned with the idea of God, the symbolism of which reveals far more about the man speaking than it does about the divinity. Several times he emphasizes the fact that in postulating an archetype of the idea of God he has no intention whatsoever of advancing this as a proof of God's objective existence.

This harping may seem unnecessarily fussy, but it was nevertheless justified by certain deep-rooted hostilities towards him. There were psychologists, unbelievers for the most part, who objected to his psychological revaluation of religion on the ground that his hypothesis of a divine archetype meant trying to establish a scientific proof of the existence of God. Jung rightly defended himself against this charge, which he did not deserve, saying that he was a psychologist, not a philosopher, and that to say that an archetype had numinous characteristics and appeared in the unconscious did not necessarily mean affirming the existence of God.

This distinction, the reader will remember, was not a new one. In 1937 he had said: "Notwithstanding the fact that I have often been called a philosopher, I am an empiricist and adhere to the phenomenological standpoint".[1] The really new thing in the introduction to *Psychology and Alchemy* is Jung's clear acknowledgement that the religious believer's point of view is a perfectly valid one.

If this had simply been something said in passing, it could not be quoted as giving the lie to his earlier observations, but he goes more deeply into the question. After saying that psychology

[1] *Psychology and Religion*, p. 1 (1937). Cf. also *Seelenprobleme der Gegenwart*, p. 371 (1926).

in itself can never prove that God exists—and how can anyone complain against this, since it is just as true of psychology as it is of all the other positive empirical sciences, mathematics and physics, chemistry and biology?—he at once goes on to say that psychology by no means excludes the existence of God. The case is very much the contrary, he seems to say: "When I say as a psychologist that God is an archetype, I mean by that the 'type' in the psyche. The word 'type' is, as we know, derived from τύπος, 'blow' or 'imprint'; thus an archetype presupposes an imprinter. Psychology as the science of the soul has to confine itself to its subject.... Should it set up a God, even as a hypothetical cause, it would have implicitly claimed the possibility of proving God, thus exceeding its competence in an absolutely illegitimate way. Science can only be science; there are no 'scientific' professions of faith".[1]

Why then does Jung keep the word "God" in his vocabulary at all? The reason is a relatively simple one: when through psychological analysis we find an archetype present, expressing itself in a kind of symbolism similar to the most widespread representations of God, we call it "God". Thus psychology has its own particular technical use of the word.

The technical meaning that Jung gives the word "God" makes things doubly difficult for those of his readers who are religious believers. In their eyes the word refers to both the "real" God and the "absolute" God. Psychology, however, eliminates both these, and the believer has therefore to remember all the time he is reading Jung that the God Jung is writing about is an abstract idea including not only the "true" God but Allah, Purusha and the Tao as well. In other words the word "God" covers all the different ideas that have been held about him throughout mankind's somewhat chequered history. Furthermore, he has to remember that Jung does not even mean the ontological reality of this God of his, but only its repercussions in the human psyche —which also appear in the experience of the numinous and the symbolic expressions of the idea of God.[2] The difficulties inherent

[1] *Psychology and Alchemy*, p. 14 (1944).
[2] See Jung's Preface to V. White, *God and the Unconscious*, p. xvii (1952).

in this kind of abstraction lie behind the misunderstandings that are to be found in so many religious analyses of analytical psychology. Unfortunately the confusion of Jung's own language has contributed to this,[1] even when the technical word "self" is substituted for the ambiguous word "God".

The faulty application of this abstraction does not mean that it is not fully justified. It is possible therefore to agree with Jung when he says: "The religious point of view, understandably enough, puts the accent on the imprinter, whereas scientific psychology emphasizes the *typos*, the imprint—the only thing it can understand. The religious point of view understands the imprint as the working of an imprinter; the scientific point of view understands it as the symbol of an unknown and incomprehensible content. Since the *typos* is less definite and more variegated than any of the figures postulated by religion, psychology is compelled by its empirical material to express the *typos* by means of a terminology not bound by time, place or milieu. . . . For this reason I have found myself obliged to give the corresponding archetype the psychological name of the 'self'."[2]

Under the pressure of often violent criticism Jung managed to drop his attitude of unreasonable hostility to non-psychological methods and to define the exact scope of his own. We must now try to look a little more closely into these two aspects of Jung's position in the matter of method.

His most important piece of writing about religious symbolism is undoubtedly *Aion*. This not only discusses the self, the cardinal factor in analytical psychology, but, what is more, it keeps scrupulously within the limits of psychological methodology. Once again Jung compares his psychological analyses with the processes of art criticism, as he had done twenty years before.[3] "The parallels I have established between Christ and the self only refer to psychological matters. There is no question of my making any incursion into metaphysics." "In principle all I aim at and all

[1] See last chapter for a further discussion of this difficulty in connection with the book *Answer to Job*.
[2] *Psychology and Alchemy*, pp. 17–18 (1944).
[3] Cf. p. 132, the quotation from *Contributions to Analytical Psychology*, p. 225 (1921).

my method aims at is to do what the historian of art does in the field of art when he tries to discover what influences lie behind some particular representation of Christ."[1] As Jung is quite aware that this method lays him open to painful misunderstandings—it can easily give the impression "of reducing the symbol Christ to a psychological image of the self"[2]—he ends by trying to explain its exact scope once again: "Psychology, as has just been said, is not in a position to come to any conclusions of a metaphysical kind. All it can say is that the symbolism of the totality coincides with the symbolism used to convey the idea of God. But it is no more able to prove that the image of God bears any relationship to God than it is to show that the self can take the place of God."[3]

The limitations that Jung imposes on his psychological method emphasize the specific value of metaphysics and theology. But here again we must be on our guard against any premature enthusiasm. Above all we must scrutinize Jung's statements with an eagle eye. It is a striking fact that in *Psychology and Alchemy* his psychological point of view is always opposed to the point of view held by the religious believer. For Jung this latter includes metaphysics as well as theology. He refers, for instance, in the same breath, to "metaphysical assertions or other professions of faith",[4] and regards "the assertions of faith" as synonymous with "metaphysical assertions".[5] In *Aion* he explains the phrase "the domain of metaphysics" by immediately adding, "i.e. of faith".[6] The religious believer's point of view which Jung finally deigns to recognize belongs in his view to the sphere of "faith", i.e., something that one accepts as true as the result of a subjective certainty. "The religious-minded man is free to accept whatever metaphysical explanations he pleases about the origin of these images; not so the intellect, which must keep strictly to the principles of scientific interpretation."[7] Since, in Jung's view,

[1] *Aion*, pp. 106 and 107 (1951).
[2] *Aion*, p. 9 (1951).
[3] *Aion*, p. 287 (1951).
[4] *Psychology and Alchemy*, p. 14 (1944).
[5] Ibid., p. 29 (1944).
[6] *Aion*, p. 106 (1951). Cf. also *Answer to Job*, p. xiv (1952).
[7] *Psychology and Alchemy*, p. 14 (1944).

metaphysics belongs to the sphere of faith, he points out in passing "the impossibility of ever proving or refuting the truth of a metaphysical assertion"—on a scientific basis, of course.[1]

This attitude proves to me beyond any shadow of doubt that Jung is an incorrigible empiricist in his search for truth. Any conviction that is without an empirical scientific basis must in his view be something freely consented to, an acquired personal conviction. This somewhat tawdry idea of metaphysics, theology and faith is not much help to him when it comes to defending his own views against critical attack. Generally speaking he avoids giving any direct answer to the charges levelled against him and contents himself with repeating that people fail to realize how modest he is, or else complains bitterly that great wrong is being done him in saddling him with aims that lie quite outside the range of his empirical point of view. All the controversies in which he has been engaged and all the correspondence that has been published show how difficult it is for him to grasp the exact significance of any method other than his own.[2] We have already seen how the agnosticism which he professed for so long and so passionately was not so much a metaphysical attitude as an almost instinctive defence mechanism to safeguard the validity of his scientific method.

If we acknowledge, then, that from 1944 onwards Jung has never failed to recognize the validity of the religious believer's point of view we can still not ignore the fact that he is really quite unable to see any difference between metaphysics, theology and faith. These three fields, so different in nature, are all put under the same single heading, "the religious point of view", and this includes everything that exists outside the field of psychology and about it the scientist knows absolutely nothing. Is it surprising then, in view of his unfamiliarity with the religious point of view, that Jung should always have been reticent about any sort of confrontation with the unknown?

In itself it is not so very important for an empirical psychologist to be familiar with metaphysics and theology or to be able to see

[1] *Psychology and Alchemy*, p. 29 (1944).

[2] Cf. the controversy with Buber in *Merkur*, May 1952, and the correspondence with Haberlandt in *Wissenschaft und Weltbild*, Feb. 1953.

how these two branches of knowledge differ from faith, but if he also chooses to make a special study of religious symbolism a very real danger lies in wait for him: he runs the risk of compromising his own branch of knowledge by his ignorance of the other branches that have been studying the same material for centuries. And this danger is increased when the empirical investigator in question feels justified in setting up his own conclusions against views already established in these other fields.

Jung's ignorance of metaphysics and theology forces us to make certain reservations. This in no way implies any denigration of Jung himself as a person, or of his works. He has had no compunction about confessing his ignorance in these matters, indeed on occasions he has even gone so far as to express a touching desire to remedy it if only he could find a suitable collaborator. "Instead of criticism which misses the target," he wrote in a letter to Fr. Victor White, "I should much prefer to have a scholarly Catholic collaborator who, with understanding and good will, would correct my inadequate theological terminology."[1] And in the preface to Fr. White's book he re-echoes his delight and gratitude for the fact "that the co-operation I had so long wished and hoped for has now become a reality".[2]

Declarations like these, whose sincerity is beyond question, show how anxious Jung is to be fair to the religious point of view. One is obliged to recognize that his inadequate knowledge of theology, metaphysics and faith must necessarily vitiate his solution of problems shortly to be discussed, but one must also remember that he tackles these problems with a real desire to estimate religious phenomena at their true value.

Jung's fundamental attitude is that of an indefatigable investigator. In the beginning he rejected all religious values absolutely. Before long, however, he was becoming more and more impressed by the part that religion has played in Western civilization and the psychic development of the human person. For many years he has had no contact whatsoever with any religious body. His knowledge of faith and dogma is self-taught. The practice of

[1] V. White, *God and the Unconscious*, p. 260 (1944).
[2] Preface to V. White, *God and the Unconscious*, p. xvi (1952).

religion, with its psychological repercussions, and its grievous distortions, had only been accessible to him through his patients. In view of this, is it surprising that he should have stuck to his scientific psychological point of view rather more firmly than he might otherwise have wished? Should we not rather be all the more delighted that his empirical observations have so often helped him to overcome the obstacles raised by a kind of mind that in the beginning was, after all, rather restricted in its scope?

Since 1935 Jung's writings have shown how important dogmatic representations are to him. But he has always immediately added that it has not been given him to "believe". Never, he says again and again, has he felt that he can accept anything which he cannot understand. For this reason he has studied the psychology of religious dogma passionately in an effort to discover some acceptable meaning in it. I sometimes wonder whether it is quite so certain as he so often suggests that he has been unable to believe because he has not been given the grace of faith. May it not be that the scientific way of thinking has taken such a hold of him that he has come to regard any kind of faith whatsoever as unacceptable? If this is so, then he was describing his own case when he wrote of the mediaeval alchemists that they "ran counter to the Church in preferring to seek through knowledge than to find through faith".[1]

The above analysis of the gradual development of Jung's religious thought helps me to state my own position towards the various conflicting criticisms that have been made of his attitude.

In the first place I am bound to acknowledge that Jung was speaking the truth when, looking back on half a century's work, he said, "I have never anywhere denied God".[2] It would be wrong to accuse Jung of being an atheist in the strict sense of the word.

The agnosticism which he flaunted so continuously during his first two periods he rejected when he realized the validity of the religious point of view. It is true that he can be accused of having a faulty conception of metaphysics, but it is quite impossible to

[1] *Psychology and Alchemy*, p. 35 (1944).
[2] Letter in V. White, *God and the Unconscious*, p. 258 (1944).

say that he ever questions the believer's right to accept, for religious reasons, the fact of God's existence and the possibility of coming to know his nature.

It is not so easy to answer a third charge. Must we agree that Jung has failed to free himself from "psychologism"? Jung himself has rejected this charge indignantly. But one cannot ignore the fact that he has his own way of defining psychologism: he simply means any theory that regards religion as being simply the transformation or sublimation of an instinct. According to such a theory, inevitably, religion must essentially be something non-genuine. Jung accuses Freud of having fallen into this error, and at once adds that his own attitude is fundamentally different from Freud's. Far from deriving the religious function from some other instinct, he has declared that it is irreducible.[1] On the other hand it is certain that critics who attack "Jung's psychologism" can quote his followers to support their allegations.[2] In so far as Jung himself is concerned, it must be said that he has tried hard to escape from "psychologism", at least during his latest period. But his ignorance of metaphysics and his incompetence in the religious field have often militated against his good intentions. The result is that it is only too easy to interpret his ideas backwards to fit in with one's own particular point of view. Some of his disciples have not been afraid to exploit his ambiguities in favour of an out-and-out psychologism. For these people God is nothing more than a psychic reality, even when they say that this reality is irreducible. I for my own part am quite convinced that Jung himself would never go so far as this, but his own words are not clear enough to settle the question outright one way or the other.[3]

Jung is not an atheist. Nor is he an agnostic. He is primarily an empirical investigator who has remained scrupulously faithful to his subject. It was almost inevitable that he should give the

[1] Cf. *The Secret of the Golden Flower*, p. 130 (1929) and *Answer to Job*, p. 169 (1952).

[2] Cf. Von Gebsattel, *Christentum und Humanismus*, p. 49, and even more, P. Dessauer, "Bemerkungen zum Verhältnis von Psychotherapie und Seelsorge," pp. 129–30.

[3] In a private conversation I had with Jung he hit off his religious attitude very neatly when he said: "It is quite clear that God exists but why are people always asking me to prove this psychologically?"

impression of falling into psychologism, for the religious side of life, which fascinated him more and more as the years went by, became the centre of his scientific interest, and only a thorough grounding in speculative thought could have enabled him to formulate his exact position with regard to theology, philosophy and faith.

His genuine interest in the religious side of life on the one hand and his self-taught study of the most difficult problems of theology and philosophy on the other made him try to bring religion and psychology together. In practice this led to the development of a profound respect for religion, even in its various dogmatic forms, but in theory it made him take up matters which in theology and philosophy had long been settled.

In the next two chapters I shall discuss these problems more fully. The inquiry will be considerably helped by the fact that we have now reached a better understanding of the development of Jung's religious thought, and have a better idea of the various criticisms that have been made of it and a better grasp of the theoretical and practical problems that he has had to cope with as a practising therapist.

VI

PSYCHOTHERAPY AND SPIRITUAL DIRECTION

For many centuries spiritual direction was the exclusive prerogative of priests and religious, but at the beginning of the present century a change set in and since then the psychotherapist has gradually taken over the direction of an ever-increasing number of patients. It is not surprising that directors of conscience resented this as a profane intrusion into a field rightly to be regarded as their own, and their unamiability has become all the fiercer the more interest the psychotherapist has shown in religion: the fact that he follows quite a different method from the priest has not pacified those who object to it. We have seen how and why Jung turned to a study of his patients' religious problems. His investigations in this field aroused a good deal of suspicion in the minds of a great number of spiritual directors, and they made no secret of the fact, and it was no real compensation to Jung that he was given a favourable reception by a handful of admirers. In vain has he insisted that he is a doctor: generally speaking he has been suspected of having secret intentions going far beyond the avowed aims of his psychotherapy.

Most spiritual directors know from experience how helpless they are when they come up against psychic troubles, and so they have tried to find a kind of solution that would provide therapist and priest with their own clearly defined spheres. This prevents overlapping, and makes any attempt at collaboration unnecessary: the "sick" are inexorably packed off to the doctor, and the priest jealously keeps all the people in good health to himself. This radical demarcation of the separate zones of influence is usually justified by a reference to the distinction between the natural and the supernatural, the former belonging to the doctor, the latter to the priest.

Unfortunately this solution, neat though it undoubtedly is, is not very effective in practice. It ignores the fact that the "sick" and the "well" do not form two quite separate categories, and that the spheres of the natural and supernatural exist one above the other and interact. Some sort of interaction between psychotherapy and spiritual direction is unavoidable, and the refusal to collaborate must inevitably lead to antagonism.

In an effort to reduce this antagonism I shall in this chapter discuss the true nature of the relationship between psychotherapy and spiritual direction, meaning by therapy the kind that is practised by Jung, and by spiritual direction what is practised by the Catholic Church. In the previous chapter I treated Jung's religious ideas independently of any outside standard of judgement, but here I shall have to compare them with the practice and teaching of the Church. In doing this I shall adopt a certain attitude towards Jung and see him from a definite point of view: I am obliged to do this because of Jung's own position even more than as a result of my own personal convictions, for when Jung discusses dogma and ritual in his writings he usually means usages and doctrines of a specifically Catholic kind such as confession, the Mass, the Assumption, the Trinity.[1] Naturally, of course, in all his inquiries his aim is to bring out the psychological significance of these rites and representations, not their objective content.

We must therefore be quite clear about the real point at issue between psychotherapy and spiritual direction. I shall try to make this clear by discussing the traditional *modus vivendi* between analysis and confession. Then we must try to grasp the exact significance of Jung's psychotherapy, and to this end I shall examine his aim and how he proposes to achieve it. Finally, I shall sketch a possible system of collaboration between the director of conscience and the therapist.

[1] He can even go so far as to say that the principle of the *privatio boni* is a *sententia communis* of the Catholic Church. (Preface to V. White, *God and the Unconscious*, pp. xviii–xix.)

I. Confession and Psychological Analysis

Let me say at once that I reject any rapprochement that is based either on external resemblances or on a wrong interpretation of the things in question. A typical example of this kind of misunderstanding occurs when psychological analysis and confession are regarded as the same thing.

In the early days Jung himself expostulated against this sort of identification because it seemed to him likely to do psychotherapy harm.[1] But as he gradually discovered that the various religions provided mankind with "the great psychotherapeutic systems of the past" he grew more and more interested in confession. Soon he was having no hesitation in saying that psychoanalysis was a logical development of confession and that his method, like Freud's, was based on the practice of confession.[2]

In point of fact such a statement misses out all that is essential in both confession and analysis and simply compares secondary structural elements. No doubt a detailed avowal of one's sins is required in confession by a formal decision of the Church. But can this be said to be the really essential element in the sacrament of penance? The indispensable element in confession is a sincere contrition for deliberate sins which the patient must enumerate to the best of his ability. This sincere contrition for sin and the priest's subsequent giving of absolution make up the sacramental act and bring forgiveness. The forgiveness is essentially sacramental, and of itself it causes no change in the penitent's state of mind that can be seen psychologically.[3]

In psychotherapy, on the other hand, the doctor is not at all concerned with conscious sins but with unconscious tendencies that are creating a conflict whose origin the patient is unable to grasp. All that is apparent is the resulting psychic disorder, and the absence of any adequate cause in the psychic consciousness

[1] *The Psychology of the Unconscious*, "The Sacrifice", pp. 237–67 (1911).

[2] "Yoga and the West", in *Brabuddha Bharata* (1936).

[3] This chapter had already been published before I happened to come across Fr. Victor White's lecture, "The Analyst and the Confessor", published in his book *God and the Unconscious*. There (pp. 165–9) will be found a detailed study of the similarities and differences between confession and analysis. Fr. White's line of argument and his conclusions are exactly the same as my own,

makes the disorder look like a "foreign body" devoid of all meaning: this is the very heart of the neurosis. It thus becomes essential to uncover the psychic motivation behind the disorder by way of dream analysis, associations or spontaneous drawings, so as to reintegrate it and guide the patient's personal development along the line of his own dispositions.

Confession and analysis are thus at opposite poles. Confession means forgiveness of intentional conscious acts that have been repented of. Analysis brings into consciousness unconscious tendencies for which the person concerned cannot be held responsible. If we ignore these radical differences and try to reconcile confession and analysis simply because they have the structural element of acknowledgement in common, we stray beyond the field of phenomenology, for phenomenology is based on the comparison of structures that are identical in meaning, and the meaning of the acknowledgement made in confession is not at all the same thing as the meaning of that which is made in psychotherapy. For this reason I cannot agree with Jung when he says that "the first beginnings of all analytical treatments of the soul are to be found in its prototype, the confessional".[1]

Actual sin, i.e., an act that is intentionally evil, does not lead to neurosis, and confession, as the sacramental forgiveness of sins, is incapable of curing neurosis even in its mildest form. Analysis, again, has no use for formal sins: it only becomes interested in sins when ignorance or repression of them causes some sort of psychic dissociation.

Naturally these clear-cut distinctions need to be qualified in actual practice. So far I have been discussing formal sins—i.e., sins that are committed deliberately, in full consciousness—and the actual sacramental act in itself, minus the psychic element that exists in every human act. The penitent who kneels down in the confessional will normally get a certain amount of moral and psychic comfort from doing so, all attributable to the fact that he is confessing; but this comfort is not the aim of confession, or its essence, and by emphasizing the psychological significance of confession to the detriment of its sacramental character the

[1] *The Practice of Psychotherapy*, p. 55 (1929).

whole point of it is missed. And any phenomenological comparison between the two immediately loses all its value.

By way of illustration, let us apply the above principles to a few imaginary cases.

Take the case, for instance, of the man who deliberately seeks sexual satisfactions to which he has no right. As he is a Christian believer he knows that he is committing sins that have to be confessed. He conforms to this rule, regretting perhaps that he cannot have the pleasure without paying for it. His whole conflict takes place on the level of consciousness: there is a conflict between his sense of moral obligation and his longing for personal satisfaction. The moment his sense of duty triumphs, his sin can be forgiven in confession. But this will not get rid of his hankering after the pleasure or its inevitable repercussions. Capitulation and repeated sin may continue, but confession will still be there to confirm the over-riding claims of duty. It is also possible that he may refuse to go to confession, which requires sincere contrition, and give way to his inclinations without any real regret. Throughout all this conscious conflict between sin and duty there is nothing in the way of neurosis. Even in the case of sins committed deliberately again and again, as on the second hypothesis, and ending in an inveterate habit, there is still no question of absence of consent and personal responsibility: there can be no doubt that we are faced with a sinner—as the person himself would in fact agree—and not someone to be regarded as neurotic or sexually obsessed. No analytical treatment would prove effective in this case because what is involved is not an unconscious chain of causality that has to be uncovered but simply a free decision of the will that has to be changed.

We can imagine a second case that would involve quite a different diagnosis and a different kind of treatment. Seen from outside it may appear to be no different from the first case, but in fact it is diametrically opposed to it. This is the case of a man who seeks sexual satisfactions because he is driven to do so by a power that seems too strong for him and which is set in motion by stimulants that seem to have no erotic connections at all. This happens in the case of the "fetishist", for instance. Assuming that, as in the first example, the man is a Christian believer, he will be convinced of the seriousness of his behaviour and acknowledge it in confession. He is torn inwardly by a conflict between what he regards as his duty and the repeated acts that he is obliged to commit against his will. Confession, far from helping him, increases his despair because of its apparent ineffectiveness psychologically, and he gives in to his obsession, imagining it to be a sin. In this case confession proves absolutely useless, and with good reason: an analysis is needed to get to the root of the obsession and to enable the person to take an objective view of what he takes to be his sin.

These are two extreme cases, of course. It is rare for a conscious, deliberate bad habit not to contain traces of neurosis, just as it is exceptional for a case of neurosis to exclude all freedom. That is why neurosis can be helped by the confessional, especially if the confessor is an understanding priest with a knowledge of the human soul; just as the sinner can gain comfort from the psychotherapist, particularly if the latter is a person of high moral standing. There is thus nothing wrong in comparing priest and therapist so far as their general human qualities are concerned, but with regard to the specific reality of confession and analysis these cannot be regarded as identical simply because they have one particular point in common.

This basic distinction seems to me to be all the more important because the neurotic as well as the sinner is tempted to exploit any confusion of the two. The neurotic often feels convinced that his sin, or what he regards as his sin, is the cause of his psychic disorder, and imagines that he can free himself from it automatically through confession without having to pay in his own person for the integration of the unconscious conflict. Unfortunately, sooner or later he discovers that this ruse is ineffective: automatic confession—putting in a sin and pulling out forgiveness—simply does not work. And then his terrible certainty is confirmed: his condition is beyond control. The sinner too often takes refuge in this confusion and tells himself that his sin is not a free act but something that simply takes possession of him, so that he has an excuse for giving way to it without making any attempt to control himself. If the priest and the psychotherapist fail to see what is involved in these two different kinds of tragedy they will find themselves unable to help their patients or penitents as they should: no method, however excellent, brings success unless it is rightly applied.

My refusal to accept any identification of psychic analysis with confession does not mean that there can be no collaboration between priest and therapist. On the contrary, it means that these two particular fields, these two different ways of treating the human soul, can be clearly defined; and then, having eliminated any ambiguity or undue interference between the two, we can be in a position to recognize the individual character of both confession and psychotherapy. Both try to remedy human distress. Both do this by asking man to acknowledge his real condition. But confession tells the sinner that he must repent of his conscious sin; analysis tells the neurotic that he must integrate an unconscious conflict.

II. The Psychotherapist's "Weltanschauung"

Jung distinguishes, in theory at least, between the psychotherapist's job and the spiritual director's job. He has said, for instance, in all sincerity, that as far as possible he sends his patients to a priest as soon as their psychic balance has been sufficiently restored.[1] In practice, unfortunately, he has often found himself in the painful dilemma of having either to refuse to treat a large number of his patients because they would have nothing to do with a spiritual director or to take over the director's job, in part at least, himself.

On the one hand he had come to see that what was required for any lasting psychic stability was a fundamentally religious attitude: "Among all my patients in the second half of life—that is to say, over thirty-five—there has not been one whose problem in the last resort was not that of finding a religious outlook on life. It is safe to say that every one of them fell ill because he had lost that which the living religions of every age have given to their

[1] *The Practice of Psychotherapy*, p. 16 (1935).

followers, and none of them has been really healed who did not regain his religious outlook."[1]

On the other hand he had very soon realized that a large number of these patients, whose difficulties centred consciously or unconsciously round the matter of religion, turned to him because they had failed to find the understanding they were looking for in their spiritual adviser.[2] These patients forced him "to spread far beyond the confines of somatic medicine and psychiatry into regions that were formerly the province of priests and philosophers".[3] As a doctor Jung did not feel that he could send away anyone who was ill without having tried all the remedies he knew. "As a doctor it is my task to help the patient to cope with life. I cannot presume to pass judgment on his final decisions, because I know from experience that all coercion . . . ultimately proved to be nothing but an obstacle to the highest and most decisive experience of all, which is to be alone with his own self. The patient has to be alone if he is to find out what it is that supports him when he can no longer support himself. Only this experience can give him an indestructible foundation. I would be only too delighted to leave this anything but easy task to the theologian, were it not that it is just from the theologian that many of my patients came. They ought to have hung on to the community of the Church, but they were shed like dry leaves from the great tree and now find themselves 'hanging on' to the treatment."[4]

This practical attitude was no new thing. In 1930 he had asked:

> But what will he do when he sees only too clearly why his patient is ill; when he sees that it arises from his having no love, but only sexuality; no faith, because he is afraid to grope in the dark; no hope, because he is disillusioned by the world and by life; and no understanding, because he has failed to read the meaning of his own existence?

[1] *Modern Man in Search of a Soul*, p. 264 (1932).
[2] Any experienced director will know that what Jung says about this is true. He will also add, however, that he knows at least as many cases in which patients have turned to a priest because their psychotherapist has let them down. I shall be returning to this point in the third section of this chapter.
[3] *The Practice of Psychotherapy*, p. 122 (1951).
[4] *Psychology and Alchemy*, pp. 27–8 (1944).

> There are many well-educated patients who flatly refuse to consult the clergyman. With the philosopher they will have even less to do, for the history of philosophy leaves them cold, and intellectual problems seem to them more barren than the desert. And where are the great and wise men who do not merely talk about the meaning of life and of the world, but really possess it? Human thought cannot conceive any system or final truth that could give the patient what he needs in order to live: that is, faith, hope, love and insight.
>
> These four highest achievements of human effort are so many gifts of grace, which are neither to be taught nor learned, neither given nor taken, neither withheld nor earned, since they come through experience, which is something *given*, and therefore beyond the reach of human caprice. Experiences cannot be *made*. They happen—yet fortunately their independence of man's activity is not absolute but relative. We can draw closer to them—that much lies within our human reach.[1]

These two passages raise a number of highly interesting points, but critics of analytical psychology will primarily condemn them as highly circumspect avowals, hedged in by all sorts of provisos, of what they suspect to be Jung's real aim—to give back to those who have lost their dogmatic faith a new religion of a higher kind—which turns out in fact to be his own psychology.

There is some truth in this, though Jung himself has always violently denied it. He rightly points out that he has never brought any pressure to bear on his patients and never attempted to do any violence to their dogmatic convictions.[2] Believers, he says, need no further help from him after they have been freed from their psychic troubles. But this is not the case "with all those people—and there are a great number of them—in whom the light of faith has gone out and the mystery has vanished and God is dead".[3] Jung wants to give all these people—and they form the majority of his patients—a real chance to recover their religious attitude—which is quite a different thing from instituting

[1] *Modern Man in Search of a Soul*, pp. 260–1 (1932).

[2] From my own acquaintance with him as a practitioner I must testify that he has always remained faithful to what he likes to call his "objectivity". There can be no doubt that some of his followers have had no compunction about departing from this "objectivity", but Jung can hardly be held responsible for their aberrations.

[3] *Psychologie und Religion*, p. 161 (1937). Cf. *Psychology and Alchemy*, pp. 33–4 (1944).

a new creed or cult. There is a certain impatience in Jung's retort to the critics who accuse him of being a religious innovator: "With a truly tragic delusion these theologians fail to see that it is not a matter of proving the existence of light, but of blind people who do not know that their eyes could see. It is high time we realized that it is pointless to praise the light and preach it if nobody can see it. It is much more needful to teach people the art of seeing . . . How this is to be done without psychology, that is, without making contact with the psyche, is frankly beyond my comprehension."[1]

Whenever, for whatever reason, the theologian fails in his purpose, Jung sees it as his function to come to his patients' help so that they can discover the real depth of their being and adopt an attitude in accordance with it. This attitude, because of its actual concrete characteristics, Jung calls religious. Psychology itself, therefore, is in no sense a religion, but it does enable unbelievers to become aware of fundamental religious values and to go on to build them up in themselves.

Let us then look a little more closely at the attitude which Jung wants the psychotherapist to adopt in his endeavour to help the patient to develop properly—the development culminating in the adoption of a religious attitude.

It must be emphasized at the outset that Jung is quite aware that the psychotherapist's personality is bound to come into the actual treatment: "People have imagined for far too long that psychotherapy can be applied in a purely 'technical' way like a kitchen recipe or a surgical method or a blueprint for making colours. A doctor can use any medical technique he likes and it does not matter what he thinks of his patient or what psychological theories or even philosophical or religious beliefs he holds personally. But psychotherapy is different: whether he likes it or not the therapist, with all his preconceived ideas, is just as much involved in it as the patient is . . . It is not the technique that is the deciding factor but the person who uses it . . . The method is designed, not for the treatment of a lifeless anatomical specimen, or an abscess, or a chemical body, but for the suffering person as

[1] *Psychology and Alchemy*, p. 13 (1944).

a whole. Therapy is concerned not with neurosis but with the person who is suffering from neurosis. A cardiac neurosis, for instance, does not come from the heart but from the sick person's psyche. Nor in fact does it come from one particular obscure corner of the unconscious, as so many psychotherapists still like to think; it comes from the life, the subjective and objective life lived by the person concerned for year after year with the whole of his being, and this includes not only his individual psychic life but his family and social life too."[1]

Today doctors themselves stress the fact that it is essential not to give any "technical" treatment to patients. On this they are to be congratulated. As regards psychotherapy, however, Jung's remarks are of vital importance. Whether the psychotherapist likes it or not, in "a fundamental discussion between 'I' and 'You' and 'You' and 'I'. . . it is almost certain that not only the patient but the doctor as well will find the situation 'getting under his skin' ".[2]

This certainty, the result of actually practising psychotherapy, obliges the doctor of the psyche to be fundamentally honest himself. He has to be an integrated person, conscious of the part played in him by his unconscious; otherwise how can he realize where unconscious reactions come from and tend to, both in the patient and in himself? It was this that made Jung insist, with the utmost firmness, that every psychotherapist should himself be analysed before practising.[3] "The doctor is as much 'in the analysis' as the patient." He must therefore have himself successfully performed the task he asks of his patient. He must have gone beyond infantilism and integrated his unconscious tendencies. "All these guiding principles of therapy make so many ethical demands, which can be summed up in the single truth: be the man through whom you wish to influence others . . . The fact of being convinced and not the things we are convinced of—that is what has always, and at all times, worked."[4]

[1] "Zur gegenwärtigen Lage der Psychotherapie", pp. 2–3 (1934).
[2] *Psychology and Alchemy*, p. 5 (1944).
[3] According to Jung Freud only required didactic analysis at Jung's own insistence. Cf. *The Practice of Psychotherapy*, p. 72 (1929).
[4] *The Practice of Psychotherapy*, pp. 72–3 (1929).

For Jung the therapist's calling means above all else that he must dedicate himself to a moral life of the utmost sincerity, for only such a life will enable him to pass on anything to others. Ideally, the psycho-therapist has an integrated personality achieved through didactic analysis and through taking an active part in the analyses to which he submits others. Jung likes to call this ideal a *Weltanschauung*.

We have already seen what Jung means by *Einstellung*, or the orientation of the personality. It means co-ordinating psychic contents through one particular unifying aim. "We can only properly speak of a *Weltanschauung* when a person has at least made a serious attempt to formulate his attitude conceptually or visibly, that is, when it becomes quite clear to him why and to what purpose he behaves and lives as he does."[1] And Jung goes on to explain what this means in the case of the psycho-therapist: "To have a *Weltanschauung* means to make an image of the world and of oneself, to know what the world is and who I am. Taken literally this would be too much. No one can know what the world is and as little also can he know himself; but *cum grano salis*, it means the best possible knowledge—a knowledge that requires wisdom and the avoidance of unfounded assumptions, arbitrary assertions and didactic opinions. For such knowledge one must seek the well-founded hypothesis, without forgetting that all knowledge is limited and subject to error."[2]

We can see again in these passages Jung's idea of the fundamental part played by hypotheses in scientific work. But here he applies it not to theories but to the practical attitude to be adopted in analytical treatment, and this makes it clear that in practice Jung's *Weltanschauung* is not so much a philosophical attitude as the distilled essence of his empirical observations.

A real *Weltanschauung* should help the psychotherapist to develop a receptive attitude towards every new observation. Whilst making full use of the personal experience he has gained through didactic analysis and subsequent analysis of his patients he should take care to avoid the dogmatic kind of attitude that

[1] *Contributions to Analytical Psychology*, p. 144 (1931).
[2] Ibid, p. 146.

has ready-made laws on how to guide and interpret the psychic process. His past experience should guide the analysis and at the same time submit to it, and he must be prepared to correct and indeed reverse it if the occasion demands. "Taken basically, psychotherapy is a dialectic relationship between the doctor and the patient. It is a discussion between two spiritual wholes, in which all wisdom is merely a tool. The goal is transformation; not indeed a predetermined, but rather an indeterminable, change, the only criterion of which is the disappearance of I-ness. No efforts on the part of the doctor force the experience. The most he can do is to make easy the path of the patient towards the attainment of an attitude which will oppose the least resistance to the decisive experience."[1]

As the therapist's attitude must conform to the patient's development it will inevitably undergo its own development in rhythm with the course of treatment. At the beginning of the analysis direct help is required. All patients are ill because they cannot find their bearings in the objective and subjective world, and the therapist in a sense shoulders a burden that they have found too heavy to bear themselves. The therapist bears this burden with them, not with the intention of taking it over permanently but to give them a breathing-space and a chance to get their strength back. This is the point of the transference at the beginning of the treatment: the therapist has to build up the invalid's personality or ego again. But it must be remembered that this transference is only justified if the therapist is ready to dissolve it as soon as he can. Jung lays great stress on this: as soon as the patient has regained his strength it is up to him to take over the struggle. And as the patient now has the main part to play, the psychotherapist must become simply an interested spectator, an umpire, an intelligent "manager". He must keep to the side lines: "My aim is to bring about a psychic state in which my patient begins to experiment with his own nature—a state of fluidity, change, and growth where nothing is eternally fixed and hopelessly petrified. . . . In handling a dream or fantasy I make it a rule never to go beyond the meaning which is effective

[1] Foreword to Suzuki, *Introduction to Zen Buddhism*, p. 25 (1939).

for the patient; I merely try to make him as fully conscious of this meaning as possible, so that he shall also become aware of its supra-personal connections."[1]

The psychotherapist's attitude cannot therefore be governed by any dogmatic certainty either as regards the sexual origin of neurosis or the absolute truth of any creed. The *Weltanschauung* imposed on him by his practice means an unconditional receptivity towards the individual evolution of the person whom he is helping to discover and develop his own life. The psychotherapist can only note the certainties that follow from such a receptivity. As all the cases that Jung was able to follow through to the end had the same result, the patient's discovery of a personal meaning to his life, he advances it as an empirical fact that life has a meaning and individual life an individual meaning.

This short sketch of the ideal psychotherapeutic attitude should have made it clear that it includes noble views and most humane aims. As what Jung says is based entirely on his own empirical observations he is unable to express his conclusions in an absolute form. He himself is glad of this, because it seems to him to make his conclusions a good deal sounder than any philosophical or metaphysical views can be. But anyone who wants to see man as an ontological as well as a psychic being must attach some importance to philosophy, and he cannot avoid the following question: is the psychotherapist's *Weltanschauung* acceptable when man is regarded as a being in search of the absolute?

As long as the psychologist restricts himself to his own special field, his methods and conclusions concern that field only. This, as a rule of any sound methodology, is beyond question. The attitude that Jung asks of the psychotherapist is essential if there is to be no danger of an *a priori* attitude that would tend to destroy the possibility of impartial observation. So far as religion is concerned, there seem to be no grounds for any disagreement with Jung in principle. Faith is a free act and is only truly itself when the individual comes to it through personal submission and not simply through an alienation of himself. In this sense a missionary only does useful work when he leads his converts to a

[1] *The Practice of Psychotherapy*, p. 46 (1929).

personal act of faith, in other words helps them to convert themselves, not when he converts them. Even more true is it that the psychotherapist—who, if he is a believer, will be personally convinced of the absolute objective value of his faith—cannot impose his own faith upon his patients from outside. He has not even the right to unsettle their minds. The patients who knock at his door are looking for psychic rehabilitation, and it would be a grave mistake on his part if he were to take advantage of his privileged position and try to inculcate truths into their minds which their subjective condition makes it impossible for them to assimilate.

We do not allow a doctor to prescribe the last sacraments for a patient who is not a believer: must we not say, likewise, that any psychotherapist who tried to effect a religious reformation in his patient without its being called for by his inner development would be a very poor psychologist?

So long as we confine ourselves to the field of psychotherapy there is no reason why we should not accept Jung's attitude. Unquestionably, however, many of his followers make use of their master's views to support their own particular brand of militant atheism. These deviations from Jung's own position should not be allowed to cloud our agreement in principle, but they should lead us to be rather prudent in actual practice.

I shall end this section by quoting a passage that provides an admirable summary of his views: "If the doctor wants to offer guidance to another, or even to accompany him a step of the way he must be in touch with this other person's psychic life. He is never in touch when he passes judgement. Whether he puts his judgements into words, or keeps them to himself, makes not the slightest difference. To take the opposite position, and to agree with the patient off-hand, is also of no use, but estranges him as much as condemnation. We can get in touch with another person only by *an attitude of unprejudiced objectivity*. This may sound like a scientific precept, and may be confused with a purely intellectual and detached attitude of mind. But what I mean to convey is something quite different. It is a human quality—a kind of deep respect for facts and events and for the person who suffers from them—a respect for the secret of such a human life. The truly religious person has this attitude. He knows that God has brought all sorts of strange and inconceivable things to pass, and seeks in the most curious ways to enter a man's heart. He therefore senses in everything the unseen presence of the divine will. This is what I mean by 'unprejudiced objectivity'. It is a moral achievement on the part of the doctor, who ought not to let himself be repelled by illness and corruption. *We cannot change anything unless we accept it.* Condemnation does not liberate, it oppresses. I am the oppressor of the person I condemn, not his friend and fellow-sufferer. I do not in the least mean to say that we must never pass judgement in the cases of persons whom we desire to help and improve. But if the doctor wishes to help a human being he must be able to accept him as he is. And he can do this in reality only when he has already seen and accepted himself as he is."[1]

III. Collaboration and Mutual Respect

Jung's requirements of the psychotherapist were the fruit of long experience. It is not for me to say whether or not they are realizable by the Protestant pastors whom Jung was addressing in the lecture "Psychotherapists or the Clergy" from which the last quotation is taken. But I can say with conviction that every Catholic director who has charge of souls endeavours to conform as far as he possibly can to Jung's ideal. "Unprejudiced objectivity that enables us to accept a man as he is because we have first of all accepted ourselves as we are" is a governing principle of all pastoral theology. Every director of conscience has to have an understanding insight into the difficulties of the people he is directing if he is to help them towards a personal religious life. No more than the psychotherapist can he attempt to impose his own personal attitude on them, for he knows that God's ways are inscrutable. And like the psychotherapist he must try not to go against the personal development of the people he is directing. Just as Jung tries not to overlook any unconscious clue to the

[1] *Modern Man in Search of a Soul*, pp. 270–1 (1932). Jung's italics.

proper development of the psyche, so the director has to keep a sharp look-out for the action of grace, so as not to hinder the development of the spiritual life.

In so far as every priest is a director of conscience his ideal attitude may well be described as "unprejudiced objectivity" towards all in whom grace is active.

Here again then, as in the case of the unburdening made in confession and analysis, we find a structural element that is common to both spiritual direction and psychotherapy. But it has a very different meaning according to which of the two it is found in. The psychotherapist is trying to re-establish psychic equilibrium by seeking out and then analysing with "unprejudiced objectivity" the unconscious dispositions that are affecting the conscious attitude adversely through some repression or faulty attitude. The director, on the other hand, is trying to promote spiritual equilibrium by studying the action of grace and respecting it with "unprejudiced objectivity".

So far we have been speaking of the priest as a person in charge of the spiritual direction of a flock. But he is also the representative of Christ, with an official mandate from the Church to preach the truth and keep the faith free from error, and as such, like the Church herself, he has to pronounce anathemas and condemn sin—which does not mean rejecting the actual people who are in error or sin. Jung himself acknowledges that "certain patients' confessions are hard even for a doctor to swallow,"[1] but he is careful not to condemn them. The priest must do the same. Often he will have to disapprove of opinions which he finds unacceptable, but at the same time he will take care not to reject the people who hold them. And here in fact the priest enjoys an undoubted advantage, for his own attitude is determined by a conviction that he is concerned not with some sort of abnormal behaviour but with a perverted form of essential truth.

It goes without saying that this twofold duty of directing souls and preaching the truth complicates the priest's task considerably. He may not fail in the first through an excess of harshness, nor omit the second from a misplaced feeling of pity. That is why

[1] *Modern Man in Search of a Soul*, p. 270 (1932).

the psychologist can only see the priest's "dogmatic intransigence", which cuts across his own exclusively therapeutic preoccupations.

The above considerations should enable us to discern a little more clearly the kind of collaboration that is possible between psychotherapist and spiritual director. It should be noted that from the beginning of this chapter I have omitted to discuss the sort of collaboration that would involve any encroachment either way. It is in fact because they both have their own specific field that they must realize which cases lie outside their own particular competence.

The spiritual director should not feel that he has to wait until psychotic or neurotic disturbances break out in any of his flock before he calls in the psychotherapist. Many problems that seem at first sight religious have in fact a psychic causation. Von Gebsattel gives two clear cases of this kind of psycho-religious failure. Quite frequently, he says, "religious practices are adopted as an escape from legitimate tendencies which for some reason or other create uneasiness". Then there begins a "religious life" which is in the strongest sense of the words simply a mask or consequence of unconscious tendencies or feelings which the person concerned refuses to admit. Religion is in this case not being sought for its own sake but as a desperate means of escape from a proper sense of responsibility. Or again, people may turn their backs on religion not so much for religious as for psychological reasons, either because they have been unable to understand it properly or because they are afraid of having to conform to certain concrete demands.[1]

More than one sort of neurosis is the result of this kind of faulty psychic attitude towards religion, and the spiritual director's efforts are all doomed to failure so long as the psychic field remains untouched. And usually he has neither the time nor the knowledge to undertake this latter task, arduous and delicate as it is, satisfactorily. Irritation on the part of the psychotherapist is fully justified when some of the spiritual director's flock are suffering from the kind of neurotic symptoms described above and he refuses to pass them over to him for analysis. For such a refusal

[1] Cf. V. von Gebsattel, *Christentum und Humanismus*, pp. 15–17.

is the result of an immoderate zeal tainted by ill-disguised egotism. Can it be surprising if the upshot is total failure, manifesting itself sooner or later in the people concerned in a lamentable state of psychic and spiritual collapse? And when people have been reduced to such an extremity it is often too late to do anything really useful for them.

On the other hand, the therapist should not forget that his function too has its limits. Even if he makes it a rule to pass on his patients' religious problems to the spiritual director—if they really want him to do this and ask him to do so in so many words—a danger still lies in wait for him: he will be tempted to corner and monopolize all those who through weakness or ignorance are unable to escape from his personal domination over them. It is quite true that he cannot send patients who are unbelievers to the priest, and the fact that in such cases Jung tries to get the people concerned to see the psychological value of religion does him great credit. Unfortunately he does not seem to realize that by doing so he in fact prevents them from grasping the objective value of religion. And yet that is the real reason why both Protestants and Catholics have condemned his psychologism. His psychological revaluation of religion is not generally speaking a first step on the road to faith but an obstacle to any deeper understanding of the real meaning of faith. Therefore, though I respectfully acknowledge Jung's impartiality in his treatment of his patients I cannot agree with his exclusively psychological revaluation of religion.

The psychotherapist is absolutely indispensable so long as it is a question of restoring sick people to psychic health. In performing this latter function he is in no sense encroaching upon the domain of the priest as a director of conscience and spiritual director; on the contrary, he is relieving the priest of a great number of desperate cases in which his zeal would be destined to failure because he has no way of coping with them. I am thinking particularly of cases that drag on in priests' parlours and the confessional—unless the people concerned definitely turn their backs on their priest—people whom the priest cannot in charity bring himself to turn away for fear of extinguishing their last gleam of hope, though in fact he can do nothing for them. In the hands of the therapist such people would find, if not certain cure, at least proper treatment.

If the psychotherapist is to succeed in his work he has to guide the people who come and ask for his advice towards the full development of their psychic dispositions. This, as Jung would readily agree, includes religious values. Now these, it is true, are only objectively present in all their fullness in the Church, but it is a different matter when we come to the question of their concrete expression in each separate individual. Here we find ourselves up against a mystery that creates one of the greatest problems in theology. Tradition, faithfully following the Gospels, tells us that in any individual case subjective sincerity is of more moment than objective truth: there is salvation for those who sincerely, even if wrongly, believe themselves to be in the truth and do their best to conform their lives to it. For these reasons the psychotherapist must respect his patient's personality, and in particular his religious convictions, on the psychic level.

Alas, if psychotherapists sometimes take advantage of their position to influence their patients' religious convictions, it is also true that priests sometimes refuse psychic help to people in need of it. They seem to hate the thought of having to take a back seat, and so they try to tackle problems which as priests they are not fitted to deal with.

On the other hand, it is just as necessary for psychotherapists to realize that priests have this sort of experience in reverse. Psychotherapists may be visited by large numbers of people who have failed to get the help they hoped for from their spiritual directors, but spiritual directors receive just as many patients who have turned away from the psychologist because he has not succeeded in giving them the help they need. Very often this failure is due to the fact that the psychotherapist has not had a proper sense of their religious needs and problems. Now this may be without the slightest fault of method on his part: what he may lack is the knowledge of religion that comes from experience, something not to be found in books or comparative studies any more than psychotherapy. And so ideally a Christian believer should undoubtedly go, not to the kind of psychotherapist who looks indulgently upon religion as a matter of family tradition or crumbling social custom, but to someone who applies his religion to life and makes it the very substance of his being.

Any collaboration between spiritual director and psychotherapist means that in the first place they must both recognize that they each have their own specific job to do. Since their activity takes place in different fields it is ridiculous to try to exalt either at the expense of the other. The psychotherapist's attitude has been carefully analysed by Jung, and I am glad to signify my agreement with what he says. But behind the non-dogmatic religious attitude which he holds up for approval there lurks a danger for all the people who with his kindly help come to realize the psychological value of religion and are then unable to go beyond this. Jung insists upon the priest's recognizing the validity of his demands as a therapist. I have tried to do this, and am happy to follow him in all that concerns his psychotherapeutic attitude. Unfortunately he himself is not sufficiently aware of the demands felt by the spiritual director, which are also valid.

VII

PSYCHOLOGY AND DOGMA

THE psychotherapist has no right to avoid any of the problems that his patients bring to him. Jung "is not a philosopher but an empirical scientist"; even less is he a theologian or "a Biblical scholar, but a layman and a doctor who has been allowed to sound the depths of the psychic life of a large number of patients". These have forced him to study a number of problems of a specifically philosophical and theological nature. The zeal he has shown in grappling with the writings of the Fathers and his passion for getting down to essentials in the matter of papal bulls and the decisions of councils command respect. But he has never taken the trouble to build up a consistent system on the basis of all this work. He has always embarked on it fortuitously, because it chimed in with some particular psychological interest of the moment, either as the result of some point raised by one of his patients or because his investigations into religious symbolism had brought up some special problem. This makes it difficult to grasp the precise significance of his conclusions, as all the scattered data referring to any particular question have first to be patiently collected together and then put in order.

This can be very interesting, however. It is after all quite natural for a psychologist to compare the data acquired through his own scientific investigations with the statements of metaphysics and theology. But he must take care not to reject anything on the one side simply because it does not seem to fit in with the other. When psychological data seem to conflict with the facts of faith the first thing to do is to make sure that there has been no misunderstanding on either side. If the conflict persists, the next thing to do is to make sure that both the psychological and the theological statements are correct. The psychological statements, which are essentially hypothetical, in the technical sense of the word, may need to be clarified still further or to be expressed rather differently. Also of course the theological statements may be relieved of non-objective elements that have simply been due to the influence of surroundings or historical circumstances and so come to be defined more clearly as a result of the further light shed on them by psychology.

There is no doubt that the Galileo controversy helped towards a clearer understanding of Biblical inspiration. Many theologians had had far too narrow an idea of this and tended to believe that it guaranteed the scientific accuracy of the sacred authors' views on astronomy. The fact that we no longer believe this today is due not to any change in the content of faith but to progress in our understanding of the precise nature of the sacred authors' aims. Such has been the result of the argument raised by discoveries made in the field of astronomy. Similarly, psychology can in its own different way help us indirectly towards a better statement of certain theological problems.

All Jung's inquiries into metaphysics and theological problems are concerned essentially with three main points which can be summed up in the following questions: What is the psychological significance of the mandala centre? What insight does analytical psychology give into the problem of evil? What psychological meaning is to be ascribed to the doctrine of the Trinity? I shall now attempt to answer these questions.

I. The Self as a Mandala Centre

In his book *Psychology and Religion* Jung devotes several pages to the first of our questions. He puts his point in the form of a syllogism. In all ages, he says, the mandala centre has been occupied by the main, essential object of the faith the mandalas express: in the Catholic Middle Ages it was Christ surrounded by the evangelists, or the Trinity Itself with the Virgin Mary; in India there was Shiva, in China the Tao. . . .[1] Now in the mandalas of all the patients Jung has had to treat the centre has always been

[1] *Psychology and Religion*, p. 97 (1937).

occupied by a symbol—star, circle, flower, precious stone, etc.—of the self.[1] Therefore the self must be the main, essential object in the religion of modern man.[2]

Jung makes no effort to conceal his own aim: he believes that his observations made it quite clear that all objectivized divinities are simply projected expression of the ultimate psychic reality, the self. As his reasoning is presented in the form of a syllogism the truth of his premise leads ineluctably to the truth of his conclusion—if the middle term really connects the major premise with the minor. Let us therefore look a little more closely at this middle term, the mandala.

For many years Jung has used the active imagination method. He was struck by the fact that his patients frequently produced drawings with a round or square pattern. Both the inner structure of these drawings and their relationship to the background developed in rhythm with the treatment. Jung was intrigued with all this, but he had no point of reference that would help him to explain these drawings; so he carefully held on to them and kept quiet. Some time later, between 1925 and 1929, his friend, Richard Wilhelm, an expert on China, brought the symbolism of Asia to his attention and he then found in the religious cultures of India, China and Tibet designs that showed a striking resemblance to the ones produced by his patients, who of course had known nothing about these cultures. As these designs are known in the East as mandalas—magic circles—Jung adopted the term himself and used it for all the drawings produced by the spontaneous imagination that had the same characteristic structure—four basic elements or components (in rare cases three or five) arranged in a circle or square. These could take on any number of different forms according to the way one was related to the other, by being repeated, interacting, etc.[3]

In the East the mandala is essentially a help to meditation or contemplation. "The true mandala is always an inner image, which is gradually built up through active imagination, at such

[1] *Psychology and Religion*, pp. 98–9.
[2] Ibid., pp. 99–101.
[3] Cf. *Psychology and Alchemy*, pp. 94–7 (1944) and *Gestaltungen des Unbewussten*, pp. 190–3 (1950).

times when psychic equilibrium is disturbed, *or when a* [religious] *thought cannot be found and must be sought for, because not contained in holy doctrine*."[1] "Historically, as we have seen, the mandala served as a symbol in order to classify the nature of the deity philosophically, or to demonstrate the same thing in a visible form for the purpose of adoration."[2] These mandalas are always inspired by religious dogma and this supplies them with their content. Their actual inner structure follows rules that have been strictly laid down.

In analytical psychology, on the other hand, mandalas are unconscious productions. They are not inspired by ideas or known representations and they do not follow any pre-established rules known to the persons who draw them. So far as these people are concerned they are an unexpected upsurge of the unconscious and they can appear whenever the grip of consciousness is relaxed, for example in dreams or visual expressions, visions or spontaneous drawings. As a result of patient observation Jung has found that the inner structure of these mandalas reveals the psychic condition of their creators. "The mandalas usually appear in times of disturbance, anguish or chaotic psychic states. Their aim at such times is to bring back order into this chaos, without the patient being aware of it. They always express order, equilibrium, totality. Often patients stress the beneficent effects of this kind of symbol. Generally the mandalas express religious, i.e., numinous ideas or representations, or else philosophical ideas, and these usually have an intuitive, irrational character. Through their symbolic value they reactivate the unconscious. For all these reasons the mandalas have a 'magical' significance and effect, in the figurative sense of the word."[3]

A comparison of eastern and medieval mandalas with mandalas produced during treatment thus seems logical and significant, and it is tempting to conclude that they proceed from the same psychic condition in each case. But we must not forget that those in the first category belong to the field of objective religion and

[1] *Psychology and Alchemy*, p. 142. Jung's italics.
[2] *Psychology and Religion*, p. 96 (1937).
[3] *Gestaltungen des Unbewussten*, p. 198 (1950). Cf. *Psychology and Alchemy*, pp. 94 and 172–5 (1944).

those in the second to the field of psychic religion. Now this makes a difference, for in the eastern and medieval mandalas the dogma organizes and governs the symbolic interpretation, whereas in the mandalas produced by patients all the symbolism is explained as a function of psychic realities assumed by hypothesis to reveal themselves in them. It seems to me therefore that in Jung's syllogism the middle term is being used in two different senses: it would only be the same sense if the dogma was simply a projection of psychic realities, or, in other words, the "objectivating" expression of a purely subjective reality. I have shown in Chapter V that this was indeed Jung's view until about 1935 or 1940; but he has never produced any conclusive proof of it, though he tries to prove it by his syllogism. As it is stated in *Psychology and Religion*, therefore, I challenge this syllogism on the ground that its middle term conceals a *petitio principii*.[1]

This criticism is directed against *Psychology and Religion*. It needs to be qualified, however, in the light of the modification of his conception of the self in *Psychology and Alchemy*. It is true, he says in this book, that the centre of the mandalas is occupied by a symbol of the self. But what in fact is the self? Is it an ultimate reality of an ontological kind? Not at all. The self is the last element that psychology can reach to—not as something directly apprehended, however, but as a psychic reality whose existence has to be postulated. We must therefore, Jung goes on, regard the self as a "*lediglich negativer Grenzbegriff*", a limiting concept about whose positive nature psychology has nothing to say. What the self may signify in metaphysics or theology is not a matter for psychology for the simple reason that the psychologist is not qualified to speak about either of these fields.

This last point does not conflict with the teachings of philosophy

[1] It also sins by the illegitimate extension of its conclusion: instead of being said to prove that the self is the object of modern man's religiosity, it should be said, of the patients treated by Jung. According to his own confession: "I have treated many hundreds of patients, the larger number being Protestants, a smaller number Jews, and not more than five or six believing Catholics" (*Modern Man in Search of a Soul*, p. 264). I do not mean to suggest that his conclusion is necessarily wrong but simply that Jung has not verified it to any worthwhile extent so far as Catholics are concerned. I am quite sure that Jung himself would have no hesitation in agreeing with me about this and there is no need for me to say anything further about it.

or theology; on the contrary Jung is reverting by a rather clumsy roundabout route to the metaphysical principle that God as he is in himself cannot be proved by scientific argument. All that psychology can say about the self, man's final, supreme value, is that it has to be postulated as a *sine qua non* condition of all other psychic realities. As such it demands unconditional submission, and once this is given there is a chance of proper development. The self is thus present in the psyche, though it is distinct from the ego and its actual essence is inaccessible. It is both immanent and transcendent—psychically speaking, of course—and cannot be identified with God in an endeavour to prove his existence or set up against him in an endeavour to disprove it.

For this reason I must state my entire agreement with Jung's position as stated in *Aion*. Discussing his investigations into the symbolism of the self he asks, "Is the self a symbol of Christ or Christ a symbol of the self?" And he gives his answer plainly: "In this study I have adopted the latter view."[1] As his decision is the result of a methodological attitude, not an ontological position, Jung is clearly prepared to grant that other people can opt for the first view with equal justification.[2] But this takes one into the field of philosophy, and it is easy to understand that Jung chose to avoid embarking upon anything so hazardous.

II. The Problem of Evil

The second problem which we must now tackle raises two difficulties. In the first place there is Jung's language: we have to try to reach a proper understanding of his views without allowing ourselves to be put off by peculiar turns of phrase or expressions that do not fit in with our traditional terminology. It is all too easy to condemn something because one has failed to understand it. And then we must not be blinded by Jung's own statement that the idea of evil as a "privation of good" is absolutely incompatible with his own observations and empirical discoveries.

[1] *Aion*, p. 107 (1951).

[2] This has been done by Zacharias in a very stimulating essay, *Die Bedeutung der Psychologie C. G. Jungs für die christliche Theologie*, which examines what conclusions can be drawn from the principle "that the self is a symbol of Christ".

Let us try to discover what Jung means by evil, what importance it has for him, and what part it plays in analytical psychology. We shall then be able to go on to examine the exact meaning of the classic saying, *Malum est privatio boni.* A comparison of the psychological and philosophical ideas involved here may help to solve an antinomy that at first sight may seem insoluble.

Jung is a psychologist, but his patients have drawn him powerfully towards the problem of evil. In point of fact, careful study of the process of psychic integration revealed from the beginning that there was some extremely powerful activity threatening the unification of the psyche. The evil that Jung is concerned with is therefore pre-eminently psychic. But we must understand what this word means. Psychic evil includes external events independent of the person suffering them, as well as the purely subjective inner realities that are hampering his development. All these evil forces are psychic in Jung's sense of the word, because they only interest him—and can only interest him—in so far as they relate to the psychic development of his patients and all who pass through the process of individuation. In the second chapter of this book I tried to define the particular object of analytical psychology, and there I stressed the special character of psychic realities. They are not things distinct from other things in the objective world, as a table is from a chair; they are simply a particular aspect of the whole of reality or in other words the whole of reality as related to the self. Psychic evil, therefore, is to be defined as anything that hinders, prevents, falsifies or distorts individuation.[1]

This should help us to see how Jung can look upon evil as a real positive force whilst at the same time saying that it is a subjective, or, to be still more precise, a relative thing. This relative character of evil is clear from the fact that it is impossible to predict whether any given action or situation will prove to be a help or a hindrance, good or evil. The loss of a beloved child may bring despair and lead to a fatal crisis in the life of a mother and those around her, but it may mean, alternatively, that an

[1] Jung often calls psychic evil a *moral* evil. In doing so he gives this latter phrase a meaning not sanctioned by the traditional terminology, which uses it to mean sin. For Jung moral evil is the evil that attacks the psyche, whilst physical evil attacks the body.

over-indulgent and possibly egoistic kind of love has been changed into wholehearted submission to a higher order. In the first case the death is an evil, in the second a great good. It all depends how the trial is accepted.

This relativity of evil does not of course mean that it is not a real and positive thing too, as Jung himself recognizes. He has no doubt about this. In point of fact if any force is to resist the psychic tendency to full development it will have to be as real and positive as the tendency itself: only realities of the same order are capable of holding each other in check and destroying each other.[1]

The psychic evil that Jung means then is both positive and relative—relative, in so far as it is created in each case by the reaction of the person whom it affects; positive, in so far as it is successful in its struggle against the tendency to full development.

Thus from this angle Jung regards the good and evil forces that appear in the course of psychic development as being both of a positive nature. This may suggest that he supports a dualistic point of view that in its own way is a sort of revival of Manicheism, and indeed this is an objection that has often been made against him. But in fact it ignores the important qualifications that Jung has added to his original statements. We have already seen that when in the course of treatment he comes up against a situation that seems insoluble he always goes on in the serene conviction that the solution will eventually appear of its own accord if he has the courage to be patient. The real dangers, in his view, come from the kind of attitude that tries to ignore evil or get round it: as soon as we face up to the adversary and look him straight in the eyes he gives in. This facing up to the problem may not supply a rational solution, but it does enable us to achieve a higher synthesis. The seemingly insoluble conflict is transcended by a new attitude that makes us its masters. The solution comes because the problem has lost the urgency that prevented us from looking at it properly and has been given its proper place in the psychic development. Good itself results from this courageous facing up to evil.

Hence Jung's merciless war against any defensive policy of

[1] *Symbolik des Geistes*, p. 401 (1948).

minimizing evil or trying to get rid of it by specious arguments.[1] From evil, experienced in all its intensity, can come the great blessing of a new development, when the patient discovers that the tunnel he has had to pass through leads to a light of unexpected brightness. The light does not do away with the tunnel, any more than the joy of having a child does away with the pangs of childbirth, but it nevertheless gives a meaning to it. From evil accepted and integrated comes good; the only sterile thing is the evil that is merely endured without any effort to recognize it for what it is.[2]

Quite clearly, then, in Jung's view, evil, which is a debilitating psychic force, does not originate from any ontological duality, for it is relative in its origin and ends by leading to a greater good. Evil comes from a false or unsatisfactory attitude, and disappears as soon as this has been corrected. In all human development evil is the way to good.

This conviction of Jung's has not been based on any ideological beliefs but on empirical fact. Throughout his observations he has seemed to see the same process repeated. And so he finds it disturbing if during a particular course of treatment this confrontation with evil fails to appear. He has however often come across cases of fierce resistance on the part of his patients in this particular respect. In spite of this—often because of it—the havoc wreaked by evil has been atrocious. When he began to try to find out what lay behind this failure to recognize something that to himself seemed almost tangible he discovered that it was a conviction which some of his patients, more familiar with the jargon of philosophy, traced back to the principle of the "privation of good". They said that this saying meant that evil was a lesser good or pure non-being, which meant that it did not exist and so there was no need to worry about it! Is it surprising that Jung should have objected with all his might to such a disconcerting explanation?[3]

[1] *Gestaltungen des Unbewussten*, p. 139 (1950).

[2] *Modern Man in Search of a Soul*, p. 278 (1932).

[3] In his preface to V. White, *God and the Unconscious*, Jung describes how he first came across the *privatio boni* principle: "I had to treat a patient, a scholarly man, who had become involved in all manner of dubious and morally questionable practices. He turned out to be a fervent adherent of the privatio boni, because it fitted in admirably with his scheme: evil in itself is nothing, a mere shadow, a trifling and fleeting diminution of good, like a cloud passing over the

Jung, knowing the explanation to be absurd, at least in the psychological field, attacked the "privation of good" theory as something that "destroyed the reality of evil",[1] wherever he met it—in Greek philosophy, and in the Church Fathers, particularly St. Augustine, whom he accuses of taking it from the Greeks to get round his own Manicheism.[2] He detects it even more in its modern forms of theosophy and anthroposophy.

Conversely, he made an enthusiastic search for any representations that emphasized the reality of evil. In this connection he has a special liking for the books of the Bible, and even more for the apocryphal writings that concentrate on the conflict between Satan and Christ. He believed that the oldest and truest view of this is to be found where Satan is presented as a "son" of God, or, to be even more precise, as his eldest son, expressing part of his nature—his "shadow"—because this brings out the reality of evil and at the same time the fact that it is complementary to good. Jung in fact believes that both good and evil must be present in God. In the third section of this chapter I shall return to this idea of his and discuss it more fully; here I need only say that according to Jung the principle that God is the supreme good follows directly from the idea of evil as a "privatio boni". By postulating that good and evil are found together in God Jung believes that he escapes from the dualism that seems inevitable when one stresses the real, positive character of evil as strongly as he does.

So far I have been simply trying to state Jung's actual ideas, and the reader will do well to suspend judgment on them, for before we can criticize them we must look a little more closely at the way philosophy solves the problem of evil.[3]

---

sun. This man professed to be a believing Protestant and would therefore have had no reason to appeal to a *sententia communis* of the Catholic Church, had it not proved a welcome sedative for his peace of mind" (pp. xviii-xix).

[1] *Aion*, p. 76 (1951).

[2] *Aion*, pp. 75–86.

[3] Jung presents the "privatio boni" principle as "a *sententia communis* of the Catholic Church" (cf. p. 163). As he equates philosophy with faith we must not be surprised if in theology itself he makes no distinction between revealed truth and the philosophical principles that are meant to help towards an understanding of revelation. "Privatio boni" is nonetheless, as all thinkers are agreed, a strictly philosophical principle, and it is as such that I shall speak of it here.

The philosopher too begins by facing squarely up to evil. He has no desire to minimize its importance or to treat it as non-existent: he wants to know it for what it is. He has no doubts about the dreadful reality of concentration camps, hell, dictators, the devil. He, too, is upset by the sight of all the evil that spreads such chaos through the world and presents him with one of his most anguishing problems. And he too is struck by the fact that in every manifestation of evil some good, however small, is hidden, and that many evils can in the end lead to a greater good.

To avoid the risk of ignoring the good hidden behind every form of evil, and of letting evil predominate over good, the philosopher tries to define these two things in a way that is universally valid. He begins by making a distinction, in every form of evil—whether it is a person or a thing, a disposition or an activity—between the being in whom the evil is so to speak rooted and what actually makes the being evil. There is no need to say, of course, that the being really exists in itself; but what makes it evil is the fact that it has turned away from, or been made to turn away from, the end for which it was created.

Evil is not in itself, therefore, being, but a deficiency or lack in some being. It is made up of the privation of what the being, by its very nature, needs. Of course evil can be regarded as something positive in the case of, say, a hump-back or a cancer, regarded as a proliferation or excess of tissue; and it can be looked upon as something negative in the case for instance of the loss of a limb; but whether positive or negative, hump-back or amputation, these are both evils because they are deformities away from the normal. And therein lies the real nature of evil.

This is even more obviously the case when what is involved is not physical, bodily evil but, in the traditional sense of the word, moral evil. In this case indeed the being itself does not seem to be affected: Lucifer is still an angel, even after his fall. But what does this mean? It means, not that his angelic nature, good and perfect as it is in its own order, has changed, but that he no longer directs it towards the end for which it was created—submission to God: he has revolted against this submission through a decision in conflict with his essential being. The religious art of the Middle Ages presented this spiritual mutilation in a very striking way: it pictured the prince of darkness with enormous bat's wings, and at the same time it presented the angels' wings with the spectra of the rainbow. The deformity is there all right, but the wings, the pictorial representation of the angelic nature, are still there too.

To say that evil is the privation of a good is not, therefore, the same thing as saying that evil is a lesser good. Evil is the absence of a good that should be there: it is a privation, in the strict sense of the word. There is no evil in the fact that an animal "lives like a beast"; on the contrary, it is a good and proper thing for it to do. And if we say that it is a lesser good as compared with man's way of living we are no longer putting ourselves in the animal's place but man's, and for man "living like a beast" would indeed be an evil because it would be going against the demands of his nature, which are that he should live like a man. In this sense the philosopher too speaks of the relativity of evil, since it only exists in so far as there is a deficiency as compared with what should be there. But it must be realized that this relative character is utterly different from the relative character that Jung attributes to psychic evil. The philosopher by no means maintains that evil is simply an absence of good, or simply non-being; he says that it involves a privation, is a deformity, a deficiency.

The crucial distinction between the being affected by evil and the deficiency which is the actual evil itself enables the philosopher to say that all beings, even bad ones, are created by God, and that nevertheless God has not directly willed evil. In point of fact what God has created is this particular being, which is good inasmuch as it exists: the fact that it turns vicious or is made evil by some other being has not been willed by God.[1]

And now, having made the necessary distinctions about this problem of evil as seen from both the philosophical and the analytical-psychological point of view, we can return to our original question, which was to discover what light analytical psychology can shed on the question of evil.

[1] It is only when seen from this angle that the saying "*omne bonum a Deo, omne malum ab homine*", which Jung condemns, takes on a meaning that is not only perfectly acceptable but very true.

It is clear to begin with that the positive character that Jung attributes to evil creates no difficulty for the philosopher. Not only because Jung restricts himself to empirical considerations and thus does nothing to involve the metaphysical viewpoint,[1] but because the reality of evil things is the primary fact from which philosophy starts. It is precisely the undeniable reality of evil that leads to the "privatio boni" theory. Unfortunately Jung has taken advantage of the apparent contradiction between his own views and those he imagines as lying behind this saying to hamstring his patients, who, failing to grasp the proper meaning of the phrase, have used it to stifle their own scruples and to justify immoral conduct. The philosopher is not trying to get rid of the fact of evil by reducing it to the level of a lesser good or by declaring it non-existent.[2] It is much to be regretted that Jung's ill-judged contempt for the phrase should have made him utter inept and irrelevant judgments about "the nonsensical doctrine of the 'privatio boni' ".[3] Even if he has since retracted this to a certain extent and confined his criticism to the purely psychic and empirical level, his statements still reveal a failure to understand the validity of the philosophical position.[4]

Nevertheless, I do not deny that his emphasis on the reality of evil is very much to the point. It is only too true that the traditional principle of the "privatio boni" has been subject to

[1] *Aion*, p. 91 (1951).

[2] I do not deny that some Fathers of the Church, some scholastic philosophers and even some modern theologians have presented the " privatio boni " in an erroneous or simple-minded way. Their interpretations of the phrase have left it wide open to criticism and in this connection I agree with all that Jung says about it. But the psychologist turned critic cannot forget that the passages from the Fathers which Jung has particularly condemned (*Aion*, pp. 67–97) are far more in the nature of exhortations or sermons to people often with very little education than scientific tracts for intellectuals and scientists. They contain a high proportion of concrete examples and figurative explanations suitable for the purposes of instruction if not necessarily enjoying the approval of strict philosophy. I am afraid that this lack of historical perspective may be one of the reasons why Jung's reading and very careful study of the Fathers has not enabled him to see the problem of evil in its proper perspective or to grasp all its implications.

[3] *Answer to Job*, p. 33n (1952).

[4] In one of his most recent writings Jung says amongst other things: "*My criticism is only valid within the empirical realm*; in the metaphysical realm, on the other hand, good can be a substance and evil a *μὴ ὄν*. I know of no empirical fact which would come anywhere near such an assertion. Therefore at this point the empiricist must remain silent " (Preface to V. White, *God and the Unconscious*, p. xx (1952)). Jung's italics.

erroneous interpretations of the kind Jung mentions, and when these occur, as frequently happens in the case of patients being analysed, it is necessary to point out to them, indeed inculcate into them, the reality of evil. But it would still be wrong to go to the opposite extreme and falsify a well-established philosophical axiom.

The second characteristic that Jung finds in evil, namely its relativity, is also not lacking from the philosopher's view of the problem. "Relativity" is a dangerous word to use however because of its ambiguity. For Jung evil is relative to the person who is not all he should be on the psychic level and so is unable to integrate it. For the philosopher it is relative to the person who is not all he should be on the ontological level. Jung has said in so many words that this latter side of the matter is not his concern. The philosopher, likewise, is not concerned with the facts of psychology in themselves. Would it not be perfectly logical, then, for each to go his own way without more ado? Far from believing this, I think that it would be a great pity if the contact that has begun to be established between the two were broken. For the philosopher is in a position to shed a certain amount of light on the discoveries made by the psychologist.

The psychologist has in fact discovered that evil is relative both at its source and in its end. This discovery saves him from an irresolvable dualism. But how can anything be both positive and relative? How can psychic forces be able to hamper the development of the psyche and at the same time capable of promoting it?

In psychology the only possible answer to these questions is the simple statement that it does, and it is a good enough answer for psychology, which only sets out to discover what is. But this is just where the philosopher can step in and draw the psychologist's attention to a particular point.

On the empirical level evil comes into existence because some particular thing fails to be integrated and this produces a psychic dissociation. The thing that is in the way does not stop the psychic activity altogether, it does not destroy the energy, but it disturbs the work that should be going on by erecting a barrier and diverting the energy from its natural course towards the development of being. It is thus not the psychic energy and the activity in themselves that are evil but their disorder or disorientation. The energy retains its full value and power but it is wrongly directed—and so the psychologist calls it evil. In suggesting all this the philosopher is not denying the value of the psychologist's empirical discoveries. Jung himself has frequently stressed the fact that the mark of psychotherapy "is not the imaginary entity known as a neurosis but the distorted totality of the human being".[1] Does not this clearly mean that psychic evil is a lack of something, in fact a privation of some good that should be there?

If this explanation of evil is right—and in my view there can be no doubt that it is—we can see at once that Jung's idea about the presence of evil in God is untenable. Jung puts good and evil into God to account for their presence in man and yet at the same time avoid any sort of dualism. But this is not necessary. Psychic evil means a disturbance in the equilibrium of the psyche, and it is a fault which will never be completely eliminated because man, being a created being, can never be perfect. It is therefore quite natural for good and evil to exist side by side in him even though their relative proportions can vary infinitely. But it does not follow from this that evil must be found in God too or must be assumed to exist in him. Jung's remarks about Satan as God's eldest son and Antichrist as the enemy of Christ, which continue for page after page, are only possible because he projects human properties on to God. Daim quite rightly condemns such a procedure as "going off the rails like the gnostics" (*eine gnostische Entgleisung*),[2] though I myself prefer not to charge Jung with gnosticism for he avoids its real error: he never, in fact, identifies human representations with ontological realities.

A comparison between Jung's views on the problem of evil and the classical doctrine of the "privatio boni" shows, quite clearly, that there is no irremediable conflict between the two. Both accept the fact of evil and make no attempt to deny its activity. But that is not all. The relative character of evil as established by Jung on the empirical level is in perfect harmony with the ontological principle that evil is the privation of a good that should

[1] "Medizin und Psychotherapie", p. 319 (1945).
[2] W. Daim, *Der Grundfehler C. G. Jungs*, p. 58.

be there. The only point on which I must make it clear that I cannot agree with Jung is where he shifts his empirical discoveries about psychic evil on to God. It matters little whether he does this bluntly or tactfully, for in both cases he projects human deficiencies on to God and brings the Creator down to the level of the creature.

III. Trinity and Quaternity

The questions raised by the problem of evil could not be solved without a careful study and close discussion of the psychological and philosophical points of view. A similar delicate understanding of the respective positions taken up by theology and psychology is necessary before we can form a proper estimate of Jung's remarks on the Trinity and what he calls "quaternity". This means, in fact, comparing the Christian dogma of the Trinity as a God in three Persons with Jung's view, based on his own empirical data, that "quaternity" is the best of all symbols of totality or the self.

To bring out the full significance of Jung's data we shall have to discuss in some detail what Jung means by quaternity.

As I pointed out in connection with the mandalas, Jung has emphasized the special part played by quaternary symbolism in psychic processes. This symbolism can take the most varied and unexpected forms, and it sometimes appears a good deal less clearly than at others: it may be perfectly apparent in the four points of the compass or the four colours of alchemy, or again it may be concealed in a four-pointed star, a four-wheeled cab or a table with four people round it. Its meaning, however, whether disguised or not, is constant: quaternary symbolism expresses or prefigures a process of integration in which the four psychic functions enter into harmonious collaboration and complement each other. Each stage, however transitory, in the simultaneous development of the four functions Jung regards as a sign of progress towards *Vollständigkeit*, i.e., the full development of the being as a whole.

Ternary symbolism on the other hand—which appears far less frequently—generally shows that the integration is not complete: one essential element at least is missing, some vital component has been inadvertently ignored or repressed. Not that this failure in one particular point means necessarily that there may not be a very great differentiation between the assumed elements: often within a particular triad the components may reach a state of extreme perfection. Jung calls this imperfect kind of perfection *Vollkommenheit*.[1]

A typical example of this perfection that is limited to a few functions is found in the over-intellectualized person. "In this case the higher function is thought, in the sense of intelligence. One or two functions of an irrational kind are also differentiated—perception, in the sense of the 'function of the real', and intuition, in the sense of perception via the unconscious. The lower function is then feeling (value-function)."[2] When this is so, feeling, like any other lower function that has not been brought into proper line, goes off into strange deviations and incomprehensible extravagances.

No particular insight is needed to discern the weak point in the "rationalized" man. It is always found in the affective sphere, and it manifests itself either as blind confidence or hopeless love, or as unreasonable bias or brutal aversion. For in this case the affective life is entirely beyond the control of thought. But such a deficiency in one particular point should not blind us to the real enrichment that can result from this kind of unilateral differentiation. "The strange dissociation which is to be found in all exclusive development does not minimize the real differentiation that in itself means a liberation of consciousness . . ." "Abstraction is a way of gaining freedom from the hold of impressions and emotions, fascinating ideas and presentiments."[3]

Jung does not say therefore that *Vollkommenheit* is valueless, but he clearly regards it as a lower form than *Vollständigkeit*. The latter alone really corresponds to a development of the whole being, because it omits none of the latent potentialities of personal development.

[1] *Vollkommenheit* can be quite simply translated as "perfection". But *Vollständigkeit* is a different matter. As they are both technical terms I have preferred to explain the meaning of the German words and then keep to them.

[2] *Symbolik des Geistes*, pp. 396–7 (1948).

[3] Ibid., p. 397 (1948).

Vollständigkeit, in fact, needs to be carefully distinguished from the non-differentiation found in children and primitives. In these the four functions are amalgamated, but in a chaotic whole. Lacking any unifying directive from consciousness, the psyche is at the mercy of all their whims. Do we not all come across "primitives" with this kind of tawdry psychology every day—people whose "thought" is tyrannized over by ungoverned feelings and their "perception" falsified by false intuitions, except when their incoherent perceptions volatilize their "intuition" and their disordered thoughts confuse their "feelings". *Vollständigkeit*, on the other hand, involves a kind of differentation that brings out the proper characteristics of the various functions and, far from reducing them to any common denominator, emphasizes their specific differences. As a result of this psychic lucidity, this state of higher consciousness, the functions culminate in a mutually beneficial interaction and complement each other perfectly.

This *Vollständigkeit*, moreover, is not limited to the functions. It also includes the unification of the various opposites. The integration of evil—i.e., of neglected or repressed psychic components—is as necessary as the integration of good: the masculine qualities need to be fused with the specifically feminine virtues and the constitutive elements of the conscious attitude have to be made to combine with the components of the unconscious. *Vollständigkeit* never means levelling down to one particular element at the expense of the others. It only comes about when there is a harmonious union of the specific differences and main oppositions as described by analytical psychology.

This *Vollständigkeit* is, of course, impossible without the complementarity of opposites and the compensation of conscious and unconscious. These two mechanisms are only possible because all the psychic elements are rooted in and unified by the self. It thus follows naturally that all the symbols that show an essentially quaternary structure, and thereby express a state of *Vollständigkeit*, should be admirably suited to signifying the self.

The purely psychological views analysed above help us to get a better view of the subject with which we are concerned here.

It is not indeed surprising that thinking about ternary and quaternary symbols should have revived childhood memories in Jung, for it will be remembered how fascinated he was one day by the question of the Trinity when he was glancing idly through his catechism to vary the monotony of an hour's religious instruction. His father's decision to ignore the paragraph concerned, because he himself could not understand it, had unfortunately disappointed his expectations, but the fascination remained, and more than fifty years later it crystallized in a straight question: why is it that quaternity is the commonest symbolic expression of the Self, i.e., the being who has reached *Vollständigkeit*, whereas the supreme being appears in ternary form in Christian dogma?

Jung imagines that the Christian believer will not ask himself this question or, if he does, will do his best to gloss it over so as not to risk laying himself open to doubts that might upset his religious convictions.[1] Well, what is his own answer to this question, as one who has not been given "the gift of faith" and has nevertheless been too deeply impressed by the psychological part played by dogma to be able to reject it outright as illusion?

Jung undertakes a twofold task. First he tries as a psychologist to understand what the dogma of the Trinity really means, then he tries to discover if there are any traces of quaternity in Christian dogma.

In Part One of "Versuch einer psychologischen Deutung des Trinitätsdogmas", he gives a list of the divine triads that were to be found, long before the Christian era began, first in Egypt and Mesopotamia and later in Greece.[2] Such a recurrence of ternary symbolism, which cannot possibly be put down to any influences of a historical kind, shows clearly in Jung's view that what is involved is in fact an archetype. The New Testament gives further proof of the existence of the same archetype in the appearance of the Trinity. "In point of fact it is not an intellectual expression of the Trinity that is revealed but the Trinitarian drama of the Redemption. . . . Leaving aside the *comma joanneum*, which is an interpolation . . . there is not a single passage in which the

[1] *Answer to Job*, p. 148 (1952).
[2] *Symbolik des Geistes*, pp. 327–50 (1948).

doctrine of the Trinity is stated systematically [*intellektuell fassbar*]."[1] The combined efforts of four centuries of Christian thinkers were needed to develop the clear, succinct, precise formula of "one Nature in three Persons". "This centuries-long development is simply the gradual maturing of the archetype in consciousness . . . This unfolding in history brought an understanding of something that had in the first place been revealed through a sudden illumination and taken a rapid hold on men."[2] "The evolution of the symbols clothed the Trinitarian suggestions in Holy Scripture with a construction of ideas [*ein Ideengerüst*]."[3]

The thing to be deciphered, then, is the psychological meaning of this archetype.

Jung believes that the Trinity, as expressed by the Christian faith in the form of Father, Son and Holy Spirit, is best regarded as a projection of the three stages through which every human being passes to Being itself. The Person of the Father is an expression of the original state of non-differentiation. At this first stage, non-differentiated being is identified absolutely with the family (or group). The child, or the primitive, thinks, lives, feels, judges, through and in the family or group, and is quite unable to take up any objective attitude towards it. Before long, however, it discovers that it possesses an independent personal existence and inevitably tries to emancipate itself. It turns its back on its mother's love, throws off its father's authority, and hurls itself into a battle for its own personality in the external world. It thus enters upon the second stage—represented, according to Jung, by the Son—and tries to free itself from its mother and father and the rest of the family. This kind of affirmation through opposition is necessary for anyone who is determined to discover his own personality, and if the process is hindered, either by dominating parents or through failure on the part of the adolescent himself, his world will harden at the infantile stage and be dominated by the figure of his father. This second period is therefore usually characterized by an exclusive tendency towards liberation and self-affirmation. This exclusive line of development needs

[1] *Symbolik des Geistes*, p. 361. [2] Ibid., p. 364. [3] Ibid., p. 373.

to be transcended in its turn, and in the third stage the grown man should unite the two preceding stages by realizing that his independence is no more absolute than the other values in his life and has no meaning unless he is prepared to submit freely to a reality that transcends him. He thus returns to the totality he had left behind him, not through any childish abdication of responsibility but as a result of an adult submission.

As the first stage is dominated by the Father and the second by the Son so the third, which unites the first two, is dominated by the Spirit, the link between Father and Son.

To conclude, then. According to Jung the archetype that lies behind the Trinity is in fact the psychic reality of the three stages that man goes through on the way to full development. Seen from this angle the Trinity is the transposition of a subjective reality on to a "metaphysical" plane, i.e., a plane "situated outside the subject".

Jung knows only too well that in saying that "the statements made in the Holy Scritures are also utterances of the soul" he runs "the risk of being suspected of psychologism",[1] and so he adds a few qualifications. His interpretation, he says, "is not an exhaustive explanation but only an analogy"[2] designed for those who, like himself, "are unable to believe what they cannot understand". Did not St. Patrick do the same when he tried to explain the doctrine of the Trinity to the Irish? He compared it to a shamrock, which is also three and one—three leaves all like each other and yet together making one leaf.

If Jung was simply trying to manufacture an analogy easily comprehensible by the modern mind we should have no right to complain. But, unlike St. Patrick, who was indeed using his analogy—and a rather inadequate one!—to help to make the Trinity acceptable to his auditors, Jung uses his to try to get rid of the dogma altogether. Jung's comparative researches have not put theology in his debt; on the contrary, they have only increased the danger, not only that the absolute transcendence of the mystery will be lost sight of, but, even more, that people will give themselves

[1] *Answer to Job*, p. xv (1952).
[2] *Symbolik des Geistes*, p. 427 (1948).

a pat on the back for having come to such a vast comprehension and understanding of the dogma that faith itself is no longer necessary.

Jung's investigations have produced an abundance of material, all presented with a highly imposing critical apparatus. Unfortunately it is wasted enthusiasm: it brings neither believers nor unbelievers a jot nearer to an understanding of the dogma. When he comes to the end of his investigation he is further away from the dogma of the Trinity than ever, despite having begun with the actual words used by the Church Councils.[1]

Jung's attempts to make the dogma of the Trinity acceptable are rotten at the root. Perhaps he had more luck with his investigations into the "quaternity" of Christianity?

From his observations Jung concluded that ternary symbols generally express a state of *Vollkommenheit* or partial perfection. He found this surprising, and the question it led him to ask was whether Western man had omitted some essential element from his representation of God. The answer he finally gave to this question was yes. In point of fact he had been strongly impressed by the part played in the process of individuation by evil, and he was astonished to find no trace of evil in the representation of God, who was always conceived of as the Supreme Good. He decided that this suppression must be the result of a generalized repression. The patients he had to treat confirmed his suspicions. Usually they seemed not to care very much when they were faced with evil, and he found this disconcerting: could it be because every kind of treatment had to begin with their facing up to their "shadow", and this had been denied because they would not recognize or admit the evil they bore within themselves?

Spurred on by these observations Jung embarked upon a comparison of various kinds of religious literature, in particular the books of the Bible. Struck by the preponderant part played in them by Satan, the spirit of evil, he found that in the oldest books this figure was presented as a son or "servant" of Jahweh. In the latter books of the Old Testament this son of Jahweh became a

[1] In his remarkable critical-historical study of this matter, Leibbrand gives a striking demonstration of this from the point of view of the history of dogma.

rebel angel, almost a malevolent despot, to whom God gave a free hand. The first centuries of Christianity had taken a further step forward and attributed greater and greater power to him.

In Jung's view the emphasis on the sovereign goodness of God, whose Fatherhood was revealed by the Son, inevitably led Christian theology to remove the power of the Prince of Darkness out of range of God's immediate control. Christian thinkers contented themselves with stating that at the end of time the divine omnipotence would manifest itself in a resounding victory that would show Lucifer and his crew the futility of their endeavours. Jung is afraid that by thus dissociating good and evil they created an irresolvable dualism, all the more dangerous from the fact that it remained unconscious. He says that this divorce between good and evil on the objective plane of divinity is symptomatic of a psychic dissociation within man himself, who is no longer prepared to recognize the lower part of his being as part of himself. The repression of the "shadow", which includes evil, explains, as Jung sees it, the two opposite attitudes that modern men take towards evil: either a guilty "couldn't care less" attitude or a frenzied revolt against it. In the first case they say that there is no evil in the world, because they imagine it to be inoperative within themselves; in the second they are exasperated by its reality in the world because they cannot see that they bear it within themselves.

Jung sees only one way of remedying these two attitudes, both equally false and sterile: both sides, the rebels and the indifferent, need to become aware of the real, positive part played by evil in the human condition. They have to begin by recognizing that they carry this evil within themselves and then do all they can to integrate it as a psychic reality instead of dismissing it from their own personal sphere. Then they will be able to come to a state of *Vollständigkeit*.

I have tried to show how Jung was led to compare the Christian doctrine of the Trinity with his ideas of *Vollkommenheit* and *Vollständigkeit*. Let me briefly sum up his line of argument. He believes that all ternary symbols indicate that some psychic component is being repressed by the person producing the symbol. Then he finds that Western man's idea of God is essentially ternary. It thus seems to follow that Western man's representation of the human ideal has missed out some essential component. As the Christian God is regarded as the Supreme Good, Jung begins to wonder whether the ignored element may not be evil. If so, *Vollständigkeit* requires the spirit of evil to be added to the Trinity to make up a quaternity. In doing this Jung hopes to avoid any sort of dualism, for evil is traced back to God, indeed into God, and this creates a quaternity reflecting the ideal that must govern any fully human development.

This brief résumé of Jung's argument brings out its weak point. What he postulates in fact as the basis for his whole line of reasoning is that God is to be identified with the ideal image that man should, and does, form of himself and then projects into the supra-human or metaphysical order. This takes Jung a thousand miles away from the actual dogma itself. For the dogma never mentions man's idea of God; it is entirely concerned with God's being, as a thing revealed. Nothing drawn from any idea of God can help to throw any light on God's being.

I am quite willing to grant that Jung has shown that in a great number of cases—but not by any means always, as, by an unjustified generalization, he likes to say—the ternary symbolism of unconscious productions reveals a psychic condition characterized by the systematic ignoring of some essential component. It is perfectly understandable that such a psychic condition should be reflected in representations made of God, and these representations tell us a great deal about their author's state of mind; but they tell us nothing whatsoever about the actual being of the Trinity as revealed in history and set forth by the Church.

Jung, of course, would be quick to retort that his remarks are all concerned solely with representations of God and not with his essential being or nature. He would repeat, with a certain touch of impatience, that by this very fact nothing that he says can possibly conflict with any dogma. When he quotes from statements drawn up at Nicæa, Constantinople or the Lateran Council, or from the inspired writings of Holy Scripture, he is only doing so, he says, "because they are utterances made by the psyche", and as such within the competence of the psychologist.

The unfortunate fact is, however, that this self-imposed restriction is of no avail towards getting Jung out of the impasse to which his reasoning has inexorably led him. For in point of fact if he wants to maintain his position he must, implicitly at least, reduce the dogma itself to "an utterance made by the psyche". But dogma—whether it be the dogma of the Trinity or any other—can no more be regarded as equivalent to any "psychic utterance" than it can to any spatial symbol or painted image. Not even the poetic visions of a Dante or Fra Angelico's heavenly paintings are to be identified with the dogmatic truths they clothe in literary or plastic form.

Jung was not content with one attempt to find quaternary symbolism in Catholic dogma. In his latest book, *Answer to Job*, he develops a new theory.

Some years before, in *Psychology and Religion*, he had referred to the medieval mandalas in which the Blessed Virgin appears along with the Trinity. These mandalas are frequently to be found in drawings and paintings, prose passages and poems, describing or depicting visions of the life of heaven. In *Answer to Job*, which was published six years after the big book on the Trinity, Jung stresses the fact that the Trinity is regarded almost entirely as a masculine thing, since it is always the Father and Son who are spoken of. But where in this case is the feminine element that should complement these masculine characteristics?

The Church herself has realized this deficiency, says Jung, and with some enthusiasm he salutes the proclamation of the dogma of the Assumption as "the most important religious event since the Reformation".[1] This dogma had been present in a latent state in the early Church, had gradually come to the fore in the liturgy and theological thought, and has at last been given official recognition in the papal decree. This gradual development of the dogma corresponds perfectly to the emergence of an archetype into consciousness as described by Jung in the earlier case of the dogma of the Trinity. And he stresses the fact

[1] *Answer to Job*, p. 169 (1952).

that the Pope based the solemn definition of the dogma on official tradition and the living faith in the hearts of the Christian masses. Jung concludes that within the actual Church, within the fold of perfect orthodoxy, a quaternity has been developed under the clear influence of archetypal components. It is true that the Blessed Virgin remains inferior in nature and dignity to the three Persons of the Trinity: her exceptional position does not deify her; nevertheless she transcends all other creatures as Heavenly Spouse and Mother of the Son himself.

Jung maintains that the singularity of her position is essential. Quaternity, in fact, as a union of opposites, does not mean absolute identity, otherwise it would end in identification pure and simple and thus eliminate the constitutive elements. In the case of the Assumption the Blessed Virgin is united in a singularly close way with the life of the Trinity but at the same time she remains a creature and as such infinitely far removed from the Creator. The fact that she is a woman, again, enables the faithful to find in the highest spheres of heaven all the feminine and maternal characteristics that a uniquely masculine representation of the divinity had not sufficiently covered. And Jung turns sharply upon Protestants for failing to see that in the new dogma "there is more . . . than papal arbitrariness"[1] and for accepting "nothing but a man's religion which allows no metaphysical representation of woman".[2]

Catholic readers who are rather out of touch with the psychological point of view will probably be somewhat taken aback, if not scandalized, by these remarks of Jung's, even though they purport to be Catholic in tone. On reflection, however, they may come to see that—in an unexpected way, it is true—Jung is putting forward ideas to which they are by no means unaccustomed. From their earliest days they have venerated the Blessed Virgin as the Mother of God. As ardent believers they have invoked her aid, believing in the all-powerfulness of her motherly intercession with her Son. In times of distress they may have chosen to turn to her as their mediator, rather than to the Father or Son direct. When they come to

[1] *Answer to Job*, p. 174 (1952). [2] Ibid., p. 170.

reflect on these things, they may see that Jung is saying nothing new when he talks of the Blessed Virgin's role as a mother—nothing, that is, except the word "quaternity". This may upset them because it seems to affront their dearest dogmatic convictions, but one can understand how Jung himself, struck by the somewhat one-sided idea of our heavenly Father held, as he himself says, by Protestants, was delighted to find that beside the all-powerful Father a loving Mother sat enthroned. And his delight was unmixed because he believes that there are sound reasons behind it, drawn from his own observations as a psychologist.

Catholics, however, can derive no benefit from Jung's views, for they explicitly minimize the truth of dogmatic statements. Nor can unbelievers be helped any further forward by them: even when they are convinced that a certain quaternary or ternary "psychic statement" is well-founded, they are brought no nearer to a real understanding of the three divine Persons or of Our Lady's assumption into heaven.

What, then, must be my final conclusions in this matter?

Jung has said often enough that he is not concerned with the ontological side of revealed truths, and I have no intention of forgetting this declaration of principle. Still, it is much to be regretted that the ambiguity of certain important passages and the woolliness of his language should have led to so much confusion and misunderstanding—which he then waxes indignant about. However, I agree with him when he says that no psychological interpretation of any dogma can ever prove or disprove the dogma concerned. Further, I accept the validity of a psychological study "of the religious person" and "of religion proper, i.e., of religious contents".[1] In itself such a study can add nothing to our intellectual understanding of dogma, nor does it help us to practise any religious ideal; it can however help us indirectly towards a better appreciation of anything non-genuine in religious attitudes and of the repercussions that psychic dispositions can have in symbolic representations of revealed truths.

On the other hand Jung is always letting himself be dragged

[1] *Answer to Job*, p. 169.

beyond the confines of his own rights and competence. Whether he is discussing the significance of mandala centres, or examining the problem of evil, or deciphering the meaning of quaternary and ternary symbols, he sets up his facts and psychological explanations against dogmatic truths, though at the same time extolling the exceptional efficacy of the latter from the psychological point of view. By proceeding in this way he undoubtedly goes beyond the field of psychology. And therefore I feel obliged to refuse to his views, thoroughly tried and tested as they have been above, any real value in connection with the study of actual dogma.[1]

[1] In thus forthrightly condemning the contradiction between Jung's explicit denials and his implicit position I am not suggesting any deliberate *parti pris*. I am convinced that Jung is a sincere seeker after truth. But his scientific preoccupations have so dominated his thought that it has been almost impossible for him to grasp the real significance of any point of view other than the psychological.

CONCLUSION

VIII

RELIGION AND ANALYTICAL PSYCHOLOGY

We have now examined in turn Jung's empirical method, his fundamental ideas and his attempts to reconcile conflicting views. Then we went on to study his ideas on religion, and compared them with the practice of spiritual direction on the one hand and the facts of dogmatic theology on the other.

I have often been able to signify my agreement with Jung; often, again, I have been obliged to make express reservations; occasionally, indeed, I have had to reject his ideas outright. All that remains to be done now to bring this study to an end is for me to assemble my conclusions around my central theme.

Jung's analytical psychology, like all empirical sciences, is based on a number of hypotheses each of which expresses one particular aspect of the fundamental intuition and special attitude that first brought the science in question into existence. Very often the scientist himself is not explicitly aware of the exact nature of this original intuition and attitude and imagines that it is an integrating part of reality and reflects the object of his researches. In this he is not entirely wrong. The intuition undoubtedly reflects an essential aspect of the object; if not, it would have remained quite sterile. It is therefore quite true that the original intuition determines and defines the specific object of any science. The scientist however must never forget that the specific object also determines and defines the intuition. If he neglects this reciprocal conditioning he will be inevitably led to "reify" his intuition and so turn it into an objective reality—unless he empties the object of all reality to such an extent that he turns it into a mere projection.

Jung's most fundamental hypothesis is undoubtedly that of the libido or psychic energy. As an undifferentiated force manifesting itself in all psychic processes, it lies at the root of all the later developments of his thought. The undeniable influence exerted by Freud's idea of the libido as something entirely sexual fades out of the picture when the question becomes how to define the exact significance of the concept of energy. But it is worth remembering that despite the oscillations of his tireless, sometimes laborious, research Jung has continually been broadening his initial hypothesis—first in his study of the different potentialities of psychic structuration, to which he gave the name of archetypes, and then in his examination of the totality that unifies all the elements in this structuration, proceeding from it and returning to it, to which he gave the name of the self.

The significant change in his terminology—in the beginning he speaks entirely of the libido and later almost entirely of the self—is symptomatic of the gradual deepening of his thought. Libido or psychic energy is in fact simply the activity or dynamic manifestation of the self, and the self is simply the actual totality of the possibilities of structuration contained in this energy. As the original intuition, the hypothesis of psychic energy, whose many implications and manifold consequences Jung only came to realize after long years of patient research, defines the exact object of analytical psychology—which is, man as a psychic being. This definition by no means implies that Jung neglects any of the human values; it simply means that he studies and adjudges them from his own particular point of view. He is therefore quite right to emphasize the fact that science, metaphysics and theology come within the scope of psychology just as much as neurotic and pathological phenomena do, because "they are all manifestations of the psyche"—to be precise, not only "because" but also "in so far as" they are manifestations of the psyche.

These extra words are of capital importance, for they introduce qualifications that no one can afford to neglect when speaking of man as a psychic being. It is possible, no doubt, to speak of the psychic forces at work in man (the libido), the possibilities of structuration in which these forces manifest themselves (the archetypes), and the psychic totality that embraces these structures (the self), but according to the hypothesis itself this does not mean that one can go on to say anything about the "real" objects towards which these psychic forces are directed, or the non-psychic causes that may influence such structurations, or the supra-psychic realities that may govern this kind of totality.

This does not mean that Jung's hypothesis is false, or even incomplete or insufficient, but it is restrictive in the way that all methodological definitions establishing the specific object of any science are restrictive. The restrictive character of its object gives the science of psychology its value and is its whole *raison d'être*: if it were removed, this would mean doing away with the whole of analytical psychology as a distinct branch of knowledge within the framework of psychology, which itself forms a whole section of scientific thought. If the various sciences were all deprived of their specific objects they would no longer be able to be distinguished from each other and by trying to include everything would end by holding nothing.

The specific object of analytical psychology is justified in practice by the fact that it undoubtedly gives results. It is also justified in theory by the specific character of Jung's scientific experience. It would thus be just as absurd to reproach Jung for not considering man from the philosophical or ontological point of view as it would be to find fault with the philosopher for not analysing human beings empirically. Anatomy studies the whole man, but it does not include the soul or the beyond. Binswanger stresses the fact that Freud is entirely concerned with *homo naturalis*, and this gives a very clear idea of the real object of all Freud's scientific work. If I say, therefore, that the object of analytical psychology is *homo psychicus*, I am not making any complaint against Jung; I am simply stating the real object of his investigations in a single word.

I have no hesitation in granting Jung that depth psychology can teach us much that is interesting about philosophy and theology. These two branches of learning are "*also* productions of the psyche"—which means to say, they have a psychic side to them. This has enabled Jung to discover characteristics of introversion in idealism and of extraversion in realism. It has also enabled him to analyse the psychological repercussions that appear in symbolic representations of certain dogmas, just as he has been able to distinguish the genuine from the non-genuine in religious attitudes. I am happy to support these conclusions, which explain or bring to our attention phenomena that may perhaps have been wrongly regarded as exclusively metaphysical, theological or religious.

Jung's contribution to philosophy, theology and religion remains nonetheless indirect. I have acknowledged his right to enter this field—he himself has not been shy of asserting it—but he in his turn should be prepared to accept the limitations which his science imposes upon him. He ought to realize that he is speaking of *homo psychicus* or the psyche, and nothing more. This psyche extends throughout the whole of human reality, it is true; but it does not cover the whole of human reality, and psychology can tell us nothing about metaphysics or theology in themselves or anything about their specific object.

This restrictive character of the actual object of analytical psychology lies behind all the difficulties and misunderstandings that Jung has had to battle against so continuously. On the one hand he has accepted the limitations of his science with a good grace, so long as he is only presenting his own point of view; and although what he says is not always free from ambiguity he has said again and again that his science is only concerned with the psychic side of man and so unable to pronounce either way upon the matter of the absolute value of religion or the objective existence of God. But on the other hand he forgets all about these self-imposed theoretical restrictions as soon as he starts subjecting religion, dogma, the existence of God, etc., to his own brand of psychological criticism.

Jung's last book but one, published significantly under the title *Answer to Job*, makes it quite clear how he proceeds. It is one of his shortest books and it provides in brief a complete outline of his religious beliefs, gathered together around a central theme which sets up Job against Jahweh, man against God. It thus gives a bird's-eye view of all the points studied so far in this book, and a discussion of its contents will be a very suitable way of bringing this study to an end.

The starting-point of the book is the conception of Jahweh[1] which is to be found in the Book of Job. As Jung has no intention of offering "a cool and carefully considered exegesis" but is proclaiming his "purely subjective reaction" (p. 4),[2] he pulls no punches in his description of Jahweh. Jahweh is an oriental despot puffed up with his own omnipotence and intentionally blind to the injustices he inflicts upon the just man, Job. He tolerates Satan's presence at his court, lends an ear to his insinuations, and allows him to try and torment the just man even though he has no doubt about his absolute loyalty. Job on the other hand is the wise man who knows that in God omnipotence must go hand in hand with wisdom, omniscience and justice. Strong in this conviction he squares up to his friends and insists that Jahweh will vindicate him. Finally Jahweh himself comes on the scene, but far from acceding to Job's requests he swamps him under a flood of dazzling descriptions of His own omnipotence, whose only standard is his own good pleasure (p. 13). Job again shows his wisdom, and before the unleashing of this violence he bows down and is silent: man has a far higher consciousness than Jahweh. But the argument has aroused disquiet in Jahweh's heart, and henceforth he is unable to conceal from himself the one-sided character of his despotic omnipotence (i.e., henceforth man is unable to hide the fact that his representation of God as a despot was onesided).

In this description of the quarrel between Jahweh and Job Jung gives free vent to his feelings. For he regards the Book of

[1] Here again Jung makes no effort to lighten his readers' task. In his preface, as usual, he stresses the fact that he will not be discussing God but only men's ideas of God, Jahweh, Christ, etc., but throughout the book he uses the words "God", "Jahweh", "Christ", without any further qualifications. He thus obliges his readers to be making continual transpositions of the actual words before him. When we come across passages like this, for instance, "Jahweh is less conscious than man", or "God is not aware of his one-sided character", we have to take them to mean, "Man imagines Jahweh as someone less conscious than himself" and "man is aware of the one-sided character of his representation of God". This "translation", which has to go on from beginning to end, makes reading the book an absolute exercise in mental gymnastics, even for people brought up on psychology.

[2] All the references in brackets are to *Answer to Job*.

Job "as a paradigm for a certain experience of God which has a special significance for us today" (p. 4). Jung in fact is speaking in the name of modern man, who, in these days when the atomic bomb threatens to destroy the whole world, can only see the arbitrariness of God's omnipotence and seeks in vain for any sign of wisdom in it. But Jung will not despair, and he seeks in the Scriptures and other religious books of the same period a response to the challenge made to Jahweh, in the hope that the answer to Job may also be found relevant by modern man.

Job has drawn Jahweh's attention to the one-sided character of his behaviour (i.e., Job has realized that his idea of Jahweh's behaviour was one-sided). Jung believes that the Scriptures contain indications of two different tendencies, one towards the integration of the other components, wisdom, omniscience and justice, the other towards remedying the wrong that Jahweh has done to Job. The tendency towards integration appears particularly in the Book of Wisdom and even more in the apocryphal book called The Wisdom of Solomon, both of which praise the Wisdom which existed in God when he was establishing the foundations of the earth (pp. 53–5). Reparation for the wrong done to Job is particularly evident in the visions of Ezekiel, Daniel and Enoch, where the "Son of Man" appears raised to the highest heaven. Is not this proof that God is becoming more "human" (i.e., that the representation of Jahweh includes, besides his all-powerful good pleasure, the other components enumerated above)?

At the Incarnation[1] these two elements, integration and reparation, come together. God's wisdom appears in the precautionary measures taken to ensure that the Incarnation itself shall escape any influence from Satan. Christ is born of a Virgin conceived without sin, the perfect realization of "Sophia" (p. 126). Christ, the Son of God, takes over Job's destiny and, like him, the just one, submits to all the trials of innocent suffering, crying out on the Cross: "My God, my God, why hast thou forsaken me?" And Jung concludes: "Yahweh's intention to become man,

[1] The German word *Menschwerdung* (" becoming man ") takes on a special meaning in Jung's use of it which cannot be rendered by " incarnation ".

which resulted from his collision with Job, is fulfilled in Christ's life and suffering" (p. 76).

The answer to Job is still incomplete, however. The precautionary measures taken by the divine wisdom so that the Incarnation shall succeed have had two results.

In the first place, "Christ, owing to his virgin birth and his sinlessness, was not an empirical human being at all" (p. 84). He was always God and by that very fact "remained outside and above mankind" (p. 84). This is why Christ promised the Apostles that he would send his Spirit "in the sense of a continuing incarnation" (p. 156). The Holy Spirit, working within men and conferring upon them the life of God, was to realize the full "human" development of God in them.

Next, the revelation of God through Christ, his "good" son, has resulted in God's being regarded as the Supreme Good. Satan, who in the Job episode still formed part of the heavenly court as Jahweh's wicked son, was taken away from it in view of the preparations being made for the Incarnation. According to the Gospels Christ saw Satan falling from heaven: thereafter the Prince of Darkness's only kingdom was on this earth. As soon as attention focussed entirely on the goodness of God, it was inevitable that Satan, who represented his evil shadow, should be forgotten. This kind of psychic element, repressed into the unconscious, remains active, however, even when its existence is unrealized. Jung believes that he has found a striking example of this kind of unconscious duality in the case of the beloved Apostle John. John is in fact the author of epistles that say again and again that God is love and that all evil comes from man. But at the same time he is the narrator of apocalyptic visions describing how the wrath of God bursts out against his enemies. Jung has no hesitation in his diagnosis. It is a clear case of enantiodromia: love, so strongly stressed by the conscious attitude, brings images of vengeance surging up from the unconscious. Nevertheless the terrible scenes of destruction are crowned by a vision full of hope announcing a kingdom lasting a thousand years, during which Christ will triumph over evil. Then a revivification of evil is predicted: the reign of Antichrist. And in the end there appears a woman in heaven, "*amicta sole, et luna sub pedibus eius*", who, unbothered by the dragon's threats, gives birth to a child.

In Jung's view this vision refers to our own day. The two thousand years of the aeon have gone. The world is in the grip of a destructive fury never before equalled, driving men to invent one atomic weapon after another. In these distressful days the solemn definition of the Assumption has raised "the woman" to heaven. This—"the most important religious event since the Reformation" (p. 169)—makes Mary "'Queen of Heaven and bride at the heavenly court'" (p. 166). With the Trinity, at whose side she sits enthroned, she is a symbol of the unification of all opposites in God. In him all the various components have risen to the surface of consciousness—masculine and feminine, divine and human, conscious and unconscious. And thus there has been realized in heaven the fullness of all human development, *Vollständigkeit*. Job's question has at last been given a satisfactory answer in history.

This process, which Jung describes on the basis of facts supplied by the Bible and the comparative history of religion, has taken place in the unconscious. For man has not been conscious of the development of his representation of God: it has been a spontaneous growth under the pressure of an inner necessity. This leads Jung to see an archetype at work here tending towards its complete development. The historic process is thus a manifestation of the evolution experienced by every thinking person. For modern man—and for Jung in particular—the starting-point is the same as Job's: confrontation with a God who shows only the capricious, despotic side of his omnipotence. But man only becomes truly adult when he manages to unite wisdom, omniscience and justice to the omnipotence of his representation: he has to allow God to become fully human in him, so that the Incarnation may be realized in "empirical men". Jung proposes to make it a practical part of his treatment, to help people to achieve this task. It is the modern answer to Job.

This analysis of *Answer to Job* shows quite clearly how Jung, in spite of the formal disclaimers in his preface, passes from psychological fact to practical religion.

How are we to account for the difference—one might say, without exaggeration, the contradiction—between Jung's theoretical attitude and the way it is applied in practice? It will not do to simply dismiss Jung as a cloudy pseudophilosopher, even though it is true that he has never had any real philosophical training and has always refused to present his ideas in systematic form. The real reason for the difference is to be found in the dual nature of his scientific work, for he is not only a scientist establishing a psychological theory; he is also a psychotherapist who wants to help his patients. And he emphasizes one or other of these two points of view according to changes of circumstance.

The unfortunate thing is that they lead to two entirely different attitudes. So long as a man devotes himself to scientific research and puts forward hypotheses on that level, it is comparatively easy for him to remain faithful to the theoretical limitations imposed upon him by the specific object of his science, in this case analytical psychology. But the moment he turns to therapeutic treatment he comes into contact not only with the psyche as a whole but with man as a whole too. How is he to avoid, then, the bonds that connect man with everything above and beyond the psyche? Jung has always been the first to acknowledge that all his inquiries into religion and God, evil and the Trinity, have been imposed upon him by his patients, who have made him face concrete attitudes even more than theoretical problems.

The interaction of psychotherapeutic practice and psychological theory is quite a different thing from the mutual conditioning of a fundamental hypothesis and a specific object. These can be narrowly defined in such a way that they respect the limits imposed by the science concerned. The former, however, exist on two different levels, for psychological theory can easily be kept within its own proper limits, but psychotherapeutic practice is obliged to come into contact with every side of the human condition, unless it is to mutilate its "experimental" object. It is thus hardly surprising that it easily lends itself to generalizations and extrapolations, seemingly self-evident but in fact quite arbitrary.

This admixture of theory on the one hand and, on the other,

practice which ignores the well-defined limits of the psychic, lies behind Jung's contradictory attitudes. He has repeated endlessly in all sincerity that he has absolutely no desire to trespass upon the field of religious faith, that he has utterly abstained from any incursions into the sphere of philosophy and theology, and that he has never cast any doubts on the existence of God. Nevertheless his opponents, and even some of his friends, have taken him to task for agnosticism, psychologism and gnosticism. In point of fact Jung has been defending his theoretical point of view with considerable heat, whilst his critics have been attacking his practical applications of it.

Anyone who wants to judge a theory and, even more, its applications, fairly, must take into account both the explicit attitude and the implicit assumptions. Is there not something significant in the fact that Jung's education was dominated by the rationalistic, materialistic spirit rampant at the end of the nineteenth century, and that nevertheless in his very first published work, in 1902, he showed himself to be attracted by the spiritual and the irrational? He felt obliged to inveigh against the rationalistic, materialistic attitude whose ravages he saw so clearly amongst his patients, for the most part unbelievers or, more precisely, people who had lost all contact with any religious society. The more he studied their problems, the more he was struck by the fact that their psychic health was greatly affected by their religious needs. Instead of dismissing these observations, which hardly fitted in with his own convictions in the matter, he made religion the centre of his psychological inquiries. As his revaluation of religion was a reaction against an excess of rationalism, he only attached importance to direct personal experience and the religious function. But as he was unable to ignore dogma, which had proved its efficacy in the past and was continuing to do so in the present, he regarded it as a useful, in fact indispensable, by-product for people who were not in a fit condition to have a direct experience of the numinous. Thereafter he was caught up in problems of a specifically philosophical and theological nature which until then he had done his best to avoid. Despite his sincere desire not to offend anyone's religious convictions, and his frequent contact with priests and layfolk thoroughly conversant with the religious point of view as held by believers, he has not managed to keep unfailingly to his unexceptionable theoretical position.

People who judge Jung by his theoretical attitude will agree with him. People who concentrate on his practical applications of it or his explicit or implicit conclusions will break with him or launch into violent criticism of him. These different ways of approaching him explain why so many discordant judgements have been pronounced on him from time to time, judgements which have all been based on his own words or his practice as a psychotherapist. But if we take a broad general view of his work and try to draw our conclusions from this, we must acknowledge how much he has given us as well as his deficiencies.

Amongst the positive things we must note first that through impartial observation he has come to recognize the specific nature of the religious function. He has never tried to reduce this to any kind of instinct. In Jung's view the religious category is *sui generis*. Furthermore, he has made a profound study of all the various representations in which this function manifests itself. Such a study cannot but be interesting: it provides empirical proof of the great resemblances that exist between all these forms, and it enables us to see the influence of psychic factors in many aberrations. Finally, he has succeeded in synthesizing all these separate elements into an imposing psychic structure whose chief corner-stone is the religious function itself. He is aware of the limited scope of his own insights, which, as he himself has acknowledged, necessarily ignore everything connected with the actual object of this function: all his positive contributions, therefore, never go beyond the sphere of the religious function, that is to say, the feeling for religion that is rooted in man and expresses itself in behaviour. Faithful to the end to the restrictive character of his own empirical method, we remain within the confines of human representations.

But as soon as anyone attempts to raise these conclusions to the level of criteria of revealed truths, which do not originate in man, or, even less, in the psyche, he becomes guilty of an unpardonable infraction of the method in question, and all his subsequent conclusions are vitiated at their root. Furthermore he endangers the genuine acquisitions that have been made, by drawing quite arbitrary and illegitimate generalizations from principles in themselves perfectly valid. For we have now left the domain of the religious function and entered the hazardous field of religion proper, something which does not originate in human dispositions and can in fact raise them to heights otherwise undreamt of. The religious function is rooted in man, but revealed truths have their source in God; and whenever these two realities come together, any confusion of them is fatal.

In an article which ignored the new scientific material provided by psycho-analysis Jung described Freud as a typical representative of the post-Victorian age. Freud, he said, a decent, conventional citizen, broke with ethical formalism, and took upon himself the ungrateful task of unmasking his contemporaries' secret vices and moral hypocrisy. Jung himself—and I have done my best to muffle the tone of malice evident in his words about Freud—is the spokesman of the attitude that has been prevalent during the last half century. Slowly but surely he has rediscovered the religious and the sacred and got rid of an overweening rationalism. On the other hand, however, religious feeling, with all its irrationality, has fascinated him to such an extent that he has banished all the intellectual elements from it; so that, despite his attempts to synthesize the two, he has only managed to achieve a compromise, and an unsatisfactory one, between dogma and the religious function.

I have stated my criticisms clearly, and they do nothing to lessen my adherence to Jung wherever possible. In this study I have tried to avoid either undue enthusiasm or systematic aversion. My only concern has been to discover the truth in Jung's empirical facts, assumptions and hypotheses.

I have intentionally avoided any "analysis" of Jung's religious attitude. As an argument *ad hominem* this can be an easy weapon to wield against the analyst-psychologist, but it is inevitably limited to one individual "case" and by using it one restricts oneself entirely to the analysis of a psychic structure, which gives us no information whatsoever about the objective values it may contain.[1]

From beginning to end of this book I have tried to understand Jung's thought "*sine ira nec studio*", so as to look for the truth along with him and, if possible, find it. Long acquaintance first with Jung's work, then with Jung himself, has convinced me of his profound love of truth and his spontaneous loyal friendship; but even so I have always had in mind the principle which he himself proclaimed when he was still a fervent admirer of Freud: "To give Freud his rights does not mean submitting to a dogma". I have tried to check my own feelings of admiration and sympathy, and it is my hope that I may have managed to recognize the value of what Jung has contributed to depth psychology, without being led away by any naïve enthusiasm into minimizing his defects or passing over his erroneous affirmations in silence.

[1] W. Daim has not been able to resist the temptation "to look for the source of Jung's faulty interpretation in his own person, as Freud has taught us to do". No doubt Daim's sketch will be followed up and deepened later, and this, if done with proper care and competence, would certainly be interesting. But when we are told that Jung's attitude towards God and religion is the result of " an ambivalent attitude towards his father, which Jung projects on to the relationship between man and God, as frequently happens ", we learn nothing about the real objective value of his attitude. Cf. W. Daim, *Der Grundfehler C. G. Jungs*, p. 66.

BIBLIOGRAPHY

Books and Articles by C. G. Jung[1]

1. *Zur Psychologie und Pathologie sogenannter occulter Phänomene*, Leipzig, Mutze, 1902, 122 pp. E. 3, 1.
2. "Ein Fall von hysterischem Stupor bei einer Untersuchungsgefangenen," *Journal für Psychologie und Neurologie*, i, 1903, pp. 110–22.
3. "Ueber manische Verstimmung," *Zeitschrift für Psychiatrie*, *lxi*, 1903, pp. 15–39.
4. "Ueber Simulation von Geistesstörung," *Journal für Psychologie und Neurologie*, ii, 1903, pp. 181–201.
5. "Aerztliches Gutachten über einen Fall von simulierter geistiger Störung," *Schweizerische Zeitschrift für Strafrecht*, xvii, 1904, pp. 55–75.
6. "Experimentelle Untersuchungen über die Assoziationen Gesunder," *Journal für Psychologie und Neurologie*, iii, 1904, pp. 55–83; 145–64; 193–215; 283–308; and iv, 1904, pp. 24–67. = 20, 1; E 5, 1.

[1] The *Jung-Festschrift* for 1935, entitled *Die kulturelle Bedeutung der Komplexen Psychologie*, published the first detailed bibliography of Jung's works. This has been repeated and kept up to date by J. Jacobi in the successive editions of her book *The Psychology of C. G. Jung*. But it is not a complete bibliography and some of the references are incorrect, and for this reason I have taken the trouble to do the whole thing all over again. An asterisk before a title means that I have been unable to check this particular work.

With regard to books: after the title comes the place of publication, then the publisher's name and the number of pages. If there have been several editions these are shown in Roman numerals, followed by the year of publication, and, in the case of any changes, the place of publication, the publisher's name and the number of pages.

With regard to articles: the full title of the magazine in which the article appeared is given, then the vol. number (in Roman numerals), the year, and the page numbers in the volume.

As Jung has re-published a large number of articles and even books in his later works, the complete reference is followed wherever necessary by references to these, as well as to the English translations. For this the following signs are used:

= : text unchanged.
± : text revised and enlarged in subsequent publication.
E : number of corresponding English translation.

7. "Ueber hysterisches Verlesen," *Archiv für die gesamte Psychologie*, iii, 1904, pp. 347–56.
8. "Analyse der Assoziationen eines Epyleptikers," *Journal für Psychologie und Neurologie*, v, 1905, pp. 73–90. = 20, 2; E 5, 2.
9. "Experimentelle Beobachtungen über das Erinnerungsvermögen," *Zentralblatt für Nervenheilkunde und Psychiatrie*, xxviii, 1905, pp. 653–66.
10. "Kryptomnesie," *Die Zukunft*, l, 1905, pp. 325–34.
11. "Ueber das Verhalten der Reaktionszeit beim Assoziationsexperiment," *Journal für Psychologie und Neurologie*, vi, 1905, pp. 1–36. = 20, 3; E 5, 3.
12. "Zur psychologischen Tatbestandsdiagnostik," *Zentralblatt für Nervenheilkunde und Psychiatrie*, xxviii, 1905, pp. 813–15.
13. "Die Hysterielehre Freuds," *Münchener Medizinische Wochenschrift*, 1906, pp. 2301–3.
14. "Die psychologische Diagnose des Tatbestandes," *Juristisch-psychiatrische Grenzfragen*, iv, 1906, no. 2, pp. 1–47. Separate publication: Halle, Marhold, 1906, 47 pp.; II, Zürich, Rascher, 1941, 47 pp.
15. "Die psychopathologische Bedeutung des Assoziationsexperiments," *Archiv für Kriminalanthropologie und Kriminalistik*, xxii, 1906, pp. 145–62.
16. "Obergutachten über zwei widersprechende psychiatrische Gutachten," *Monatschrift für Kriminalpsychologie und Strafrechtreform*, ii, 1905–6, pp. 691–8.
* 17. "On Psychophysical Relations of the Association Experiment," *Journal of Abnormal Psychology*, i, 1906.
18. "Psychoanalyse und Assoziationsexperiment," *Journal für Psychologie und Neurologie*, vii, 1906, pp. 1–24. = 20, 4; E 5, 4.
* 19. "Statistisches von der Rekrutenaushebung," *Korresp. Blatt für Schweizer Aerzte*, xxxvi, 1906.
20. *Diagnostische Assoziationsstudien*, vol. i, Leipzig, Barth, 1906, 281 pp.; II, 1911; III, 1915. E 5.
    1. "Experimentelle Untersuchungen über die Assoziationen Gesunder." = 6.
    2. "Analyse der Assoziationen eines Epyleptikers." = 8.
    3. "Ueber das Verhalten der Reaktionszeit beim Assoziationsexperiment." = 11.
    4. "Psychoanalyse und Assoziationsexperiment." = 18.
21. "Associations d'idées familiales," *Archives de Psychologie*, vii, 1907, pp. 160–8. E 3, 2.
22. Petersen, F., and Jung, C. G.: "Psychophysical Investigations with the Galvanometer and the Pneumograph in

Normal and Insane Individuals," *Brain*, cxviii, 1907, pp. 153–218.

* 23. Riksher and Jung, C. G.: "Further Investigations on the Galvanic Phenomenon and Respiration in Normal and Insane Individuals," *Journal of Abnormal Psychology*, ii, 1907.

24. "Ueber die Reproduktionsstörungen beim Assoziationsexperiment," *Journal für Psychologie und Neurologie*, ix, 1907, pp. 188–97. = 36, 2; E 5, 6.

25. *Ueber die Psychologie der Dementia Praecox*, Halle, Marhold, 1907, 139 pp. E 1.

26. "Die Freudsche Hysterietheorie," *Monatschrift für Psychologie und Neurologie*, xxiii, 1908, pp. 310–22.

27. Bleuler, E. and Jung, C. G.: "Komplexe und Krankheitsursachen bei Dementia Praecox," *Zentralblatt für Nervenheilkunde und Psychiatrie*, xxxi, 1908, pp. 220–7.

28. "Le nuove vedute della psicologia criminale," *Rivista di psicologia*, iv. 1908, 20 pp.

29. *Der Inhalt der Psychose*, Vienna, Deuticke, 1908, 26 pp.; II, 1914, 44 pp. E 3, 13.

30. "Die Bedeutung des Vaters für das Schicksal des Einzelnen," *Jahrbuch für psychoanalytische und psychopathologische Forschungen*, i, 1909, pp. 154–73.
Separate publication: Vienna, Deuticke, 1909, 21 pp; II, 1927; III, Zürich, Rascher, 1949, 38 pp. E 3, 3.

31. "L'analyse des rêves," *Année psychologique*, xv, 1909, pp. 160–7.

32. "Randbemerkungen zu dem Buch von Wittels, 'Die sexuelle Not'," *Jahrbuch für psychoanalytische und psychopathologische Forschungen*, ii, 1910, pp. 312–15.

33. "Referate über psychologische Arbeiten Schweizerischer Autoren," *Jahrbuch für psychoanalytische und psychopathologische Forschungen*, ii, 1910, pp. 356–88.

34. "Ueber Konflikte der kindlichen Seele," *Jahrbuch für psychoanalytische und psychopathologische Forschungen*, ii, 1910, pp. 33–58.
Separate publication: Vienna, Deuticke, 1910, 26 pp.; II, 1916; III, Zürich, Rascher, 1939. = 182, 2; E. 3, 2 and 23, 1.

35. "Zur Kritik über Psychoanalyse," *Jahrbuch für psychoanalytische und psychopathologische Forschungen*, ii, 1910, pp. 743–6.

36. *Diagnostische Assoziationsstudien*, vol. ii, Leipzig, Barth, 1910, 222 pp.; II, 1911; III, 1915.
1. "Assoziation, Traum und hysterisches Symptom."
2. "Ueber die Reproduktionsstörungen beim Assoziationsexperiment." = 24.

37. "Buchanzeige von E. Hitchmanns 'Freuds Neurosenlehre',"

Jahrbuch für psychoanalytische und psychopathologische Forschungen, iii, 1911, p. 481.

38. "Ein Beitrag zur Kenntnis des Zahlentraumes," *Zentralblatt für Psychoanalyse*, i, 1910–11, pp. 567–72. E. 3, 5.
39. "Ein Beitrag zur Psychologie des Gerüchtes," *Zentralblatt für Psychoanalyse*, i, 1910–11, pp. 81–90. E. 3, 4.
40. "Kritik über E. Bleuler 'Zur Theorie des schizophrenen Negativismus'," *Jahrbuch für psychoanalytische und psychopathologische Forschungen*, iii, 1911, pp. 469–74. E. 3. 6.
41. "Morton Prince's 'Mechanism and Interpretation of Dreams'," *Jahrbuch für psychoanalytische und psychopathologische Forschungen*, iii, 1911, pp. 309–28.
42. "Wandlungen und Symbole der Libido," *Jahrbuch für psychoanalytische und psychopathologische Forschungen*, iii, 1911, pp. 120–227, and iv, 1912, pp. 162–464.
    Separate publication: Vienna, Deuticke, 1912, 413 pp.; II, 1925; III, 1938. ± 205; E. 4.
43. "Neue Bahnen der Psychologie," *Raschers Jahrbuch für Schweizer Art und Kunst*, iii, 1912, pp. 236–72. ± 53; E. 3, 14; 21, 3.
44. "Zur Psychoanalyse," *Wissen und Leben*, v, 1912, pp. 711–14. E. 3, 8.
45. "Contribution à l'étude des types psychologiques," *Archives de psychologie*, xiii, 1913, pp. 289–99. E. 3. 11.
46. "Psychoanalysis," *The Transactions of the Psycho-Medical Society*, iv, 1913, 19 pp. E. 3, 7.
47. "Versuch einer Darstellung der psychoanalytischen Theorie," *Jahrbuch für psychoanalytische und psychopathologische Forschungen*, v, 1913, pp. 307–441.
    Separate publication: Vienna, Deuticke, 1913, 135 pp. E. 2.
48. "On the Importance of the Unconscious in Psychopathology," *The British Medical Journal*, 1914 (5 Dec.), pp. 964–6. E. 3, 10.
49. Loy, R. and Jung, C. G.: *Psychotherapeutische Zeitfragen*, Vienna, Deuticke, 1914, 51 pp. E. 3, 9.
50. *Psychologische Abhandlungen I*, Vienna, Deuticke, 1914, 211 pp.
51. "On Psychological Understanding," *The Journal of Abnormal Psychology*, 1915, pp. 385–99.
52. "La structure de l'inconscient," *Archives de psychologie*, xvi, 1916, pp. 152–79. ± 72; E. 3, 15; 21, 4.
53. *Die Psychologie der unbewussten Prozesse*, Zürich, Rascher, 1917, 135 pp.; II, 1918, 149 pp. ± 43; E. 3, 14.
54. "Ueber das Unbewusste," *Schweizerland*, iv, 1918, pp. 540–58.
55. "Instinct and the Unconscious," *The British Journal of Psychology*, x, 1919–1920, pp. 15–23. = 73, 3 and 189, 5; E. 6,10
56. "On the Problem of Psychogenesis in Mental Diseases,"

Proceedings of the Royal Society of Medicine, xii, 1919, Section of Psychiatry, pp. 63–76.

57. "The Psychological Foundations of the Belief in Spirits," *Proceedings of the British Society for Psychical Research*, lxxix, 1919, pp. 75–93. = 73, 4 and 189, 6; E. 6, 9.

58. *Psychologische Typen*, Zürich, Rascher, 1921, 704 pp. (+ index), II, 1925; III, 1930; IV, 1937; V, 1942; VI, 1946; VII, 1949; VIII, 1950 (page numbering different), 718 pp. E. 7.

58a. "The Therapeutic Value of Abreaction," *British Journal of Psychology*, Medical Section, ii, 1921, pp. 13–22. E. 6, 11 and 22, 10.

59. "Ueber die Beziehungen der analytischen Psychologie zum dichterischen Kunstwerk," *Wissen und Leben*, xiv, 1921–1922, pp. 914–25 and 964–75. = 97, 2; E. 6, 8.

60. "Psychologische Typen," *Zeitschrift für Menschenkunde*, i, 1925, pp. 45–65. E. 6, 12.

61. "Die Ehe als psychologische Beziehung," *Das Ehebuch, herausgegeben von H. Keyserling*, Celle, Kampmann, 1925, pp. 294–307. = 97, 10; E. 6, 6 and 23, 8.

* 62. "Geist und Leben," *Form und Sinn*, 1926. = 97, 13; E. 6, 2.

63. *Analytische Psychologie und Erziehung*, Heidelberg, Kampmann, 1926, 95 pp.; II, Zürich, Rascher, 1936. = 182, 1; E 6, 13 and 23, 4.

64. *Das Unbewusste im normalen und kranken Seelenleben*, Zürich, Rascher, 1926, 166 pp.; II, 1936. ± 53 and 170; E. 8, 1 and 21, 1.

65. "Die Erdbedingheit der Psyche," H. Keyserling, *Mensch und Erde*, Darmstadt, Reichl, 1927, pp. 83–137. = 97, 6; E. 6, 3.

66. "Die Frau in Europa," *Europäische Revue*, iii, 1927, pp. 481–99. Separate publication: Zürich, *Europäische Revue*, 1929, 45 pp.; II, 1932; III, Zürich, Rascher, 1948. E. 6, 5.

* 67. "Geisteskrankheit und Seele," *Berliner Tageblatt*, 1927.

68. "Das Seelenproblem des modernen Menschen," *Europäische Revue*, iv, 1928, pp. 700–15. = 97, 14; E. 11 and 13, 10.

69. "Die Bedeutung der Schweizerischen Linie im Spektrum Europas," *Neue Schweizer Rundschau*, xxi, 1928, pp. 469–79.

70. "Die Struktur der Seele," *Europäische Revue*, iv, 1928, pp. 27–37 and 125–35. ± 97, 5.

* 71. "Psychoanalyse und Seelsorge," *Ethik*, v, 1928.

72. *Die Beziehungen zwischen dem Ich und dem Unbewussten.* Darmstadt, Reichl, 1928, 208 pp.; II, Zürich, Rascher, 1935; III, 1938; IV. 1945. ± 52; E. 8, 2 and 21, 2.

73. *Ueber die Energetik der Seele* (*Psych. Abhandlungen*, vol. ii), Zürich, Rascher, 1928, 224 pp.

1. "Ueber die Energetik der Seele." = 189, 1; E. 6, 1.
2. "Allgemeine Gesichtspunkte zur Psychologie des Traumes." = 189, 3.
3. "Instinkt und Unbewusstes." = 55 and 189, 5; E 6, 10.
4. "Die psychologischen Grundlagen des Geisterglaubens." = 57 and 189, 6; E 6, 9.

* 74. "Der Gegenstaz Freud und Jung," *Kölnische Zeitung*, April, 1929. ± 97, 3.
75. "Die Bedeutung von Konstitution und Vererbung für die Psychologie," *Die Medizinische Welt*, 1929, 7 pp.
76. "Die Kunst das menschliche Leben zu verlängern," *Europäische Revue*, v, 1929, pp. 530–42. ± 81.
77. "Die Probleme der modernen Psychotherapie," *Schweizerisches medizinisches Jahrbuch*, 1929, pp. 74–86. = 97, 1; E 13, 2 and 22, 5.
78. "Paracelsus," *Der Lesezirkel*, xvi, 1929, 9 pp. = 120, 4.
* 79. "The Complications of American Psychology," *Forum*, 1929.
80. "Ziele der Psychotherapie," *Bericht über den IV allgemeinen ärztlichen Kongress für Psychotherapie in Bad-Nauheim*, 1929, pp. 1–14. = 97, 4; E 13, 3 and 22, 4.
81. Jung, C. G., and Wilhelm, R., *Das Geheimnis der goldenen Blüte*, Munich, Dorn-Verlag, 1929, 161 pp.; II, Zürich, Rascher, 1938; III, 1944, xviii pp. + 150 pp. = 76; E 10.
82. "Der Aufgang einer neuen Welt, Besprechung von H. Keyserling, 'America Set Free'," *Neue Zürcher Zeitung*, 7 Dec. 1930.
83. "Die Lebenswende," *Neue Zürcher Zeitung*, 14 and 16 Mar. 1930. ± 97, 9.
84. Introduction, W. M. Kranefeldt, *Die Psychoanalyse*, Berlin, W. de Gruyter, 1930, pp. 5–16; II, *Therapeutische Psychologie*, Berlin, W. de Gruyter, 1950, pp. 5–17.
85. Introduction, F. Wicke, *The Inner World of Childhood*, New York, London, Appleton, 1930, pp. xiii–xiv. ± 95a.
86. "Nachruf für R. Wilhelm," *Neue Zürcher Zeitung*, 6 Mar. 1930.
87. "Psychologie und Dichtung," E. Ermatinger, *Philosophie der Literaturwissenschaft*, Berlin, Junker und Dünnhaupt, 1930, pp. 315–30 = 198, 1; E 9 and 13, 8.
88. "Some Aspects of Modern Psychotherapy," *Journal of State Medicine*, xxxviii, 1930, pp. 348–54. E 22, 3.
* 89. "Your Negroid and Indian Behaviour," *Forum*, lxxxiii, 1930.
90. *Dream-Analysis*. Seminar Reports, Zürich, 1928–1930. (Privately circulated.)
91. "Der archäische Mensch," *Europäische Revue*, vii, 1931, pp. 182–203. ± 97, 8.

92. "Die Entschleierung der Seele," *Europäische Revue*, vii, 1931, pp. 504–22. = 120, 1; E 13, 9.

93. "Die praktische Verwendbarkeit der Traumanalyse in der Psychotherapie," *Bericht des allgemeinen ärztlichen Kongresses für Psychotherapie*, vi, 1931, pp. 136–42. ± 120, 3.

94. Foreword, R. Aldrich, *The Primitive Mind and Modern Civilization*, London, Kegan Paul—New York, Harcourt Brace, 1931, pp. xv–xvii.

* 95. Foreword, H. Schmid-Guisan, *Tag und Nacht*, Zürich, Rhein-Verlag, 1931.

*95a. Foreword, F. Wicke, *Analyse der Kinderseele*, Stuttgart, Hoffmann, 1931. ± 85; E 23, 2.

96. *Interpretation of Visions*. Seminar Reports, Zürich, 1930–1. (Privately circulated.)

97. *Seelenprobleme der Gegenwart* (*Psych. Abhandlungen*, vol. iii), Zürich, Rascher, 1931, 435 pp.; II, 1933; III, 1939; IV, 1946; V, 1950 (page numbering different) 388 pp.
   1. "Probleme der modernen Psychotherapie." = 77.
   2. "Ueber die Beziehungen der analytischen Psychologie zum dichterischen Kunstwerk." = 59.
   3. "Der Gegensatz Jung-Freud." ± 74; E 13, 6.
   4. "Ziele der Psychotherapie." = 80.
   5. "Die Struktur der Seele." ± 70.
   6. "Seele und Erde." = 65.
   7. "Psychologische Typologie." E 13, 4.
   8. "Der archaische Mensch." ± 91; E 13, 7.
   9. "Die Lebenswende." ± 83; E 13, 5.
   10. "Die Ehe als psychologische Beziehung." = 61.
   11. "Analytische Psychologie und Weltanschauung." E 6, 4.
   12. "Komplex und Mythos." (W. M. Kranefeldt).
   13. "Geist und Leben." = 62.
   14. "Das Seelenproblem des modernen Menschen." = 68.

98. *Zur Psychologie der Individuation*, Seminar Reports, Zürich, 1930–1 (Privately circulated).

99. "Die Hypothese des kollektiven Unbewussten," *Vierteljahrschrift der Naturforschenden Gesellschaft in Zürich*, lxxii, 1932, pp. iv–v.

100. "Picasso", *Neue Zürcher Zeitung*, 13 Nov., 1932. = 120, 7.

101. "Psychological Types," *Problems of Personality. Studies Presented to Dr. Morton Prince*, New York, Harcourt Brace—London, Kegan Paul, 1932, pp. 287–302.

102. "Sigmund Freud als kulturhistorische Erscheinung," *Charakter*, i, 1932, pp. 65–50. = 120, 5; E 12.

103. "Ulysses," *Europäische Revue*, viii, 1932, pp. 547–68. = 120, 6.

*104. Foreword, O. A. Schmitz, *Märchen aus dem Unbewussten*, Munich, Hanser Verlag, 1932.

*105. "Wirklichkeit und Ueberwirklichkeit," *Querschnitt*, xii, 1932.

106. *Die Beziehungen der Psychotherapie zur Seelsorge*, Zürich, Rascher, 1932, 30 pp.; II, 1948, 39 pp. E 13, 11.

107. "Besprechung von G. R. Heyer, *Der Organismus der Seele*," *Europäische Revue*, ix, 1933, p. 639.

108. "Bruder Klaus," *Neue Schweizer Rundschau*, New Series, i, 1933, pp. 223–9.

109. Introduction, M.E. Harding, *The Way of All Women*, New York, London, 1933, pp. ix–xiii.

110. "Ueber Psychologie," *Neue Schweizer Rundschau*, i, 1933, pp. 21–8 and 98–106. ± 120, 2.

111. "Allgemeines zur Komplex-theorie," *Kultur- und Staatswissenschaftliche Schriften der E. T. H.*, 1934, 20 pp. = 189, 2.

112. "Besprechung von H. Keyserling, *La révolution mondiale*," *Basler Nachrichten*, 13 May, 1934.

113. Introduction, G. Adler, *Entdeckung der Seele*, Zürich, Rascher, 1934, pp. vii–viii.

114. Preface, C. L. Schleich, *Die Wunder der Seele*, Berlin, Fischer, 1934, pp. 3–11.

115. "Seele und Tod," *Europäische Revue*, x, 1934, pp. 229–38. = 120, 9.

116. *Ueber Träume. Bericht über das Berliner Seminar*, 1934 (Privately circulated).

117. "*Zeitgenössisches.* Entgegnung auf Dr. Bally's Deutschstämmige Psychotherapie," *Neue Zürcher Zeitung*, 27 February 1934.

118. "Zur Empirie des Individuationsprozesses," *Eranos-Jahrbuch*, 1933, Zürich, Rhein-Verlag, 1934, pp. 201–14. ± 198, 3; E 15, 2.

119. "Zur gegenwärtigen Lage der Psychotherapie," *Zentralblatt für Psychotherapie und ihre Grenzgebiete*, vii, 1934, pp. 1–16.

120. *Wirklichkeit der Seele* (*Psych. Abhandlungen*, vol. iv), Zürich, Rascher, 1934, 409 pp.; II, 1939.

1. "Das Grundproblem der gegenwärtigen Psychologie." = 92.
2. "Die Bedeutung der Psychologie für die Gegenwart." ± 110.
3. "Die praktische Verwendbarkeit der Traumanalyse." ± 93; E 13, 1 and 22, 11.
4. "Paracelsus." = 78.
5. "Sigmund Freud als kulturhistorische Erscheinung." = 102.
6. "Ulysses." = 103.

7. "Picasso." = 100.
8. "Vom Werden der Persönlichkeit." E 15, 6 and 23, 7.
9. "Seele und Tod." = 115.
10. "Der Gegensatz von Sinn und Rhythmus im Seelischen Geschehen" (W. M. Kranefeldt).
11. "Ein Beitrag zum Problem des Animus" (Emma Jung).
12. "Ewige Analyse" (W. M. Kranefeldt).
13. "Der Typengegensatz in der jüdischen Religionsgeschichte" (H. Rosenthal).

121. Preface, *Zentralblatt für Psychotherapie und ihre Grenzgebiete*, viii, 1935, pp. 1–5.

122. Introduction and Psychological Commentary, W. Y. Evans-Wentz, *Das Tibetanische Totenbuch: der Bardo-Thodol*, Zürich, Rascher, 1935, pp. 15–35; II, 1936; III, 1937; IV, 1947; V, 1948.

123. "Grundsätzliches zur praktischen Psychotherapie," *Zentralblatt für Psychotherapie und ihre Grenzgebiete*, viii, 1935, pp. 66–82. E 22, 1.

124. "Ueber die Archetypen des kollektiven Unbewussten," *Eranos-Jahrbuch*, 1934, Zürich, Rhein-Verlag, 1935, pp. 179–229. ± 208, 1; E 15, 3.

*125. Foreword, R. Mehlich, *J. H. Fichtes Seelenlehre*, Zürich, Rascher, 1935.

126. Foreword, O. von Koenig-Fachsenfeld, *Wandlungen des Traumproblems von der Romantik bis zur Gegenwart*, Stuttgart, Enke Verlag, 1935, pp. iii-iv.

127. "Was ist Psychotherapie?", *Schweizerische Aerztezeitung*, xvi, 1935, pp. 335–9. E 22, 2.

128. "Fundamental Psychological Conceptions," Report on the Seminar in the Institute of Medical Psychology, London, 1935 (Privately circulated).

129. *Psychologischer Kommentar zu Hauers Seminar über den Tantra-Yoga.* Seminar Reports, Zürich, 1935 (Privately circulated).

130. *Psychological Analysis of Nietzsche's Zarathustra.* Seminar Reports, Zürich, 1934–5 (Privately circulated).

131. "Besprechung von G. R. Heyer 'Praktische Seelenheilkunde'," *Zentralblatt für Psychotherapie und ihre Grenzgebiete*, ix, 1936, pp. 184–6.

132. "Psychological Factors Determining Human Behaviour," *Factors Determining Human Behaviour*, Cambridge (U.S.A.), Harvard University Press, 1936, 15 pp.
Reprint: Ibid., Id., 1936, 15 pp.

133. "Psychologische Typologie," *Süddeutsche Monatshefte*, xxxiii, 1936, pp. 264–72.

*134. "The Concept of the Collective Unconscious," *St. Bartholomew's Hospital Journal*, 1936.

135. "Traumsymbole des Individuationsprozesses," *Eranos-Jahrbuch*, 1935, Zürich, Rhein-Verlag, 1936, pp. 13–133. ± 172, 2; E 15, 4.

136. "Ueber den Archetypus mit besonderer Berücksichtigung des Anima-Begriffes," *Zentralblatt für Psychotherapie und ihre Grenzgebiete*, ix, 1936, pp. 259–74. ± 208, 2.

137. "Yoga and the West," *Brabuddha Bharata*, India, 1936, 7 pp.

138. "Wotan," *Neue Schweizer Rundschau*, 1936, pp. 657–69. = 179, 1; E 14 and 17, 2.

139. "Die Erlösungsvorstellungen in der Alchemie," *Eranos-Jahrbuch*, 1936, Zürich, Rhein-Verlag, 1937, pp. 13–111. ± 172, 3; E 15, 5.

140. *Kinderträume und ältere Literatur über Traum-Interpretation.* Seminar Report, Zürich, 1936–7 (Privately circulated).

141. *Ueber die Archetypen.* Seminar Report, Berlin, 1937 (Privately circulated).

142. "Einige Bemerkungen zu den Visionen Zosimos," *Eranos-Jahrbuch*, 1937, Zürich, Rhein-Verlag, 1938, pp. 15–54. ± 208, 4.

143. *Psychology and Religion*, New Haven, Yale University Press, 1938, 131 pp. = 156.

144. "Bewusstsein, Unbewusstes und Individuation," *Zentralblatt für Psychotherapie*, xi, 1939, pp. 257–70

145. "Die psychologische Aspekten des Mutterarchetypus," *Eranos-Jahrbuch*, 1938, Zürich, Rhein-Verlag, 1939, pp. 403–43. ± 208, 3.

146. Preface, D. T. Suzuki, *Die grosse Befreiung. Einführung in den Zen-Buddhismus*, Leipzig, Weller, 1939, pp. 9–37. = E 18, a.

147. "On the Psychogenesis of Schizophrenia," *Journal of Mental Science*, lxxxv, 1939, pp. 999–1011.

148. "Sigmund Freud. Ein Nachruf," *Basler Nachrichten*, 1 Oct. 1939.

149. "The Dreamlike World of India," *Asia*, xxxix, 1939, pp. 5–8.

150. "What India can Teach Us," *Asia*, xxxix, 1939, pp. 97–8.

151. *Kinderträume.* Seminar Report, Zürich, 1938–9 (Privately circulated).

152. "Die verschiedenen Aspekten der Wiedergeburt," *Eranos-Jahrbuch*, 1939, Zürich, Rhein-Verlag, 1940, pp. 399–447. = 198, 2.

153. Preface, J. Jacobi, *Die Psychologie von C. G. Jung*, Zürich, Rascher, 1940, pp. 17–18.

154. *Exercitia spiritualia of S. Ignatius of Loyola*. Seminar Report, Zürich, 1940 (Privately circulated).

155. *Das göttliche Kind*, Leipzig, Pantheon-Verlag, 1940, 124 pp. = 161; E 19.

156. *Psychologie und Religion*, Zürich, Rascher, 1940, 190 pp. = 143.

157. "Paracelsus als Arzt," *Schweizerische Medizinische Wochenschrift*, lxxi, 1941 (7 Sept.) pp. 1153–8. = 165, 1.

158. "Rückkehr zum einfachen Leben," *Du*, ii, 1941, pp. 6–7.

159. *Alchemy*. Seminar Report, Zürich, 1940–1 (Privately circulated).

160. *Das Göttliche Mädchen*, Amsterdam-Leipzig, Pantheon-Verlag, 1941, 109 pp. = 161; E 19.

161. *Einführung in das Wesen der Mythologie*, Amsterdam-Leipzig, Pantheon-Verlag, 1941, 251 pp. = 155 + 160; E 19.

162. "Das Wandlungssymbol in der Messe," *Eranos-Jahrbuch*, 1940–1, Zürich, Rhein-Verlag, 1942, pp. 67–155. ± 208, 5.

163. "Human Behaviour," *Science and Man*, New York, Harcourt Brace, 1942, pp. 423–35.

164. "Zur Psychologie der Trinitäts-Idee," *Eranos-Jahrbuch* 1940–1, Zürich, Rhein-Verlag, 1942, pp. 31–64. ± 188, 4.

165. *Paracelsica*, Zürich, Rascher, 1942, 188 pp.
   1. "Paracelsus als Arzt." = 157.
   2. "Paracelsus als geistige Erscheinung."

166. "Der Begabte," *Schweizer Erziehungs-Rundschau*, xvi, 1943, pp. 3–8. = 182, 3; E 23, 5.

167. "Der Geist Mercurius," *Eranos-Jahrbuch*, 1942, Zürich, Rhein-Verlag, 1943, pp. 179–236. ± 188, 2.

168. "Psychotherapie und Weltanschauung," *Schweizerische Zeitschrift für Psychologie und ihre Anwendungen*, i, 1943, pp. 157–64. = 180, 3; E 17, 4 and 22, 6.

169. "Zur Psychologie östlicher Meditation," *Mitteilungen der Schweizerischen Gesellschaft der Freunde Ostasiatischer Kultur*, v, 1943, pp. 33–53. ± 188, 5, E 18.

170. *Ueber die Psychologie des Unbewussten*, Zürich, Rascher, 1943, 213 pp. ± 64.

171. "Ueber den Indischen Heiligen," H. Zimmer, *Der Weg zum Selbst*, Zürich, Rascher, 1944, pp. 11–24.

172. *Psychologie und Alchemie* (*Psych. Abhandlungen*, vol. v). Zürich, Rascher, 1944, 696 pp. E 20.
   1. "Einleitung in die Religionspsychologischen Problematik der Alchemie."
   2. "Traumsymbole des Individuationsprozesses." ± 135.
   3. "Die Erlösungsvorstellungen in der Alchemie." ± 139.

173. "Das Rätsel von Bologna," *Festschrift A. Oeri*, Basle, 1945, 15 pp. E 16.

174. "Der philosophische Baum," *Verhandlungen der Naturforschenden Gesellschaft in Basel*, lvi, 1945, pp. 411–23. ± 208, 6.

175. "Die Psychotherapie in der Gegenwart," *Schweizerische Zeitschrift für Psychologie und ihre Anwendungen*, iv, 1945, pp. 3–18. = 180, 4; E 17, 3 and 22, 8.

176. "Medizin und Psychotherapie," *Bulletin der Schweizerischen Akademie der medizinischen Wissenschaften*, i, 1944–6 pp. 315–28. E 22, 7.

177. "Nach der Katastrophe," *Neue Schweizer Rundschau*, New Series, xiii, 1945, pp. 67–88. = 180, 4; E 17, 5.

178. "Vom Wesen der Träume," *Ciba-Zeitschrift*, ix, 1945, pp. 3546–57. = 189, 4.

179. "Zur Psychologie des Geistes," *Eranos-Jahrbuch*, 1945, Zürich, Rhein-Verlag, 1946, pp. 385–448. ± 188, 1.

180. *Aufsätze zur Zeitgeschichte*, Zürich, Rascher, 1946, 147 pp.
   1. "Wotan." = 138.
   2. "Die Psychotherapie in der Gegenwart." = 175.
   3. "Psychotherapie und Weltanschauung." = 168.
   4. "Nach der Katastrophe." = 177.

181. *Die Psychologie der Uebertragung*, Zürich, Rascher, 1946, 283 pp. E 22, 12.

182. *Psychologie und Erziehung*, Zürich, Rascher, 1946, 203 pp.
   1. "Analytische Psychologie und Erziehung." = 63.
   2. "Ueber Konflikte der kindlichen Seele." = 34.
   3. "Der Begabte." = 166.

183. "Der Geist der Psychologie," *Eranos-Jahrbuch*, 1946. Zürich, Rhein-Verlag, 1947, pp. 385–480. ± 208, 7.

184. "Individual and Mass Psychology," *Chimaera*, v, 1947. E 17, 1.

185. "Psychologie und Spiritismus," *Neue Schweizer Rundschau*, New Series, xvi, 1948, pp. 430–5.
   Foreword, S. White, *Uneingeschränktes Weltall*, Zürich, Origo-Verlag, 1948.

186. "Schatten, Animus, Anima," *Wiener Zeitschrift für Nervenheilkunde und deren Grenzgebiete*, i, 1948, pp. 295–307. ± 200.

*187. Foreword, M. E. Harding, *Das Geheimnis der Seele*, Zürich, Rhein–Verlag, 1948.

188. *Symbolik des Geistes* (*Psych. Abhandlungen*, vol. vi), Zürich, Rascher, 1948, 500 pp.
   1. "Zur Phänomenologie des Geistes im Märchen." ± 179.
   2. "Der Geist Mercurius." ± 167.
   3. "Die Gestalt des Satans im Alten Testament" (R. Scharf).

4. "Versuch einer psychologischen Deutung des Trinitätsdogmas." ± 164.
5. "Zur Psychologie östlicher Meditation." = 169.

189. *Ueber psychische Energetik und das Wesen der Träume*, Zürich, Rascher, 1948, 311 pp.
1. "Ueber die Energetik der Seele." = 73, 1.
2. "Allgemeines zur Komplex-theorie." = 112.
3. "Allgemeine Gesichtspunkte zur Psychologie des Traumes." = 73, 2.
4. "Vom Wesen des Traumes." = 178.
5. "Instinkt und Unbewusstes." = 55 and 73, 3.
6. "Die psychologischen Grundlagen des Geistesglaubens." = 57 and 73, 4.

190. "Geleitwort zum ersten Band der *Studien aus dem Jung-Institut*," C. A. Meier, *Antike Inkubation und moderne Psychotherapie*, Zürich, Rascher, 1949, 2 pp.

191. Preface, M. E. Harding, *Frauen-Mysterien einst und jetzt*, Zürich, Rascher, 1949, pp. viii–xii.

192. "Ueber das Selbst," *Eranos-Jahrbuch*, 1948, Zürich, Rhein-Verlag, 1949, pp. 285–315. ± 200.

193. Foreword, E. Neumann, *Ursprunggeschichte des Bewusstseins*, Zürich, Rascher, 1949, pp. 1–2.

194. Foreword, L. Abegg, *Ostasien denkt anders*, Zürich, Atlantis-Verlag, 1949, pp. 3–4.

195. *De Sulphure*, pp. 27–40.

196. Foreword, H. G. Baynes, *Analytical Psychology and the English Mind*, London, Methuen, 1950, p. v.

197. Foreword, F. Moser, *Spuk*, Baden-Zürich, Gyr-Verlag, 1950, pp. 9–12.

198. *Gestaltungen des Unbewussten* (*Psych. Abhandlungen*, vol. vii). Zürich, Rascher, 1950, 616 pp.
1. "Psychologie und Dichtung." = 87.
2. "Ueber Wiedergeburt." = 152.
3. "Zur Empirie des Individuationsprozesses." ± 118.
4. "Ueber Mandala-Symbolik."
5. "Bilder und Symbole aus E. T. A. Hoffmans Märchen 'Der Goldne Topf' " (A. Jaffé).

199. "Grundfragen der Psychotherapie," *Dialectica*, v, 1951, pp. 8–24. E 22, 9.

200. *Aion. Untersuchungen zur Symbolgeschichte*, (*Psych. Abhandlungen*, vol. viii), Zürich, Rascher, 1951, 561 pp.
pp. 22–43 = 186; pp. 44–110 = 192.

201. "Religion und Psychologie," *Merkur*, vi, 1952, pp. 467–73.

202. "Ueber Synchronizität," *Eranos-Jahrbuch*, 1951, Zürich, Rhein-Verlag, 1952, pp. 271–84. ± 204, 1.
203. *Antwort auf Hiob*, Zürich, Rascher, 1952, 169 pp. E 24.
204. *Naturerklärung und Psyche*, Zürich, Rascher, 1952, 194 pp.
   1. "Synchronizität als ein Prinzip akausaler Zusammenhang." ± 202; E 25, 1.
   2. "Der Einfluss archetypischer Vorstellungen bei Kepler" (W. Pauli).
205. *Symbole der Wandlung*, Zürich, Rascher, 1952, 821 pp. ± 42.
206. Foreword, F. Fordham, *An Introduction to Jung's Psychology*, London, Penguin, 1953, p. 10.
207. Foreword, V. White, *God and the Unconscious*, London, Harvill Press, 1953, pp. xiii–xxv.
208. *Von den Wurzeln des Bewusstseins*,[1] (*Psych. Abhandlungen* vol. ix), Zürich, Rascher, 1954, 681 pp.
   1. "Ueber die Archetypen des kollektiven Unbewussten." ± 124.
   2. "Ueber den Archetypus mit besonderer Berücksichtigung des Animabegriffes." ± 136.
   3. "Die psychologischen Aspekten des Mutter-Archetypus." ± 145.
   4. "Die Visionen des Zosimos." ± 142.
   5. "Das Wandlungssymbol in der Messe." ± 162.
   6. "Der philosophische Baum." ± 174.
   7. "Theoretische Ueberlegungen zum Wesen des Psychischen." ± 183.
209. *Mysterium Coniunctionis* (*Psych. Abhandlungen*, vol. x). Zürich, Rascher, 1955, 284 pp.

English Translations[2]

1. *The Psychology of Dementia Praecox*, tr. Brill and Peterson, New York, 1909 (= 25).
2. *The Theory of Psychoanalysis*, New York, Nervous and Mental Diseases Publishing Company, 1915 (= 47).
3. *Collected Papers on Analytical Psychology*, tr. C. E. Long, London, Baillière, Tyndall and Cox, 1916, 392 pp.; II, 1922, 492 pp. New York, Moffat, 1917, 492 pp.
   1. "On the Psychology and Pathology of So-called Occult Phenomena." (= 1).
   2. "The Association Method." (= 21 and 34).

[1] These two latest of Jung's works only appeared after my own book had been published, but as Jung had kindly told me what they contained earlier, I have been able to make use of them though without direct quotation.

[2] In the case of these English translations, only the first date of publication is given. The figure in brackets refers to the original.

3. "The Significance of the Father in the Destiny of the Individual." (= 30).
4. "A Contribution to the Psychology of Rumour." (= 39).
5. "On the Significance of Number Dreams." (= 38).
6. "A Criticism of Bleuler's Theory of Schizophrenic Negativism." (= 40).
7. "Psychoanalysis." (= 46).
8. "On Psychoanalysis." (= 44).
9. "On Some Crucial Points in Psychoanalysis." (= 49).
10. "On the Importance of the Unconscious in Psychopathology." (= 48).
11. "A Contribution to the Study of Psychological Types." (= 45).
12. "The Psychology of Dreams."
13. "The Content of the Psychoses." (= 29).
14. (in I.) "New Paths of Psychology." (= 43).
(in II.) "The Psychology of the Unconscious Processes." (= 53).
15. (in II.) "The Conception of the Unconscious." (= 52).

4. *Psychology of the Unconscious*, tr. B. M. Hinkle, London, Kegan, Trench, Trubner and Co., 1919, 566 pp.—New York, Moffat, 1916, 566 pp. (since 1931: Dodd, Mead and Co.). (= 42).
5. *Studies in Word-Association*, tr. Dr. Eder, London, Heinemann, 1918; New York, Moffat, 1919. (= 20 and 36).
1. "The Associations of Normal Subjects." (= 6).
2. "Analysis of the Associations of an Epileptic." (= 8).
3. "Reaction-time in Association-Experiments." (= 11).
4. "Psychoanalysis and Association-Experiments." (= 18).
5. "Association, Dreams and Hysterical Symptoms." (= 36, 1).
6. "On Disturbances in Reproduction in Association-Experiments." (= 24).

6. *Contributions to Analytical Psychology*, tr. C. F. Baynes, London, Kegan Paul, 1928, 410 pp.; New York, Harcourt Brace, 1928.
1. "On Psychical Energy." (= 73, 1).
2. "Spirit and Life." (= 62).
3. "Mind and the Earth." (= 65).
4. "Analytic Psychology and Weltanschauung." (97, 11).
5. "Woman in Europe." (= 66).
6. "Marriage as a Psychological Relationship." (= 61).
7. "On the Love Problem of the Student."
8. "On the Relation of Analytic Psychology to Poetic Art." (= 59).
9. "The Psychological Foundations of the Belief in Spirits." (= 57).

10. "Instinct and the Unconscious." (= 55).
11. "The Question of the Therapeutic Value of Abreaction."
12. "Psychological Types." (= 60).
13. "Analytic Psychology and Education." (= 63).
14. "The Significance of the Unconscious in Individual Education." (= E 23, 6).

7. *Psychological Types*, tr. H. G. Baynes, London, Kegan Paul, 1923, 654 pp; New York, Harcourt Brace, 1923, 654 pp. (= 58).
8. *Two Essays on Analytical Psychology*, tr. H. G. Baynes, London, Baillière, 1928, 280 pp.; New York, Dodd, Mead, 1928, 280 pp.
 1. "The Unconscious in the Normal and the Pathological Mind." (= 64).
 2. "The Relation of the Ego to the Unconscious." (= 72).
9. "Psychology and Poetry", tr. E. Jolas, *Transition*, 1930. (= 87).
10. *The Secret of the Golden Flower*, London, Kegan Paul—New York, Harcourt Brace, 1931. (= 81).
11. "The Spiritual Problem of Modern Man", *Brabuddha Bharata*, 1931, 15 pp. (= 68).
12. "Sigmund Freud in His Historical Setting" tr. C. F. Baynes, *Character and Personality*, i, 1932, pp. 48–55. (= 102).
13. *Modern Man in Search of a Soul*, tr. W. S. Dell and C. F. Baynes, London, Kegan Paul—New York, Harcourt Brace, 1933, 282 pp.
 1. "Dream-Analysis and its Practical Application." (= 93).
 2. "Problems of Modern Psychotherapy." (= 77).
 3. "Aims of Psychotherapy." (= 80).
 4. "A Psychological Theory of Types." (= 97, 7).
 5. "The Stages of Life." (= 97, 9).
 6. "Freud and Jung, Contrasts." (= 97, 3).
 7. "Archaic Man." (= 97, 8).
 8. "Psychology and Literature." (= 87).
 9. "The Basic Postulates of Analytical Psychology." (= 92).
 10. "The Spiritual Problem of Modern Man." (= 68).
 11. "Psychotherapists or the Clergy. A Dilemma." (= 106).
14. "Wotan," *Saturday Review of Literature*, 1937. (= 138).
15. *The Integration of the Personality*, tr. S. Dell, New York, Farrar and Rinehart, 1939, 305 pp.; London, Kegan Paul, 1940, 305 pp. (plus index).
 1. "The Meaning of Individuation."
 2. "A Study in the Process of Individuation." (= 118).
 3. "Archetypes of the Collective Unconscious." (= 124).
 4. "Dream Symbols of the Process of Individuation." (= 135).
 5. "The Idea of Redemption in Alchemy." (= 139).
 6. "The Development of the Personality." (= 120, 8).
16. "The Bologna Enigma," *Ambix*, 1946. (= 173).

17. *Essays on Contemporary Events*, tr. E. Welsh, B. Hannah, M. Briner, London, Kegan Paul, 1947, 90 pp.
  1. "Introduction: Individual and Mass Psychology." (= 184).
  2. "Wotan." (= 138).
  3. "Psychotherapy To-day." (= 175).
  4. "Psychotherapy and a Philosophy of Life." (= 168).
  5. "After the Catastrophe." (= 177).
  6. "Epilogue."
18. "On the Psychology of Eastern Meditation," tr. C. Baumann, *Art and Thought, a Volume in Honour of the late Dr. Ananda K. Coomaraswami*, London, Lussac, 1948. (= 169).
18a. Foreword, D. T. Suzuki, *Introduction to Zen Buddhism*, London, Rider, 1949. = 146).
19. Jung, C. G., and Kereney, C., *Introduction toa Science of Mythology*, tr. R. F. C. Hull, London, Routledge and Kegan Paul, 1951. (= 161).
20. *Psychology and Alchemy*, tr. R. F. C. Hull, London, Routledge and Kegan Paul—New York, Bollingen Series, 1953, 563 pp. (— 172).
21. *Two Essays on Analytical Psychology*, tr. R. F. C. Hull, London, Routledge and Kegan Paul—New York, Bollingen Series, 1953, 392 pp.
  1. "The Unconscious in the Normal and the Pathological Mind." (= 64).
  2. "The Relation of the Ego to the Unconscious." (= 72).
  3. "New Paths in Psychology." (= 43).
  4. "The Structure of the Unconscious." (= 52).
22. *The Practice of Psychotherapy*, tr. R. F. C. Hull. London, Routledge and Kegan Paul—New York, Bollingen series, 1954, 369 pp.
  1. "Principles of Practical Psychotherapy." (= 123).
  2. "What is Psychotherapy?" (= 127).
  3. "Some Aspects of Modern Psychotherapy." (= 88).
  4. "The Aims of Psychotherapy." (= 80).
  5. "Problems of Modern Psychotherapy." (= 77).
  6. "Psychotherapy and a Philosophy of Life." (= 168)
  7. "Medicine and Psychotherapy." (= 176).
  8. "Psychotherapy To-day." (= 175).
  9. "Fundamental Questions of Psychotherapy." (= 199).
  10. "The Therapeutic Value of Abreaction." (= 58a).
  11. "The Practical Use of Dream-Analysis." (= 120, 3).
  12. "Psychology of the Transference." (= 181).
23. *The Development of Personality*, tr. R. F. C. Hull, London, Routledge and Kegan Paul—New York, Bollingen Series, 1954, 225 pp.

1. "Psychic Conflicts in a Child." (= 34).
2. "Introduction to Wicke's *Analyse der Kinderseele*" (= 95a).
3. "Child Development and Education." (E 6, 13).
4. "Analytical Psychology and Education." (= 63).
5. "The Gifted Child." (= 166).
6. "The Significance of the Unconscious in Individual Education." (E 6, 14).
7. "The Development of Personality." (= 120, 8).
8. "Marriage as a Psychological Relationship." (= 61).

24. *Answer to Job*, tr. R. F. C. Hull, London, Routledge and Kegan Paul, 1954, 194 pp. (= 203).
25. *The Interpretation of Nature and the Psyche*, tr. R. F. C. Hull, London, Routledge and Kegan Paul, New York, Bollingen Series, 1955, 247 pp.
1. "Synchronicity: An Acausal Connecting Principle." (=204, 1).
2. "The Influence of Archetypal Ideas on the Scientific Theories of Kepler" (W. Pauli).

LITERATURE[1]

BACHELARD, G., *L'air et les songes. Essai sur l'imagination du mouvement*, Paris, José Corti, 1943, 307 pp.
La psychanalyse du feu, Paris, Gallimard, 1949[9], 219 pp.

*BERNET, W., *Inhalt und Grenze der religiösen Erfahrung*, Bern, Haupt, 1955, 223 pp.

*BAUDOUIN, C., *De l'instinct à l'esprit*, Paris, Desclée de Brouwer, 1950, 308 pp.

*BEIRNAERT, L., "Jung et Freud au regard de la foi chrétienne," *Dieu vivant*, no. 26, 1954, pp. 95–100.

BINSWANGER, L., *Ausgewählte Vorträge und Aufsätze*, Bern, Francke, 1947, 217 pp.
Grundformen und Erkenntnis menschlichen Daseins, Zürich, Niehaus, 1942, 726 pp.

*BOSS, M., *Der Traum und seine Auslegung*, Bern, Stuttgart, Huber, 1953, 239 pp.

* "Ueber Herkunft und Wesen des tiefenpsychologischen Archetypus-Begriffes," *Psyche* (*Zeitschrift für Tiefenpsychologie*), vi, 1952–3, pp. 584–97.

*BRUNETON, J. L., "Jung: l'homme, sa vie, son caractère," In: *Revue d'Allemagne*, vii, 1933, pp. 673–89.

*BRUNNER, A., "Theologie oder Tiefenpsychologie?" *Stimmen der Zeit*, lxxviii, 1952–3, pp. 401–15.

[1] Books marked by an asterisk are devoted to Jung, either wholly or in part.

*CARP, E. A., *De analytische behandelingsmethode volgens Jung*, Amsterdam, Meulenhoff, n.d., 173 pp.
*CARUSO, I., "Das Symbol in der Psychotherapie," *Studium Generale*, vi., 1953, pp. 296–302.
*CORBIN, H., "La Sophia éternelle," *Revue de Culture Européenne*, iii, 1953, pp. 11–44.
*CORRIE, J., *C. G. Jungs Psychologie im Abriss*, Zürich, Rascher, 1929, 99 pp.
*DAIM, W., "Der Grundfehler C. G. Jungs." *Wissenschaft und Weltbild*, vi, 1953, pp. 58–66.
*DESSAUER, P., "Bemerkungen zum Verhältnis von Psychotherapie und Seelsorge," *Anima* vii. 1952, pp. 112–30.
ELIADE, M., *The Myth of the Eternal Return*, London, Routledge and Kegan Paul, 1955, 195 pp.
Traité de l'histoire des religions. Morphologie du Sacré, Paris, Payot, 1949, 405 pp.
*FORDHAM, F., *An Introduction to Jung's Psychology*, London, Penguin, 1953, 128 pp.
*FREI, G., "Die Methode und die Lehre C. G. Jungs," *Annalen der philosophischen Gesellschaft Innerschweiz und Ostschweiz*, 1948.
FREUD, S., *Gesammelte Werke* (18 vols.), London, Imago Publishing Company, 1938–52.
*FRISCHKNECHT, M., *Die Religion in der Psychologie C. G. Jungs*, Bern, P. Haupt, 1945, 29 pp.
FROBENIUS, L., *Das Zeitalter des Sonnengottes*, Berlin, Reimer, 1904, 420 pp.
*GEBSATTEL, V. E. von, *Christentum und Humanismus*, Stuttgart, Klett, 1947, 168 pp.
*GLOVER, E., "Freud or Jung," *Horizon*, xviii, 1948, pp. 225–58 and 303–18; xix, 1949, pp. 209–28.
* *Freud or Jung*, London, Allen and Unwin, 1950, 207 pp.
*GOLDBRUNNER, J., *Die Tiefenpsychologie von C. G. Jung und christliche Lebensgestaltung*, Freiburg im Breisgau, 1940, 66 pp.
* *Individuation*, London, Hollis and Carter, 1955, 204 pp.
* *Personale Seelsorge*, Freiburg, Herder, 1954, 135 pp.
*HABERLANDT, H., "Diskussion um Hiob," *Wissenschaft und Weltbild*, vi, 1953, pp. 52–8.
HEIDEGGER, M., "Sein und Zeit," *Jahrbuch für Philosophie und phänomenologische Forschung*, viii, 1927, pp. 1–438.
*JACOBI, J., *The Psychology of C. G. Jung*, London, Routledge and Kegan Paul, 1951[5], 204 pp.
* "Komplex, Archetypus und Symbol," *Schweizerische Zeitschrift für Psychologie und ihre Anwendungen*, iv, 1945, pp. 276–313.
KERENYI, K., "Antike Religion und Religionspsychologie," *Apollon*,

Studien über antike Religion und Humanität, Wien, Amsterdam, Leipzig, F. Leo, 1937, pp. 15–36.

LEEUW, G. van der, *Religion in Essence and Manifestation*, London, Allen and Unwin, 1938.

*LEIBBRAND, W., "C. G. Jungs Versuch einer psychologischen Deutung des Trinitätsdogmas," *Zeitschrift für Religions- und Geistesgeschichte*, iii, 1951, pp. 122–34.

* "Das tiefenpsychologische Werk C. G. Jungs," *Hochland*, xlvii, 1955, pp. 444–51.

*LEONARD, A., "La psychologie religieuse de Jung," *Supplément de la Vie Spirituelle*, v., 1951, pp. 325–34.

MARÉCHAL, J., "Empirical Science and Religious Psychology," *Studies in the Psychology of the Mystics*, London, Burns Oates and Washbourne, 1927, pp. 1–54.

*MICHAELIS, E., "Le livre de Job interprété par C. G. Jung," *Revue de Théologie et de Philosophie*, iii, 1953, pp. 183–95.

*MULLAHY, P., *Oedipus: Myth and Complex*, New York, Hermitage Press, 1948, 538 pp.

OTTO, R., *The Idea of the Holy*, O.U.P., 1950.

*PROGROFF, I., *Jung's Psychology and its Social Meaning*, New York, Julian Press, 1953, 299 pp.

RAHNER, H., *Griechische Mythen in christlicher Deutung*, Zürich, Rhein-Verlag, 1945, 499 pp.

RORSCHACH, H., *Psychodiagnostik*, Bern, Huber, 1946[5], 277 pp.

*RUDIN, J., "Antwort auf Hiob," *Orientierung*, 1953, pp. 41–4.

* "Die Tiefenpsychologie und die Freiheit des Menschen," *Orientierung*, 1954, pp. 169–73.

*RÜMKE, H. C., "Aantekeningen over het instinct, de archetypus, de existentiaal," *Pro Regno, Pro Sanctuario, Feestbundel voor Prof. G. van der Leeuw*, Nijkerk, Callenbach, 1950, pp. 451–67.

SARTRE, J. P., *L'imaginaire, Psychologie phénoménologique de l'imagination*, Paris, Gallimard, 1948[23], 246 pp.

L'imagination, Paris, Presses de France, 1936, 162 pp.

"La structure intentionnelle de l'image," *Revue de Métaphysique et de Morale*, 1938, pp. 542–609.

*SCHAER, H., "C. G. Jung, und die Deutung der Geschichte," *Schweizerische Theologische Umschau*, xxii, 1952, pp. 91–6.

* *Erlösungsvorstellungen und ihre psychologischen Aspekte*, Zürich, Rascher, 1950, 702 pp.

* *Religion und Seele in der Psychologie C. G. Jungs*, Zürich, Rascher, 1946, 273 pp.

SCHOTTE, J., "Remarques sur l'exercice de la connaissance d' autrui dans la situation psychothérapeutique et psychiatrique ou psychologique en général," *Actes du XI Congrès international de Philosophie*, suppl. vol., pp. 189–201.

*SCHULTZ-HENCKE, H., "Ueber die Archetypen," *Zentralblatt für Psychotherapie*, ix, 1936, pp. 335–43.

*SIERKSMA, F., *Phaenomenologie der religie en complexe psychologie*, Assen, Van Gorcum, 1950, 256 pp.

SILBERER, H., *Probleme der Mystik and ihrer Symbolik*, Vienna, Leipzig, Heller, 1914, 283 pp.

STERN, K., *The Third Revolution. A study in Psychiatry and Religion*, New York, Harcourt Brace and Co., London, Michael Joseph, 1955, 306 pp.

SZONDI, L., *Schicksalsanalyse*, Basel, Benno Schwabe, 1948, 422 pp.

Experimentelle Triebdiagnostik, Text-Band, Bern, Huber, 1947, 308 pp.

*THOMPSON, C., *Psychoanalysis, Evolution and Development*, London, Allen and Unwin, 1952, 252 pp.

*TRÜB, H., *Heilung aus der Begegnung*, Stuttgart, Klett, 1951, 124 pp.

*TUINSTRA, C., L., *Het symbool in de psychanalyse*, Amsterdam, Paris, 1933, 231 pp.

*WHITE, V., *God and the Unconscious*, London, Harvill Press, 1953, 277 pp.

"The Scandal of the Assumption," *Life of the Spirit*, v, 1950, pp. 199–212.

* "Answer to Job," *Blackfriars*, 1955, pp. 52–60.

*WOLFF, T., "Exposé d'ensemble de la doctrine", *Revue d'Allemagne*, vii, 1933, pp. 709–43.

*ZACHARIAS, P., "Die Bedeutung der Psychologie C. G. Jungs für die christliche Theologie," *Zeitschrift für Religions- und Geistesgeschichte*, v, 1953, 13 pp.

* *Psyche und Mysterium*, Zürich, Rascher, 1954, 171 pp.

COMPOSITE AUTHORSHIP

* *Die kulturelle Bedeutung der Komplexen Psychologie. Festschrift zum 60 Geburtstag C. G. Jungs*, Berlin, Springer, 1935, 625 pp.

* "C. G. Jung," Special Number, *Le Disque vert*, 1955, 390 pp.

* *Studien zur analytischen Psychologie C. G. Jungs. Festschrift zum 80 Geburtstag von C. G. Jung*, Zürich, Rascher, 1955, 2 vols., 396 and 397 pp.

NAME INDEX

SUBJECT INDEX